Learning Alteryx

A beginner's guide to using Alteryx for self-service analytics and business intelligence

Renato Baruti

Packt

BIRMINGHAM - MUMBAI

Learning Alteryx

First published: December 2017

Production reference: 1221217

Published by Packt Publishing Ltd.
Livery Place
35 Livery Street
Birmingham
B3 2PB, UK.

ISBN 978-1-78839-265-5

www.packtpub.com

Credits

Author
Renato Baruti

Reviewer
Mayur Ravindra Narkhede

Commissioning Editor
Sunith Shetty

Acquisition Editor
Tushar Gupta

Content Development Editor
Aaryaman Singh

Technical Editor
Dinesh Chaudhary

Copy Editor
Safis Editing

Project Coordinator
Manthan Patel

Proofreader
Safis Editing

Indexer
Tejal Daruwale Soni

Graphics
Tania Dutta

Production Coordinator
Shantanu Zagade

About the Author

Renato Baruti is an Alteryx Certified Professional and the Tampa Bay Alteryx User Group leader, strengthening the self-service analytics community by bringing professionals closer together to share the endless data-driven insights that Alteryx has to offer.

Professionally, he is a senior systems analyst with over 6 years of experience in healthcare analytics and over 12 years of healthcare experience.

After graduating with an economics degree from the University of South Florida, Renato continued with that interest as a certified Six Sigma Black Belt. His experience has ranged across data structure and design using SQL, building intuitive Alteryx workflows to answer complex business problems, and finishing with expressive data visualizations by developing Interactive Tableau dashboards to revolutionize not just how individuals work, but how the entire organization works.

Renato believes in learning by understanding and loves teaching everything he learns! He has a passion for using Alteryx that grows exponentially day after day, identifying relationships in data and solving problems in minutes.

I would like to thank the entire team at Packt for believing in my work and for their patience and guidance. I am grateful for my friends who have always supported and pushed me to the challenge on and off the soccer field. To my co-workers, thank you for defining what teamwork is every day. I am thankful to my love, Valentina, who supported and encouraged me to write this book along the journey. I am also so thankful to my students whose challenges and feedback have given me new ideas to write this book. Finally, I would like to acknowledge with gratitude, the love and support of my family—my parents, Petrit and Majlinda, and my sister, Stephanie. This book would not have been possible without them because they have always been there for me from the very beginning.

About the Reviewer

Mayur has a good blend of experience in data science. He is a researcher with educational qualifications of a BTech in computer science and an MTech in CSE with an artificial intelligence specialization. He has core experience in building automated solutions. He is proficient at applying technology, AI, ML, data mining, and design thinking for better understandings and predictions to improve business functions and desired requirements with growth profitability.

Mayur has worked on multiple advanced solutions, such as an asset health monitoring, a batch process performance analysis, a smart metering for water utility clients, and predictive model development for oil and gas customers, and a big data platform for asset intensive industries.

He has core expertise in implementing machine learning techniques in various domains of asset-intensive industries, prediction techniques for transportation, and clustered graph laying out algorithms for Life Sciences. He has also worked with transportation clients in developing traffic prediction algorithms. He has played a key role in setting up the Data Science and Big Data labs.

Mayur is a sportsman and plays cricket, badminton, carom. He is also a vivid traveler who likes to explore new places. Beside this, he is a good reader and has a hunger to learn evolving technologies and implement them in simpler ways.

Customer Feedback

Thanks for purchasing this Packt book. At Packt, quality is at the heart of our editorial process. To help us improve, please leave us an honest review on this book's Amazon page at `https://www.amazon.com/dp/1788392655`.

If you'd like to join our team of regular reviewers, you can email us at `customerreviews@packtpub.com`. We award our regular reviewers with free eBooks and videos in exchange for their valuable feedback. Help us be relentless in improving our products!

Table of Contents

Preface

Alteryx is a platform that allows analysts to prepare, blend, and analyze all their data using workflows. Different business groups involved in marketing, sales, and healthcare find it difficult to quickly study and analyze data. Alteryx solves this problem using the different tools it has to offer for gathering, cleaning, and joining data.

A leading data blending and analytics platform, Alteryx needs no coding and provides a very user-friendly environment, with the names of the tools that are used given names that are relevant to the function they carry out, making it easier for users to exploit the different functions Alteryx has to offer.

Apart from being user friendly, it's the efficiency of this platform that makes it one of the leading business intelligence platforms in the world at the moment. What makes Alteryx attractive as a data intelligence platform? Well, this platform will help you to derive insights from data, which means a huge volume of data and also how to share these derived insights without any coding.

What this book covers

`Chapter 1`, *Getting Started with Alteryx*, introduces us to Alteryx as a platform and also shows how to download and install the Alteryx Designer. It looks inside the Alteryx Designer architecture and helps us understand how the Alteryx Engine drives data processing in a repeatable workflow.

`Chapter 2`, *Workflow Optimization*, focuses on workflow optimization concepts and gives us information about best practices for the application of runtime selections and to speed up execution. Workflow design is vital to ensure that the workflow runs efficiently, allowing for optimum processing.

`Chapter 3`, *Data Preparation and Blending*, explains the processes of data preparation, blending, and joining, which are the most powerful capabilities of Alteryx. Data analysts have found themselves struggling to get the best results from their data using Microsoft Excel or other tools. You'll be sent on a journey to discover self-service analytics and build a quick and reliable dataset for business decision making.

`Chapter 4`, *Writing Fast and Accurate Expressions*, introduces various tools in Alteryx that allow a broad variety of calculations. You will utilize multiple expressions to create new data columns, update existing columns, and reference data to qualifying rows. You will move through more rigorous expressions to maximize the potential of the Formula, Multi-Field Formula, and Multi-Row Formula tools. The goal is to gain a solid foundation in the different types of formulas to write with these tools.

`Chapter 5`, *Transforming Data*, helps us to arrange and transpose data in Alteryx that can be developed to ensure the dataset best fits the needs of how the output data should be analyzed. You'll learn the pivot orientations of the Transpose and Cross tab tools, and how they help guide the pathway to a visual representation of your data. Once your data has been aligned to meet the business needs, you will dive into summarizing your data to perform various numeric, and string actions.

`Chapter 6`, *Data Parsing Techniques*, explains the Parse tool palette, which offers parsing options that will save you time by having the tools do it all for you. The Text to Columns tool allows you to split text from one field to multiple columns or rows. Not to forget, the numerous times a file comes in with a string-formatted field and it should be a date-formatted field. This issue is solved by utilizing the DateTime tool.

`Chapter 7`, *Creating Data-Driven Custom Reports*, helps us understand the suites of reporting tools used to create high quality data-driven reports and deliver them into customers. These tools have been designed with the Alteryx design paradigm in mind creating snippets in each of the tools. You will create a report from start to finish, with the best design output, which will help organizations to make informed business decisions. Whether it's developing a data table or visual representation, the reporting tools suite will help you produce presentation-quality reports.

`Chapter 8`, *Using Macros in Workflows*, explains that a macro workflow has the flexibility to run as a single tool within another workflow. There are various macro types, which are built by using Interface Tools with the Interface Designer. Batch macros are designed to run repeatedly in the context of a workflow. The ability to run a single tool through every record, and loop the records back through the workflow until a condition is met, can be accomplished by creating an Iterative Macro.

`Chapter 9`, *Sharing Your Insights*, explains how to publish, schedule, and share workflows through Alteryx Server and Alteryx Public Gallery. Alteryx Server empowers teams to collaborate on data-driven decisions quickly and easily through a scalable platform. You'll identify how data can be deployed through effective and secure collaboration across teams. Alteryx Public Gallery is an analytics cloud platform that delivers a consumer-based analytics experience. Organizations look to cloud business intelligence to deliver faster deployment.

`Chapter 10`, *Best Practices*, takes a look at the data necessary to make critical business decisions, which is best consumed by streamlined workflows. You will learn best practice solutions on building efficient workflows, reviewing data exploration techniques, and handling data sources. These best practice guidelines, along with tips and tricks will save you valuable time in the business decision making process.

What you need for this book

The technical specifications are key to ensuring that the system requirements are met before installation. Alteryx Analytics 11.0, which is what we will install for this book and the future versions, is only available for 64-bit machines with a Windows operating system of 7 or later.

The following chart illustrates the minimum system requirements:

Machine requirements	**Operating system requirements**	**Chip**	**Processor**	**Ram**	**Disk size**
64-bit	Microsoft Windows 7 or later	Quad core i7	2.5 GHz	8 GB RAM	500 GB - 1 TB

Who this book is for

This book is for aspiring data professionals who want to learn to implement self-service analytics from scratch, without any coding. Those who have some experience with Alteryx and want to gain more proficiency will also find this book to be useful. A basic understanding of data science concepts is all you need to get started with this book.

Conventions

In this book, you will find a number of text styles that distinguish between different kinds of information. Here are some examples of these styles and an explanation of their meaning.

Code words in text, database table names, folder names, filenames, file extensions, pathnames, dummy URLs, user input, and Twitter handles are shown as follows: "The next lines of code read the link and assign it to the `open` function."

A block of code is set as follows:

```
IF Contains([DataValueUnit],'%') &&
 !IsNull([DataValue]) THEN [DataValue] + '%'
 ELSE [DataValue]
 ENDIF
```

New terms and **important words** are shown in bold.

Words that you see on the screen, for example, in menus or dialog boxes, appear in the text like this: "In order to download new modules, we will go to **Files** | **Settings** | **Project Name** | **Project Interpreter**."

Warnings or important notes appear like this.

Tips and tricks appear like this.

Reader feedback

Feedback from our readers is always welcome. Let us know what you think about this book-what you liked or disliked. Reader feedback is important for us as it helps us develop titles that you will really get the most out of. To send us general feedback, simply email `feedback@packtpub.com`, and mention the book's title in the subject of your message. If there is a topic that you have expertise in and you are interested in either writing or contributing to a book, see our author guide at `www.packtpub.com/authors`.

Customer support

Now that you are the proud owner of a Packt book, we have a number of things to help you to get the most from your purchase.

Downloading the color images of this book

We also provide you with a PDF file that has color images of the screenshots/diagrams used in this book. The color images will help you better understand the changes in the output. You can download this file from `https://www.packtpub.com/sites/default/files/downloads/LearningAlteryx_ColorImages.pdf`.

Errata

Although we have taken every care to ensure the accuracy of our content, mistakes do happen. If you find a mistake in one of our books-maybe a mistake in the text or the code-we would be grateful if you could report this to us. By doing so, you can save other readers from frustration and help us improve subsequent versions of this book. If you find any errata, please report them by visiting `http://www.packtpub.com/submit-errata`, selecting your book, clicking on the **Errata Submission Form** link, and entering the details of your errata. Once your errata are verified, your submission will be accepted and the errata will be uploaded to our website or added to any list of existing errata under the Errata section of that title. To view the previously submitted errata, go to `https://www.packtpub.com/books/content/support` and enter the name of the book in the search field. The required information will appear under the **Errata** section.

Piracy

Piracy of copyrighted material on the internet is an ongoing problem across all media. At Packt, we take the protection of our copyright and licenses very seriously. If you come across any illegal copies of our works in any form on the internet, please provide us with the location address or website name immediately so that we can pursue a remedy. Please contact us at `copyright@packtpub.com` with a link to the suspected pirated material. We appreciate your help in protecting our authors and our ability to bring you valuable content.

Questions

If you have a problem with any aspect of this book, you can contact us at `questions@packtpub.com`, and we will do our best to address the problem.

1
Getting Started with Alteryx

Alteryx Analytics is a tremendous platform allowing analysts to easily prep, blend, and analyze all their data using a repeatable workflow. Many business groups, such as marketing, finance, healthcare, and sales find it difficult to quickly analyze data they can act upon instantly using legacy approaches, such as Microsoft Excel and other platforms. Alteryx solves these problems with a seamless process, by using tools to gather, cleanse, and join data from different sources. This repeatable workflow for self-service data analytics delivers deeper insights in hours, not weeks.

You will be accomplishing the task of building and publishing analytic models by using tools in a drag-and-drop environment within the same intuitive user interface. You'll learn data preparation and data cleansing from spreadsheets and other sources to determine key insights and how share those key insights.

In this chapter, we'll focus on the following foundation topics:

- Downloading and installing Alteryx Designer
- An introduction to Alteryx Designer and what makes it such a powerful self-service analytics platform
- A look inside the Alteryx Designer architecture and understanding how the Alteryx Engine drives data processing in a repeatable workflow

- An overview of the workflow configurations, ensuring indispensable selections are met to create an optimal workflow
- Exploring the tool palettes filled with endless tools within various tool palettes (Getting familiar with the tool palettes will provide quick and easy access to designing your workflow)
- The Favorites tools to categorize and save most utilized tools

Installation and setup

In this section, we will learn how to install Alteryx Designer to begin using the ultimate platform for self-service analytics. There are a few key items to note before Alteryx Designer is installed.

No licensing action is required when upgrading the Alteryx software. The existing Alteryx license will continue to function when a new version is installed. Due to compatibility concerns, workflows developed in a newer version will not launch in the previous versions and workflows in the older versions will continue to work when a newer version is installed. Lastly, the technical specifications are key to ensure system requirements are met before installing. Alteryx Analytics 11.0, which is what we will install for this book and future versions, is only available for 64-bit machines with operating system Microsoft Windows 7 or later. Following is a chart that illustrates the minimum system requirements:

Machine Requirements	**Operating System Requirements**	**Chip**	**Processor**	**Ram**	**Disk Size**
64-bit	Microsoft Windows 7 or later	Quad core i7	2.5 GHz	8 GB RAM	500GB - 1TB

We'll now walk through the steps of downloading and installing Alteryx Designer. Before we get started, make sure to close all instances of Alteryx that you may have open:

1. Navigate to the Alteryx **Downloads** site `http://downloads.alteryx.com/` to download the software and select the **Alteryx Designer** option.

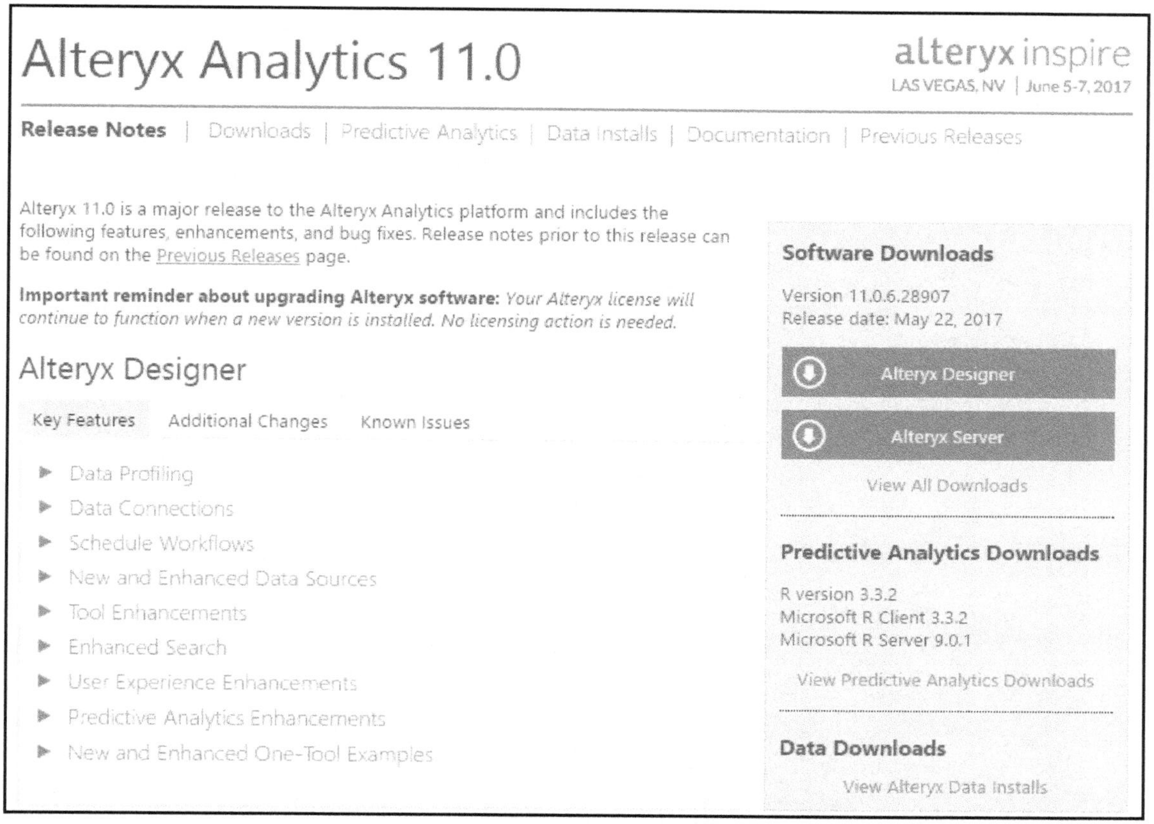

2. Once the **Alteryx Designer** option is selected, the option for application download will appear at the bottom of your browser. Select this download.
3. The open file dialog will appear. Select **Run**.

4. Two options will appear for the **Download Manager**. The first is the typical option that includes non-predictive tools. We will cover Predictive Analytics in this book, so we will select the second option, advanced.

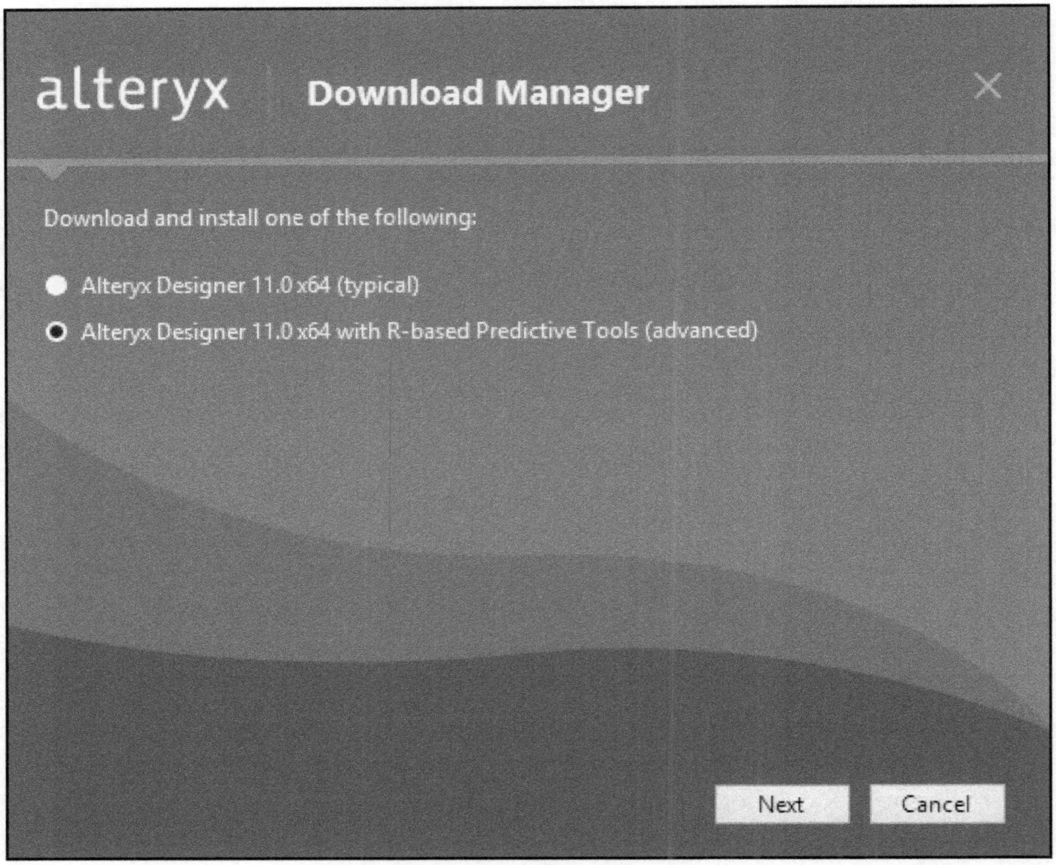

5. The **User Account Control** will prompt. Select **Yes** to begin the installation.

6. The **Install** dialog will appear where the Setup begins. The previous versions will be uninstalled. Select **Next** to install the pre-requisites.

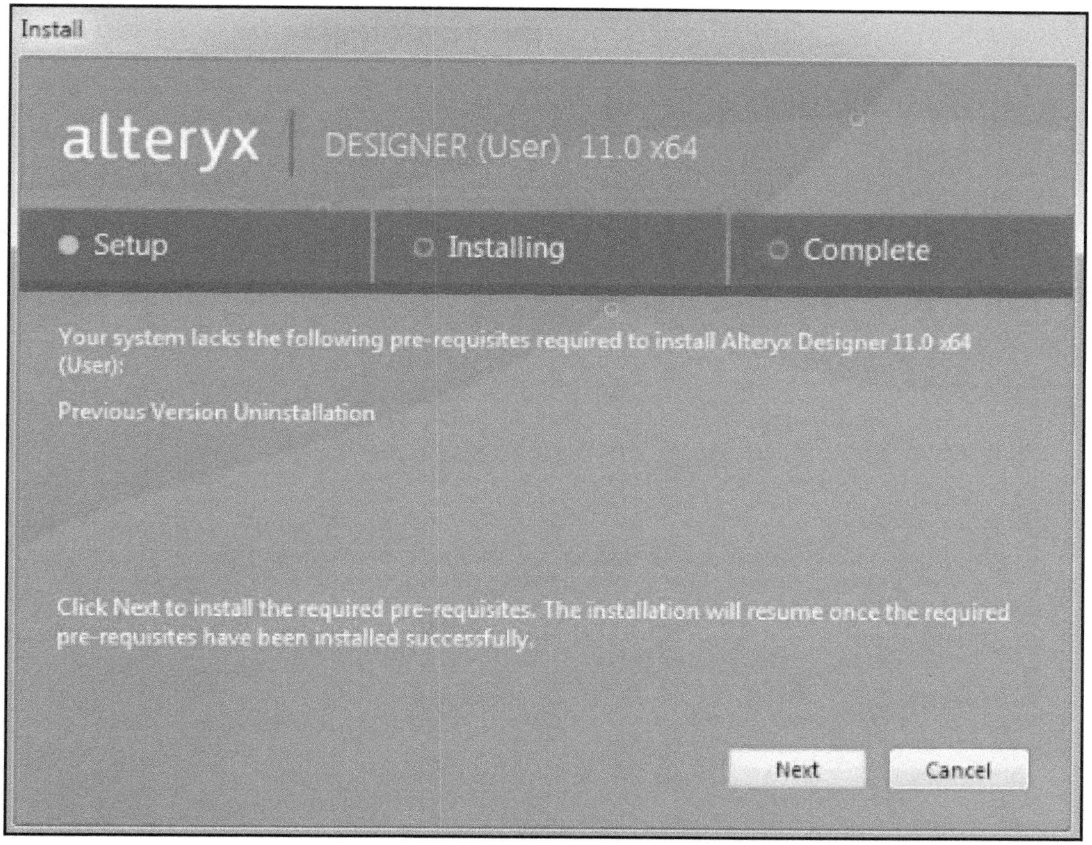

7. The installation process begins by selecting **Next** when necessary. Read and accept the license agreement and select **Next** to continue.

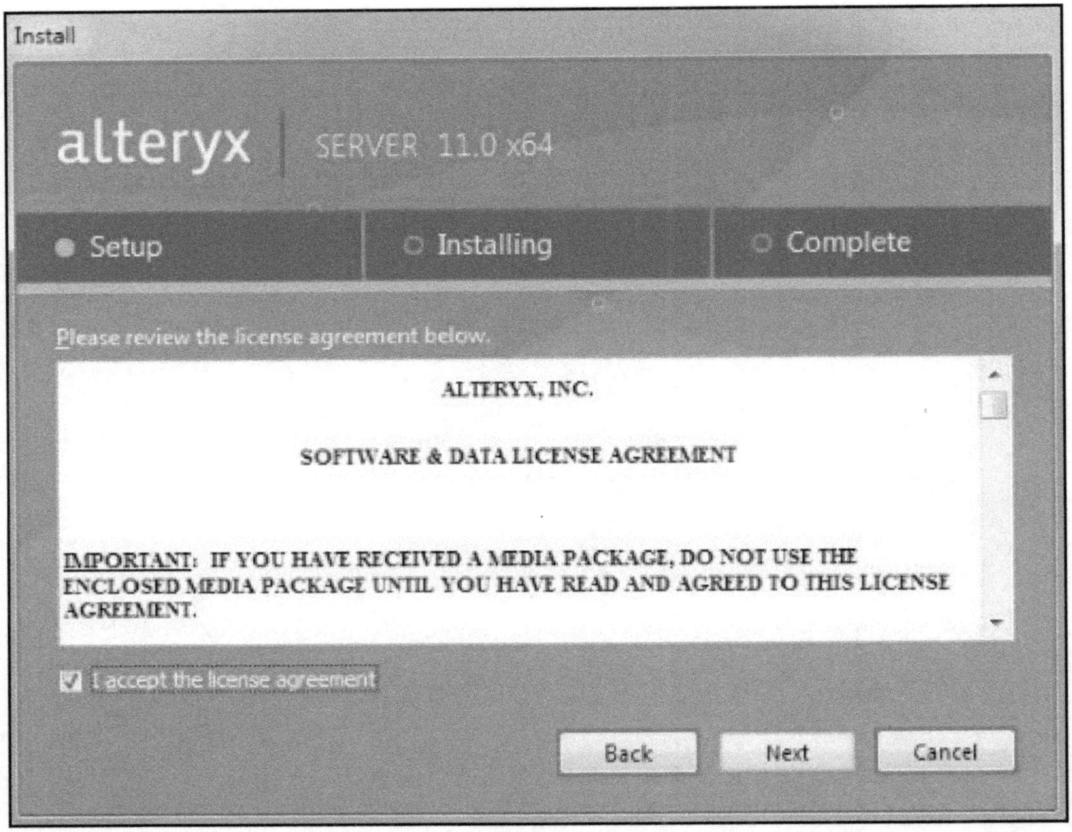

8. Select **Finish** to complete the installation.

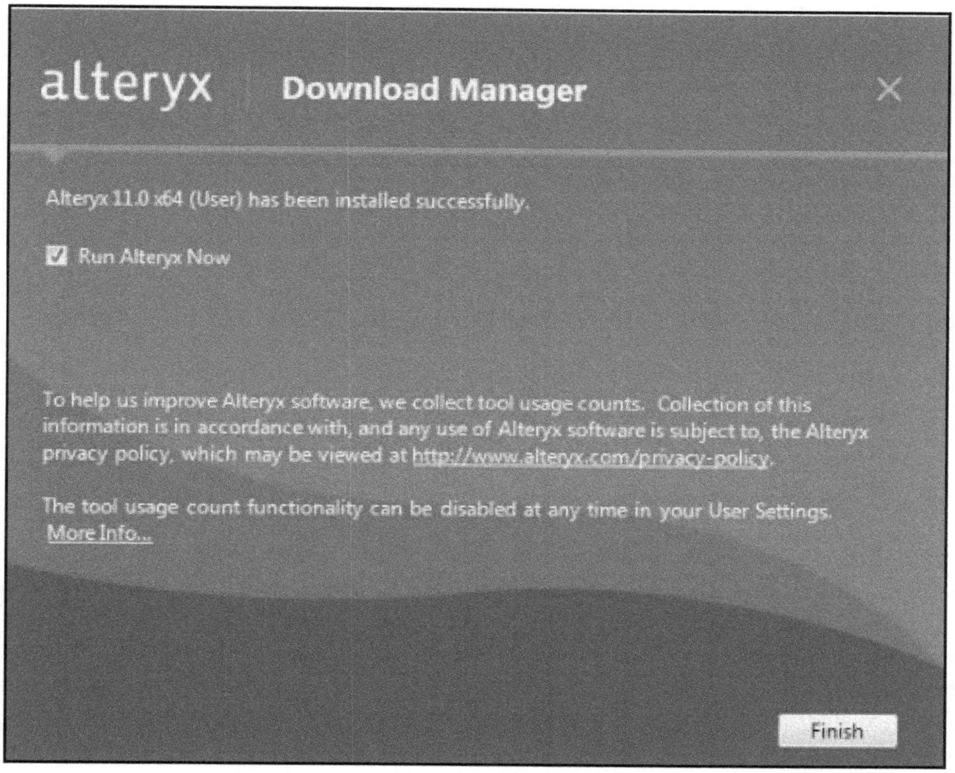

The Alteryx Designer architecture

The Alteryx Designer is an intuitive drag-and-drop user interface for users to drag tools from a Tool Palette onto the canvas. These tools can be used to create Alteryx workflows, macros, and applications. This allows the users to run workflows instantly to process data. Alteryx Designer processes workflows from a local instance of the Alteryx Engine and is written primarily in C#. Users may publish their workflows, macros, and applications to the Alteryx Analytics gallery, where others can download and run them. Workflows can be scheduled at fixed times or at recurring intervals through the Alteryx Server deployment. Alteryx Designer has a Scheduler interface located within it to execute scheduled workflows.

The Alteryx Engine, written in C++, runs a workflow and produces the output from a workflow built in Alteryx Designer. The Engine processes the data sources in-memory once the workflow is running. Processing will be written to temporary files on a disk and deleted once the processing is complete after surpasses memory limitations. We installed Alteryx by selecting the option to install the suite of R tools used for predictive analysis.

Alteryx installs the R tools, used for statistical computing and graphics, through the R program and provides a connection between the Alteryx Engine and the R Engine. This allows for the tools to function in the workflow. A command line is used by the Alteryx Engine to communicate with the R Engine.

The Alteryx Engine may execute the following tasks depending on the workflow:

- Read or write input/output files and one or more databases
- Process external runtime commands
- Send email to the email server through SMTP
- Upload or download data from the web

Let's dive a little deeper into the Alteryx Engine on how it gets deployed across multiple servers. The Alteryx Service, written in C++ and C# wrappers, allows the Alteryx Engine to deploy the execution of workflows, management, and scheduling. This is accomplished by using a Controller-Worker architecture. The server utilizes the Controller to manage the jobs scheduled to run and the Worker performs the work. The Alteryx application files and job queues are stored by the Alteryx Persistence tier to perform the operations of the Alteryx Service.

The **Alteryx Service Controller** is responsible for the delegation of work and management of the service settings to the Alteryx Service Workers. When jobs are received from the Scheduler, the Controller views them within the persistence layer, where all queued jobs are maintained, and then delegates the jobs to the workers. This is where **Alteryx Service Worker** comes into action, as the Worker runs the job and produces the output. The system performance determines how many Workers are needed to run the jobs.

The Controller's name or the IP address and the security token for that Controller must be specified for the Controller-Worker to communicate if the Worker is not the same machine as the Controller.

The Alteryx architecture process flow diagram begins from the drag-and-drop workflow tools to executing results through the Alteryx Engine:

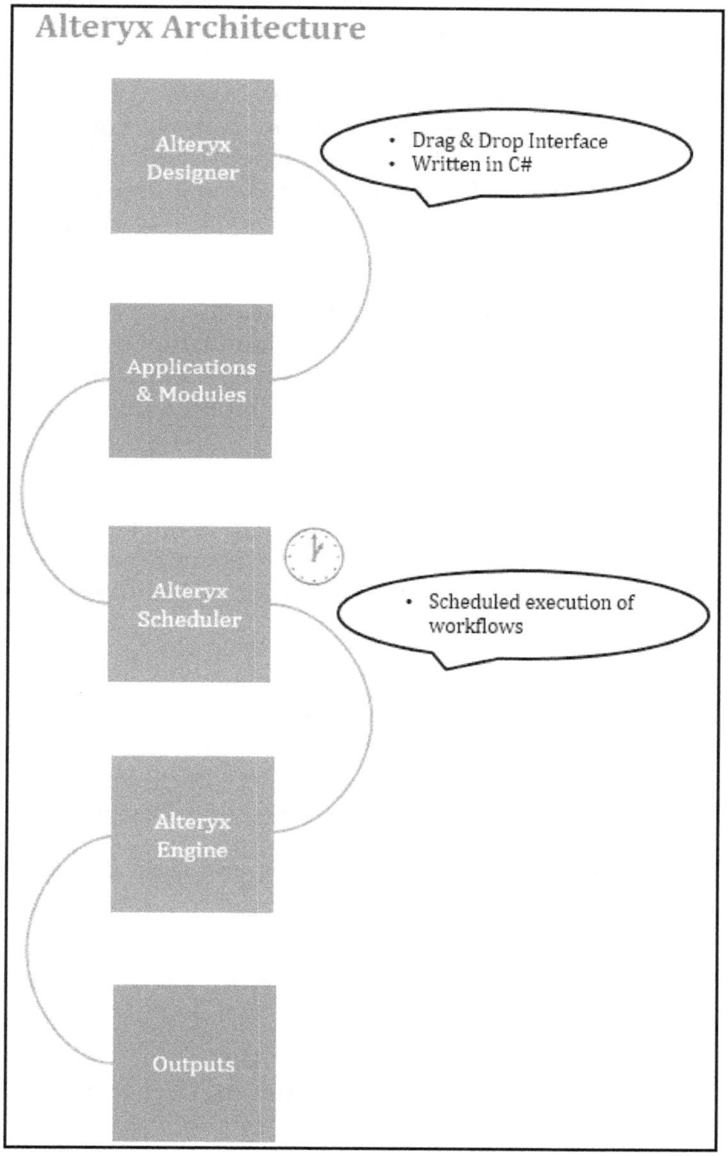

Introduction to Alteryx Designer

Alteryx provides the capability to quickly prepare and blend your data in a repeatable workflow, without the need for data science programming skills. The data acquisition is spreading rapidly across organizations with an opportunity to join millions of rows of data from multiple data sources. Traditional platforms, like Microsoft Excel, aren't designed to handle such volume of data. In addition, the drag-and-drop workflow offers the data cleansing techniques that take minutes to produce, whereas the traditional tools would take weeks to produce the same output. This traditional tools will slow down the turn-around time for an analyst to solve business problems, and in today's market, business leaders demand quicker deeper insights.

The **ETL** (**Extract, Transform, and Load**) blueprint that Alteryx provides is superior to tools like Excel, Access, and SQL. It gives the analysts the foundation to help the business move forward without time lags. Moreover, predictive analytic models built within Alteryx can be quickly expressed with visualization tools such as Tableau, Power BI, and QlikView.

The modern approach to business intelligence is in unlocking the power of data to meet strategic decision-making. The data models Alteryx generates are vital to producing a normalized data structure, as it's not about how much data can be processed but about how much data makes a meaningful impact. The executive layout reports can be easily created in Alteryx, all within the reporting Tool Palette, which we will thoroughly cover in `Chapter 7`, *Creating Data-Driven Custom Reports*.

Data can help you drive towards the objective view of how to seize opportunities and meet your data-driven goals. Meeting such goals is important for the mission of an organization. The data analysis possibilities are limitless when the focus is on core analytical outcomes. Now that we understand what Alteryx can produce, let's begin building a culture of self-service analytics by going through what's inside the Alteryx Designer.

The main menu includes the File, Edit, View, Options, and Help dropdowns.

Let's view the available Main Menu drop-down selections:

- **File**: New Workflow, Open Recent, Open Workflow, Open Autosaved Files, Save, Save As, Print, Print Settings, and Exit
- **Edit**: Undo, Redo, Cut, Copy, Paste, and Delete
- **View**: Toolbar, Tool Palette, Overview, Results, Configuration, Interface Designer, and Find Tool

- **Options**: Run Workflow, Schedule Workflow, View Schedules, Run Analytic Apps, Export Workflow, Activate License Key, Manage Licenses, User Settings, Advanced Options, and Download Predictive Tools
- **Help**: Alteryx Help, What's New, Getting Started, Sample Workflows, Community, Check for Updates, Alteryx Downloads, and About

The toolbar is where we can open a new or an existing workflow, save a workflow, copy, cut, paste, undo, redo, add a workflow to a schedule, zoom in, zoom out, and run a workflow.

All tools in Alteryx appear at the top within different tool palettes. They are divided into groups based on their function:

Once you open Alteryx Designer, you are presented with a blank canvas. This is where you build your process to transform and analyze your data with a set of tools:

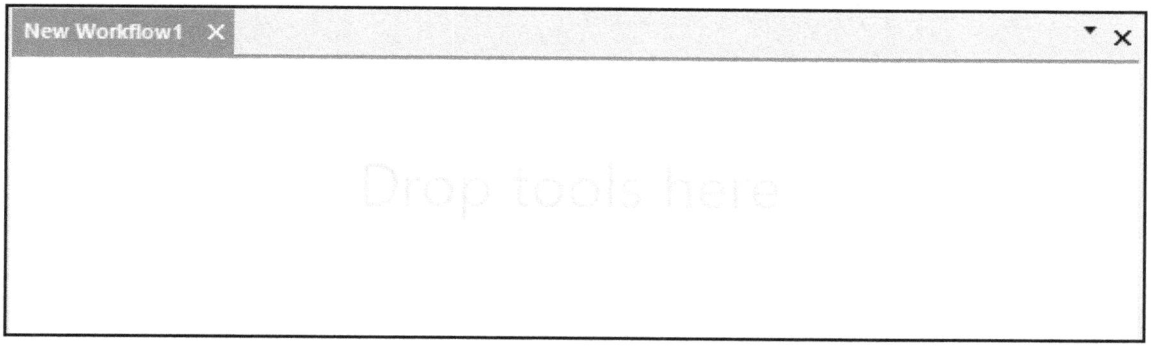

An overview of the workflow configurations

The **Canvas section** can be used to set the layout direction, either Horizontal or Vertical. We'll be using the horizontal layout throughout this book. Annotations drop down can be selected to Hide, Show, or Show w/ Tool Names.

The Connection Progress will show the downstream processing size and record count. This can be selected to Hide, Show, or Show Only When Running.

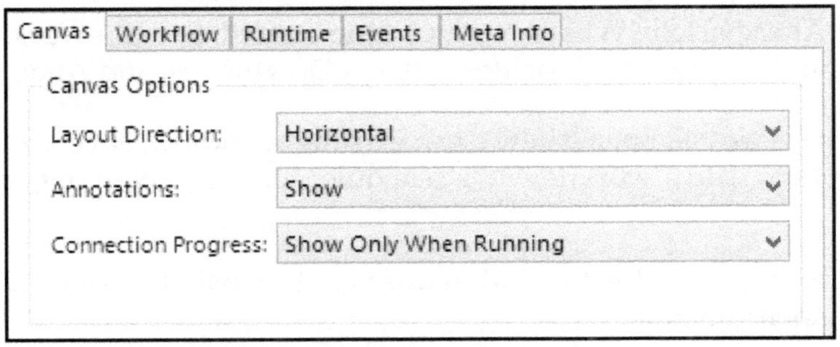

The **Workflow** section provides engine information and can be used to set the type of workflow: Standard, Analytic App, or Macro. We will cover more details on these types of workflows in the upcoming chapters.

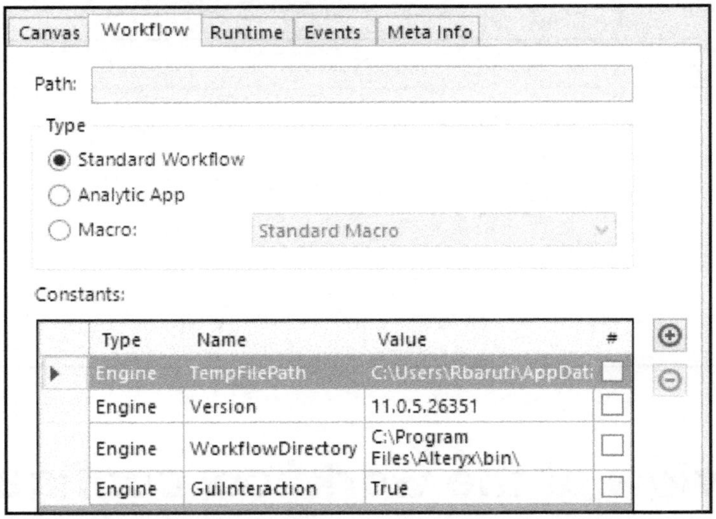

The **Runtime** section allows for memory usage settings, location of temporary files, limiting conversion errors, and different options that will help in creating an efficient workflow.

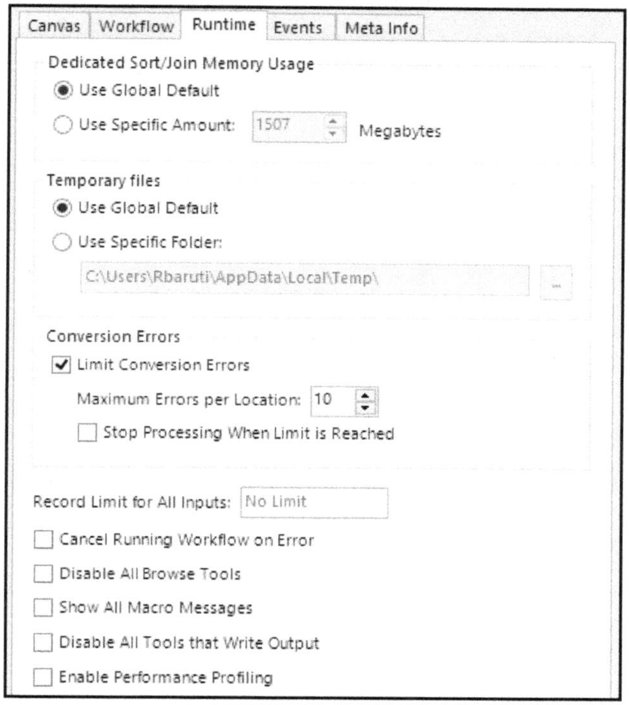

The **Events** section can be used for documenting events and sending notifications by email.

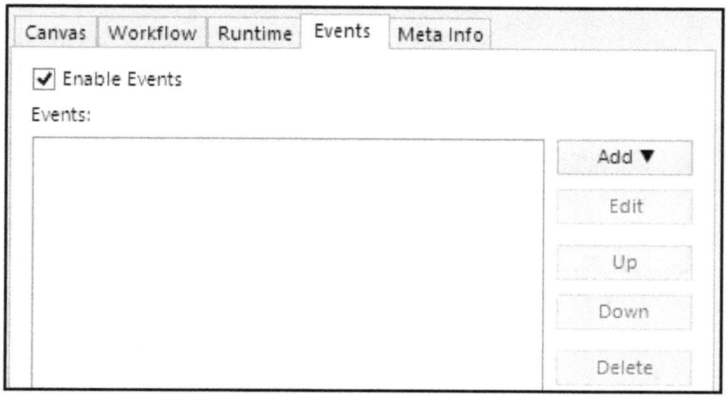

The **Meta Info** section allows setting custom demographics to your workflow.

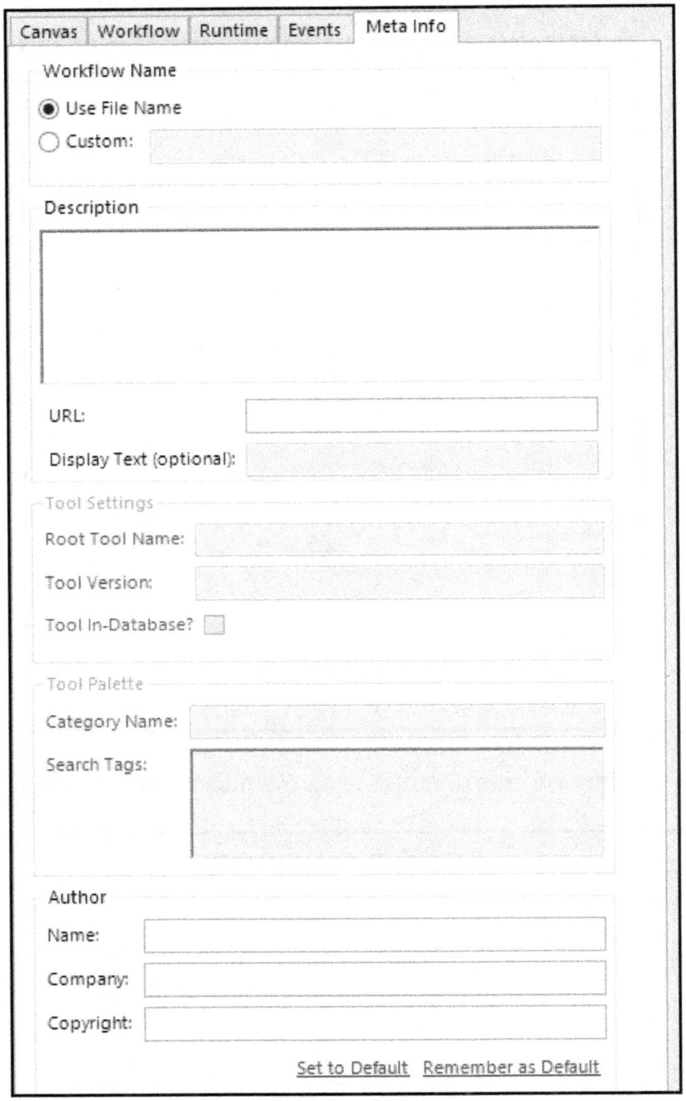

The following table lists the shortcuts that can be used to show and hide tools and navigate around the canvas.

The Undo and Redo and Copy and Paste shortcuts:

Undo and Redo, Copy and Paste	
Action	**Shortcut**
Undo	Ctrl + Z
Redo	Ctrl + Y
Copy	Ctrl + C
Cut	Ctrl + X
Paste	Ctrl + V
Move and Delete Tools	
Action	**Shortcut**
Move selected tool	Arrow key
Move selected tool by one	Ctrl + Arrow key
Delete selected tool	Delete
Scroll and Pan the Canvas	
Action	**Shortcut**
Scroll vertically	Scroll Function
Scroll horizontally	Shift + Scroll Function
Move up, down, left or right	Arrow Keys
Skip up, down, left or right	Shift + Arrow Keys
Jump to top or bottom	Home or End
Jump to left or right	Shift + Home or End
Pan	Space Bar + Left Click
Pan	Hold mouse center button

The Select and Align Tools shortcuts:

Select and Align Tools	
Action	**Shortcut**
Select all items	Ctrl + A
Deselect all selected items	Ctrl + D
Align tools vertically	Ctrl + Shift + +
Align tools horizontally	Ctrl + Shift + -
Zoom In and Out of the Workflow	
Action	**Shortcut**
Zoom in or out	Ctrl + + or -
Zoom to or from cursor	Ctrl + Scroll Function
Zoom to entire workflow	Ctrl + 0
Zoom to entire workflow	Double-click mouse center button
Jump to selection	Ctrl + 0
Jump in or out	Ctrl + 1 through 5
Zoom to area	Right-click & drag to select with

The Show and Hide Tools, Windows, Run, Open, Save, and Switch Workflows shortcuts:

Show and Hide Tools and Windows	
Action	**Shortcut**
Show Toolbar	Ctrl + Alt + B
Show Tool Palette	Ctrl + Alt + T
Show Overview	Ctrl + Alt + V
Show Results Window	Ctrl + Alt + R
Show Configuration	Ctrl + Alt + C
Reopen the Configuration	Double-click the canvas or any
Show the Interface	Ctrl + Alt + D
Show the Find Tool window	Ctrl + F
Run, Open, Save, and Switch Workflows	
Action	**Shortcut**
Run workflow; stop	Ctrl + R
Open workflow	Ctrl + O
Close active workflow	Ctrl + F4
Save workflow	Ctrl + S
New workflow	Ctrl + N
Move between active	Ctrl + Tab

Exploring the Tool Palettes

The tools are organized into tool categories called Tool Palettes. This is quite helpful when building a workflow, as viewing a category at a glance quickly facilitates suitable workflow development. For instance, to build a workflow that is focused primarily on data cleansing and renaming of fields, swiftly select the **Preparation Tool Palette** to use the applicable tools for the workflow. We'll explore more on these types of tools and how to best utilize them in `Chapter 3`, *Data Preparation and Blending*. In this section, our goal is to add and remove tool palettes and pin them, so you can easily access them, which will help streamline your workflow.

Let's see how to select the tool categories to view the tools available. Select the **Add/Remove Tools** icon  next to categories. The **Configure Tool Palette** window will appear, allowing you to:

- Select a configured **Preset** option
- Show/hide tool categories by selecting or deselecting various tool categories on the left side
- Select a Tool Palette on the left side, and then on the right side select/deselect tools to show/hide the tools

The following snapshot shows the Configure Tool Palette window:

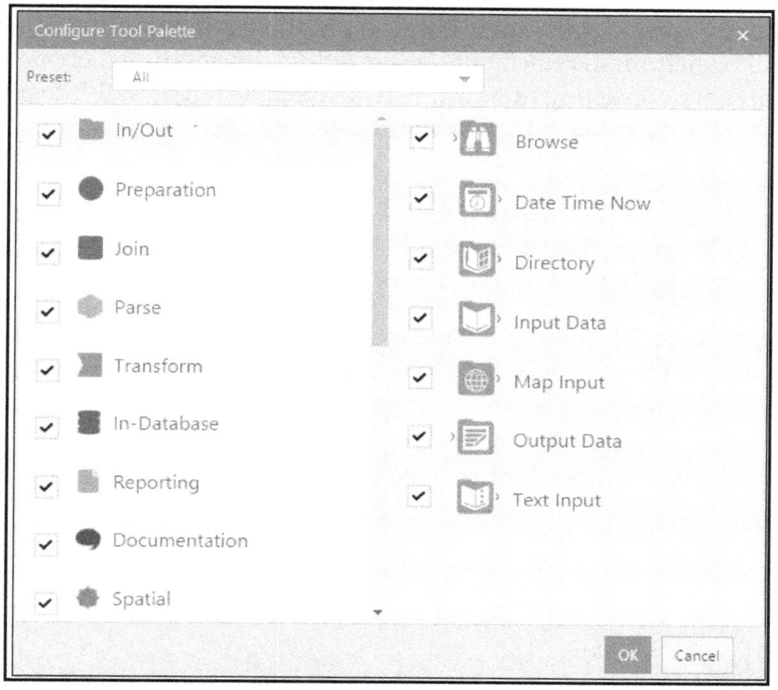

A tool category can be locked by right clicking on a tool palette and selecting **Pin** [Category]. In this case, the **Spatial** category will be pinned. The unlocked categories will remain to the right of the Favorites tool category, which by default is automatically pinned:

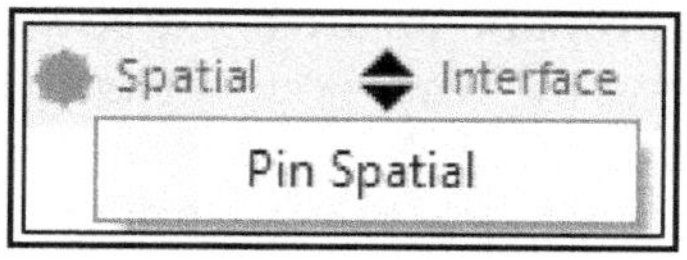

To unpin a tool category and return it to its original position, right click on the tool category and select **Unpin** [Category] or **Unpin All Groups**.

The Favorites tools

The most frequently used tools in a workflow are in the **Favorites** category. Assigning a tool as a favorite will be helpful in building your workflow. Furthermore, create your personal tool category consisting of multiple tools from different tool categories. Alteryx has preconfigured 13 tools under the **Favorites** category that are used most often by many users.

The **Favorites** tools consist of: Browse, Filter, Formula, Input, Join, Output, Sample, Select, Sort, Summarize, Comment, Text Input, and Union. It is vital to get used to using these tools, since they are widely used in workflows.

There are currently over 200 tools available in Alteryx, and becoming familiar with the Favorites tools will be the first building block to building an effective production workflow.

TIP

Add a tool to the Favorites category by selecting the gray star to the right of the tool icon. The yellow star indicates it's a Favorite tool.

Summary

The Alteryx drag-and-drop interface allows for a seamless repeatable workflow to rapidly process and analyze data. The chapter kicked off with installing Alteryx Designer to begin building a successful workflow. You've taken the first steps towards understanding how Alteryx works behind the scenes, through the architecture of the Alteryx Engine and Alteryx Service. These two key components are horsepower for data processing by managing and running jobs. Along the way, you learned the foundation of Alteryx Designer and its workflow configurations by understanding data preparation and data blending. This can be quickly processed within an analytic workflow to deliver insights in hours, not weeks. You also got acquainted with the Tool Palette, consisting of multiple tools grouped in categories, which can be added or removed based on the workflow design you set out to achieve. You also learned that having the Favorites tools will help you expedite your workflow development.

In the next chapter, we'll explore how to develop an efficient workflow by resource and design. You will learn the best practices around resource optimization, speed processing, and utilizing the performance profiling to identify potential gaps in efficiently processing data. We'll go through how to connect to data and what type of connections can be made, and get familiar with a variety of Alteryx file types. You will be prepared to develop optimal workflows and gain deeper insights within hours, not weeks.

2

Workflow Optimization

Alteryx processes hundreds of billions of rows. The workflow design is vital to ensuring that the workflow runs efficiently, allowing for optimum processing. This chapter focuses on the foundational workflow optimization concepts and applying runtime selections to speed execution. A multitude of essential selections can be made to enhance your workflow. You will learn how to apply resource optimization to process data faster. Furthermore, you'll discover how your workflow is performing by using performance profiling.

The topics we'll examine include:

- Resource optimization and speed processing
- Performance profiling
- Connecting to data
- Alteryx file types

The ability to optimize workflow will set the platform for a powerful data preparation and data blending venture that we will cover in the next chapter.

Resource optimization and speed processing

Resource optimization is important to allocate and eliminate resources that may prevent your workflows running at optimal speed. The Select, Filter, and Auto Field tools can be utilized to process records downstream in your workflows at a faster rate. Let's go through what factors may contribute to resource optimization and speed processing.

Resource optimization

Alteryx balances the memory, CPU use, and disk I/O to optimize its resources and run at peak levels. There are options we will review that can control resource utilization. This will help identify areas in your workflow where applying various settings could be very useful in processing data faster. The system, user, and workflow level are the three options to limit the amount of memory that is used. Let's look at the various settings.

The **Engine sort/join** memory setting focuses on the minimum allocated memory the engine will expend when operations such as sorts and joins are performed. Other tools forge ahead with long maximum times, using memory outside the sort/join domain.

Most users don't need to change the default sort/join memory settings, depending on resource expenditure within the workflow and resource location, where resources are driven from memory, CPU use, and disk I/O. Set your sort/join memory usage higher or lower depending on your workflow and computer usage. The sort memory derives from the sort tool and other tools to reorder your data. Any processes within your workflow that contain joins, such as utilizing the join tool and the join multiple tool, refer to the join memory. If your workflow contains in-depth sorting, then increase the memory usage, and if your workflow doesn't have intensive sorting, then decrease the memory usage.

TIP: A sort will run faster if it is run entirely in memory instead of using temp files; but if it must switch to using virtual memory, performance will decrease, which is why the setting should not be too high.

The system level settings for the global default sort/join memory usage option can be located at **Alteryx** | **Options** | **Advanced Options** | **System Settings** | **Engine** | **Default Sort/Join Memory Usage** (MB). The snapshot for the system settings screen is as follows:

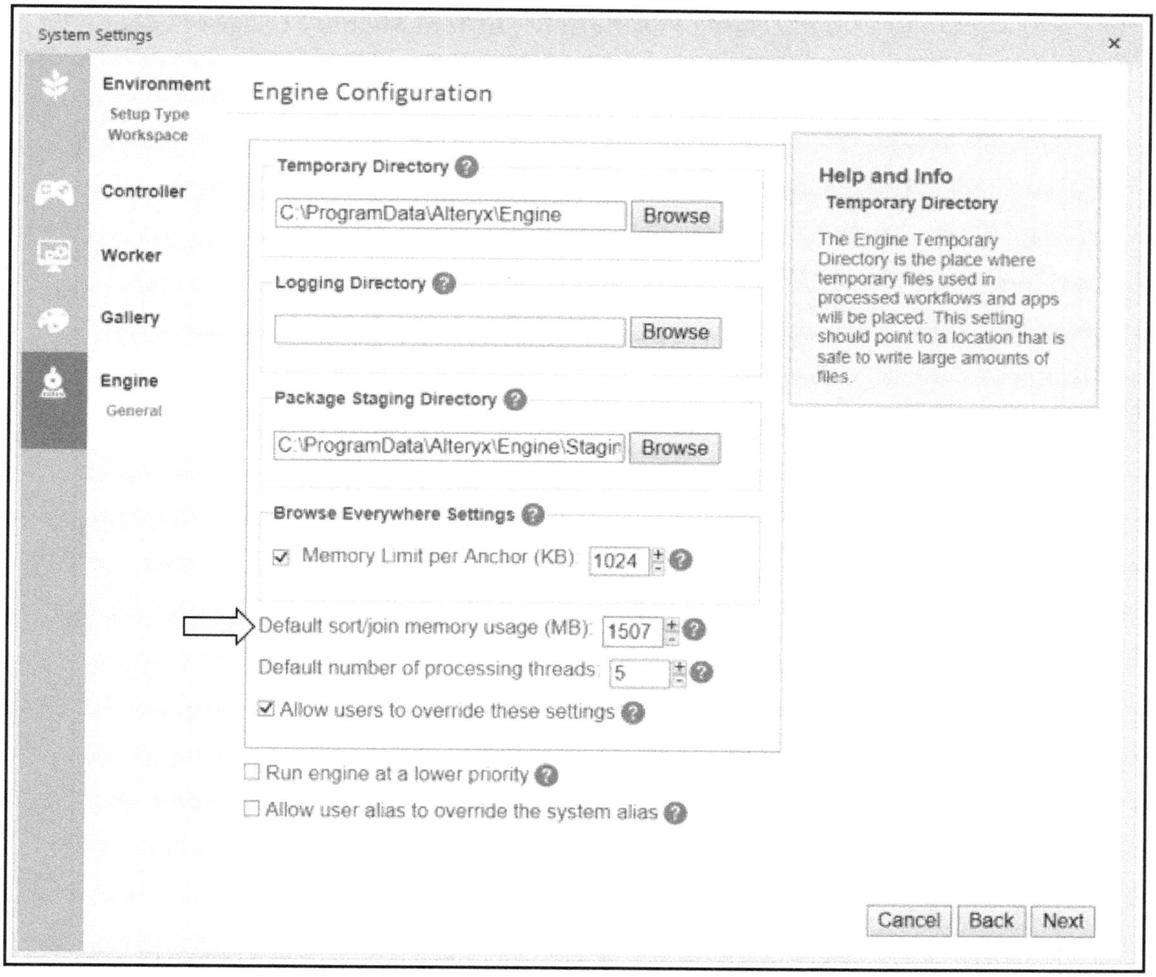

An alternative to edit the **Default Dedicated Sort/Join Memory Usage** can be found under the user settings once the option **Override System Settings** is selected in the **Engine** settings.

The user level settings for the **Default Dedicated Sort/Join Memory Usage** option can be found at the **Options** | **User Settings** | **Edit User Settings** | **Defaults** tab. The snapshot for the user settings screen is as follows:

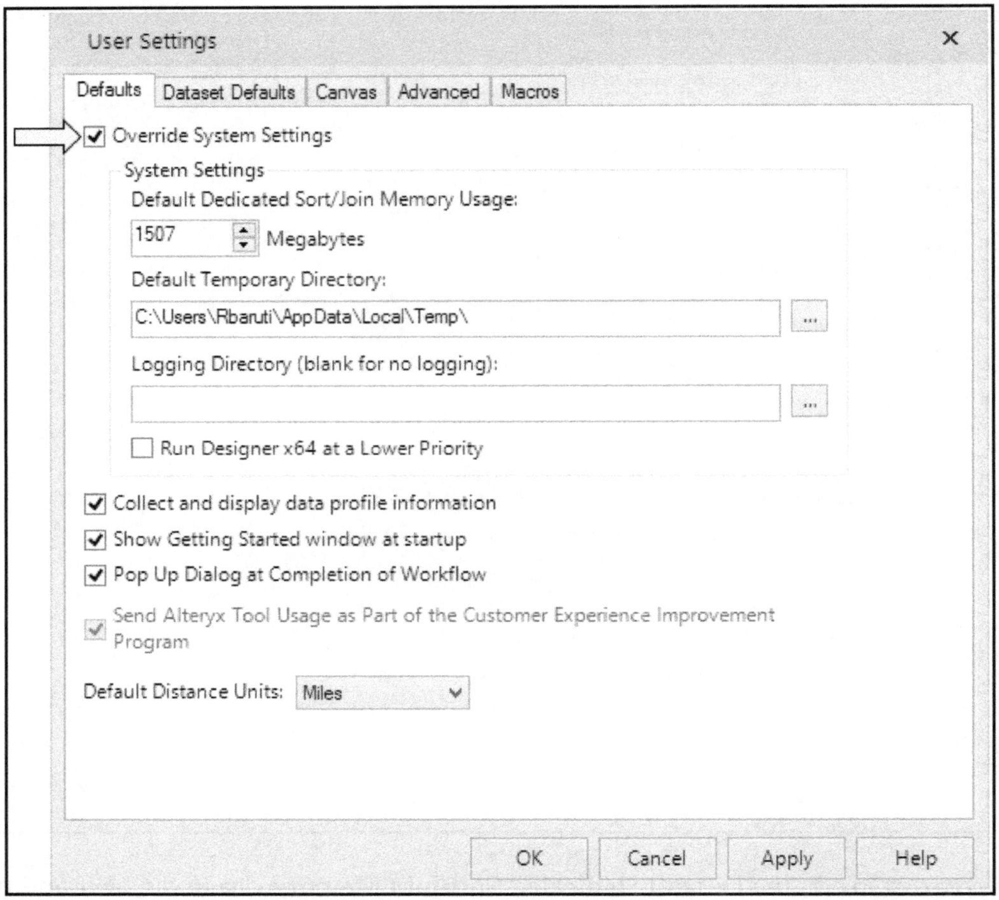

The last option to manage sort/join memory is at the workflow level. Navigate to **Workflow Configuration** | **Runtime** tab | **Dedicated Sort/Join Memory Usage** | **Use Specific Amount**. The following is the snapshot for managing the sort/join memory:

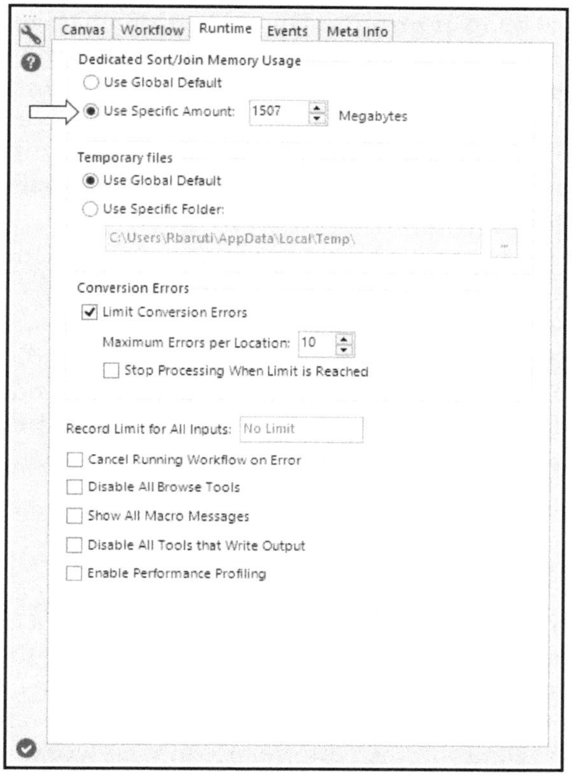

Resource optimization best practices

Resource optimization is a best practice that should be always kept in mind when running workflows. The following resource optimization topics will help your workflows run at optimal levels:

- **Shared servers**: For a shared server, the system owner/IT person should set the memory to no more than (total memory-2 GB)/(Number of Users). This way, if all the users are running workflows at the same time, the system won't go into virtual memory, which significantly slows things down.
- **Web servers**: Set the memory usage to the smallest possible setting without impacting the performance too much when running Alteryx on a web server. A system memory setting of 64 MB, increasing the memory on a per workflow basis as needed, is recommended. The web service typically runs as a separate system user, so the user setting for memory usually has no impact.

- **Run Alteryx at a lower priority**: This will ensure that the Alteryx Engine runs at a lower priority than all the other applications running on the same machine. By doing so, even the Alteryx GUI will remain responsive when you are running a large workflow in the background. This is an especially good idea for a shared server and recommended for a server hosting a gallery. The setting can be reached by navigating to **Alteryx** | **Options** | **Advanced Options** | **System Settings** | **Engine**.
- **Background processing**: It is best to run a workflow with less memory any time you are planning to run a workflow in the background while continuing to do other work.
- **Temporary Directory:** It is best to have the temporary directory point to a physical hard drive separate from your boot drive. If your temp drive points to `C:\temp` and you run a workflow that consumes hundreds of GB of temp space, your system may become unstable.

Speed processing

Speed processing is when tools are utilized to process records at a faster rate downstream. The tools covered in this section are to be used in certain areas of the workflow development to increase data processing speed. The **Select** tool is used to remove fields from your data. Some other tools, like Join, Join Multiple, Find Nearest, and Spatial Match, have select functionality. Optimize the performance of your workflow by removing fields that won't be utilized downstream for the output. Data removed upfront will process data more quickly downstream.

Another best practice to optimize workflow performance is to use the **Filter** tool to remove needless rows. The filter tool allows for two different data streams from the output: True and False. Limit your data whenever possible, as less data processed downstream will help speed up processing. For example, let's say we have healthcare data with **Emergency Department** (**ED**) visits by year and our data set starts from 2007. We are only interested in analyzing data from 2012 forward. Use the **Filter** tool to limit data downstream to 2012 forward from the True stream. We will focus more on the Filter tool and other preparation tools in `Chapter 3`, *Data Preparation and Blending*. The following snapshot illustrates only data for the Year 2012 will be processed downstream:

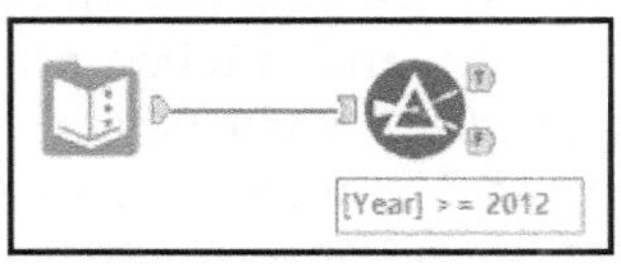

> **TIP**
> If you are reading large database inputs or bulk loading Excel/CSV files, it is in most cases best to write it to an Alteryx Database, data stored in a text file that can be saved with the file type `.yxdb` and continue to work with that Alteryx Database until the flow is done. This is also the case when using the download tool. Save the data locally and work from there.

The **Auto Field** tool sets the field type to the smallest possible size from all the records it reads through an input. It is a good rule of thumb to use the **Auto Field** tool right after your **Input Data** tool to assign the most efficient size and data type to your fields. String fields with large sizes can be a heavy burden when processing data downstream. They will carry the large field sizes with them and will slow down your workflow. The following is an example of sizes and data types before and after the **Auto Field** tool.

The following illustrates the metadata input before using the Auto Field tool. Notice, all fields are assigned the default V_String data type with a size of 254:

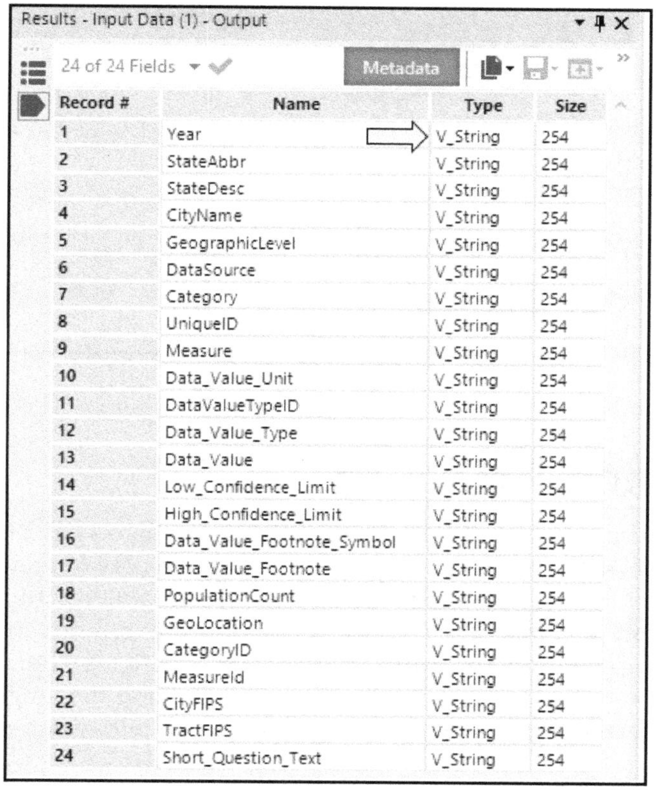

Record #	Name	Type	Size
1	Year	V_String	254
2	StateAbbr	V_String	254
3	StateDesc	V_String	254
4	CityName	V_String	254
5	GeographicLevel	V_String	254
6	DataSource	V_String	254
7	Category	V_String	254
8	UniqueID	V_String	254
9	Measure	V_String	254
10	Data_Value_Unit	V_String	254
11	DataValueTypeID	V_String	254
12	Data_Value_Type	V_String	254
13	Data_Value	V_String	254
14	Low_Confidence_Limit	V_String	254
15	High_Confidence_Limit	V_String	254
16	Data_Value_Footnote_Symbol	V_String	254
17	Data_Value_Footnote	V_String	254
18	PopulationCount	V_String	254
19	GeoLocation	V_String	254
20	CategoryID	V_String	254
21	MeasureId	V_String	254
22	CityFIPS	V_String	254
23	TractFIPS	V_String	254
24	Short_Question_Text	V_String	254

The following illustrates the metadata output after using the Auto Field tool. Notice, fields are now assigned the most efficient sizes and data types:

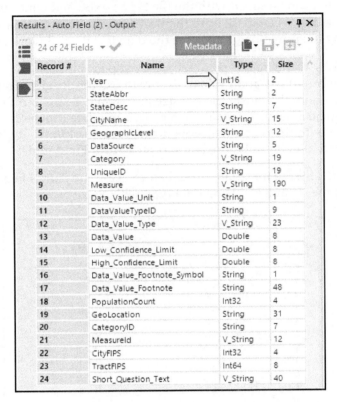

Results - Auto Field (2) - Output

24 of 24 Fields   Metadata

Record #	Name	Type	Size
1	Year	Int16	2
2	StateAbbr	String	2
3	StateDesc	String	7
4	CityName	V_String	15
5	GeographicLevel	String	12
6	DataSource	String	5
7	Category	V_String	19
8	UniqueID	String	19
9	Measure	V_String	190
10	Data_Value_Unit	String	1
11	DataValueTypeID	String	9
12	Data_Value_Type	V_String	23
13	Data_Value	Double	8
14	Low_Confidence_Limit	Double	8
15	High_Confidence_Limit	Double	8
16	Data_Value_Footnote_Symbol	String	1
17	Data_Value_Footnote	String	48
18	PopulationCount	Int32	4
19	GeoLocation	String	31
20	CategoryID	String	7
21	MeasureId	V_String	12
22	CityFIPS	Int32	4
23	TractFIPS	Int64	8
24	Short_Question_Text	V_String	40

Performance Profiling

Performance Profiling is an investigation technique focusing on which tools take the longest time to process. The tools and their runtimes are displayed in a descending order, found in your output log. Review the output log to identify where processing is degraded in your workflow and then improve your workflow to make it more efficient. Although the output takes resources and inhibits processing, it is not enabled by default. It should be enabled only when necessary, to determine what tool is taking the longest to process and also the difference between running the same workflow on two different computers.

The Performance Profiling can be found under **Workflow Configuration** | **Runtime** | **Enable Performance Profiling**:

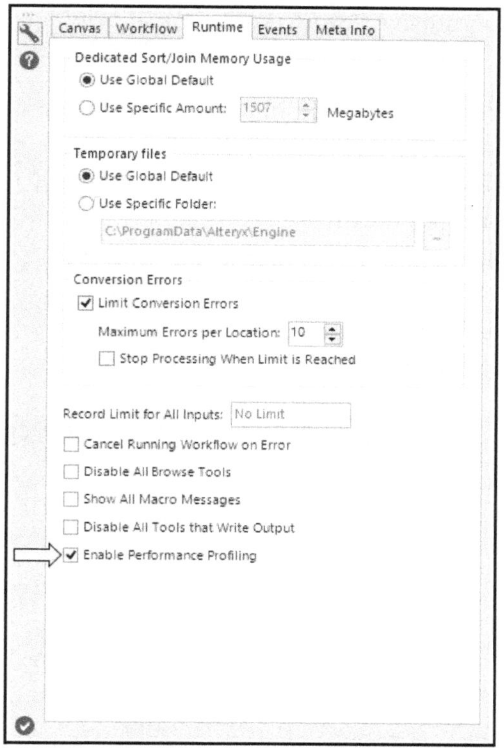

Connecting to data

The first step to bring data into Alteryx is connecting to it. There are four connection options we will review that will prepare you to connect to a variety of files and databases. These include the following tools, **Input Data**, **Text Input**, **Map Input**, and **Connect In-DB** as shown in the following image:

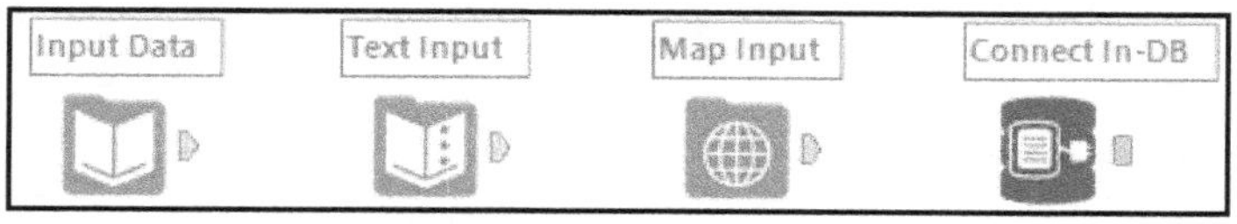

Input Data

The **Input Data** tool can be found under the In/Out tool palette. Connect to a file or database to bring data into your workflow. Let's look at how we can connect to a file by configuring the tool:

1. Open Alteryx. You should see a blank canvas with the tool palettes at the top and the workflow configuration on the left.
2. Drag the **Input Data** tool from the In/Out tool palette onto the canvas.
3. In the Configuration window, select a file.
4. In the **Open** dialogue box, navigate to the `\Learn Alteryx\Chapter 02\` directory and select the `Florida Local Data for Better Health.csv` file.
5. You will now see that you are connected to the file, with the Options and Preview sections populated as shown in the following image:

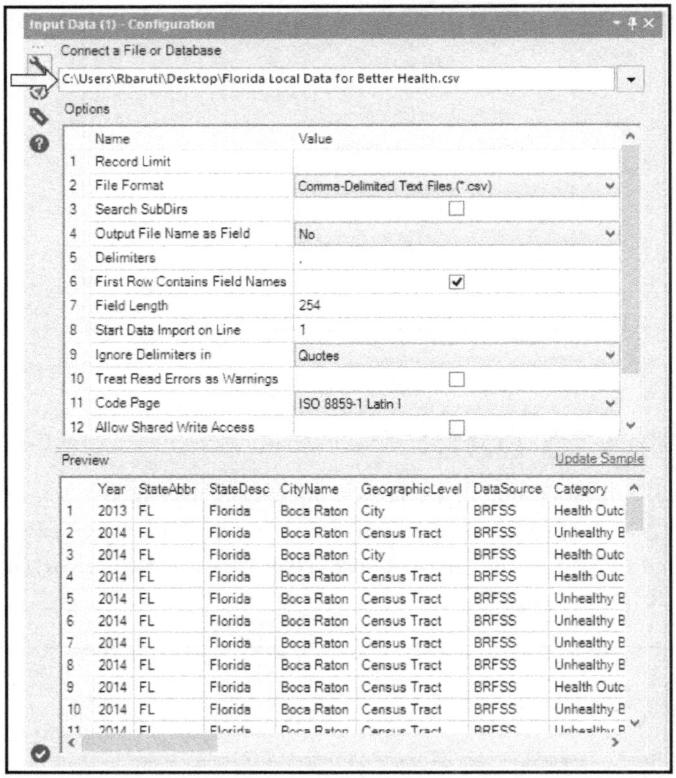

> **TIP**
> Select **Update Sample** in the **Configuration** window once you update a file, rather than reconnecting to the file through the **Input Data** tool.

Text Input

The **Text Input** tool can also be found in the In/Out tool palette. The main function of the **Text Input** tool is to manually add data by inserting columns and rows to make a user-specified data file. This is a great tool for creating lookup tables that you can join with another data file. Workflows shared with other users will contain the **Text Input**, as the inputted data will be saved with the workflow.

To configure the **Text Input** tool, click on cells to manually add data. **Field Names** can be created and renamed by typing in the header box. There is a variety of options when configuring the Text Input tool. These options include:

1. **Import**: Browse to an existing data file. The user can then manually add columns or rows of data.
2. **Copy**: Copies selected values onto the clipboard.
3. **Paste**: Pastes from the clipboard into a cell.
4. **Delete**:
    - **All**: Deletes all the data in the grid.
    - **Rows**: Deletes the selected, highlighted row(s).
    - **Column**: Deletes the selected, highlighted column(s).
5. **Insert**: Row or column insertion.

The following image shows the available options when configuring the Text Input tool:

Map Input

The **Map Input** tool provides the capability to draw or select a map object to bring into a workflow. You can draw or select a line, point, or polygon from the map that is displayed as a reference base map, such as **TomTom**. **Draw Mode** and **Select Mode** are the two options for configuring the Map Input tool:

- **Draw Mode**: Draw points, lines, or polygons on the map. A reference file containing spatial objects can be viewed and noted with a label. The label and the spatial object data will pass downstream.
- **Select Mode**: The reference layer allows for selecting points and polygons. Any point and polygon can be used as the input for the workflow as shown in the following image:

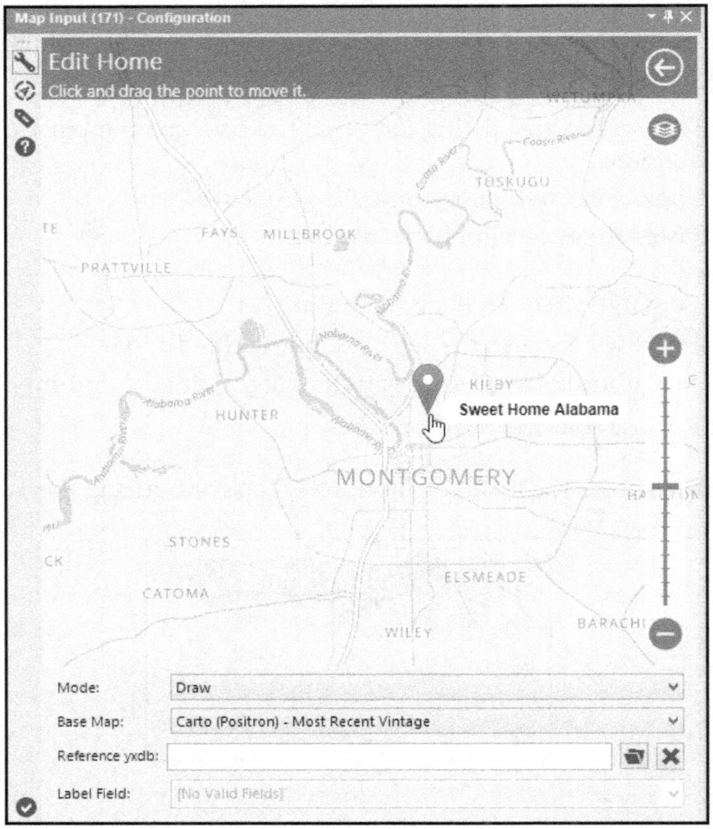

The **Base Map** display has reference layers to include within the map image. These can be selected from the drop-down list, which includes currently installed layer sets and map files. Spatial objects can be displayed on the map with an existing Alteryx Database yxdb file by selecting the file from the **Reference yxdb** option. This will provide an automatic zoom to the degree of the layer. The user can draw their own objects or pass them through the tool. You can select a field to display on the map through the **Label Field** drop-down from the **Reference yxdb**.

Connect In-DB

Alteryx can create an in-database connection in a workflow through the **Connect In-DB** tool. Use the tool to establish a new or existing connection. It is best practice to use the **Connect In-DB** tool if you are working with large data sets to analyze and blend your data. The heavy work to process data is on the database and not in the memory.

TIP

If you are bringing in bulk loading flat files or large database inputs, write it to an Alteryx Database `.yxdb` and continue to work with that Alteryx Database within your workflow. You will notice significant performance improvements, as data will be saved locally. This performance tip can also be used for the download tool.

Let's go through on how to setup a database connection.

1. Click the **Connection Name** drop-down arrow in the **Configuration** window and select an option:
    - **Manage Connections**: Create a new connection or use an existing connection
    - **Open File Connection**: Browse to a saved database connection file
2. The Table or Query displays the name of the selected database table once the connection is made.
3. Click **Query Builder** to select tables and develop queries. This is optional; however, it is recommended if you want to bring in only a select number of fields within your workflow. For instance, if a database table has 30 fields and you are only interested in 10 fields, then constructing a query to bring in only those 10 fields is optimal. As we reviewed earlier, unnecessary fields only degrade performance.

The following image shows the options available under the Connection Name drop-down:

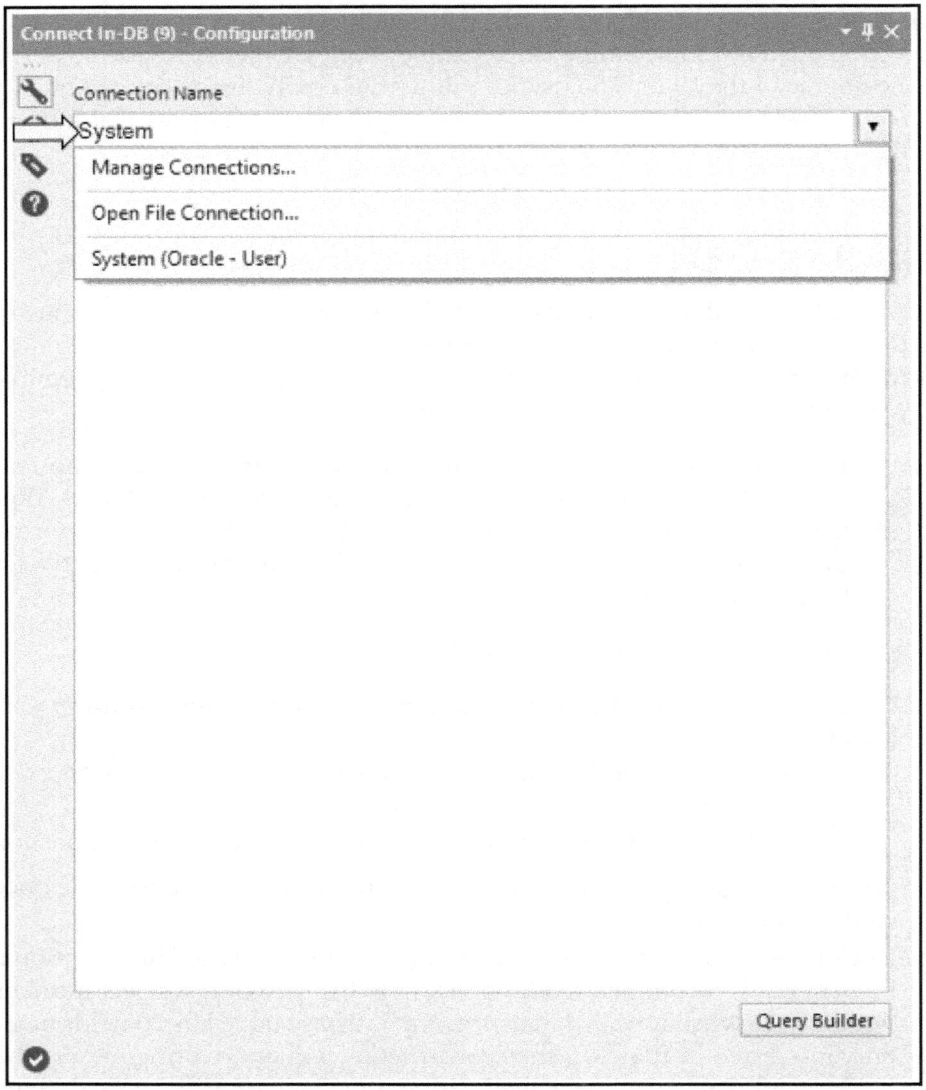

Alteryx file types

Alteryx connects to a variety of files and databases. This includes flat files, such as text files and Excel; relational databases, such as Oracle and SQL Server; and cloud-based data sources, such as Google Big Query. The following image shows the file types that Alteryx connects to:

File Types	
Alteryx Database	.yxdb
Alteryx Calgary	.cydb
Alteryx Spatial Zip	.sz
Apache Hadoop Avro	.avro
ASCII Flat	.flat
Autodesk	.sdf
Comma Separated Values	.csv
dBase	.dbf
ESRI GeoDatabase	.gdb
ESRI Personal GeoDatabase	.mdb
ESRI Shapefile	.shp
GIS	.grc, .grd
Google Earth/Maps	.kml
IBM SPSS	.sav
JSON	.json
MapInfo Professional Interchange	.mid, .mif
MapInfo Professional Table	.tab
Microsoft Access 2000-2003	.mdb
Microsoft Excel 1997-2003	.xls
Microsoft Excel 2007, 2010, 2013, 2016	.xlsx
Microsoft Excel Macro Enabled	.xlsm
Microsoft Office Access 2007, 2010, 2013, 2016	.accdb
OpenGIS	.mgl
QlikView	.qvx
SAS	.sas7bdat
SQLite	.sqlite
SRC Geography	.geo
Text	.txt, .asc
XML	.xml
Zip Files	.zip

The following image shows the databases that Alteryx connects to:

Databases	
Amazon	Amazon Aurora
	Amazon Redshift
Apache Hadoop	Cassandra
	Hadoop Distrubted File System (HDFS)
	Hadoop Hive
	Spark
Cloudera	Impala
	Hadoop Distributed File System (HDFS)
	Hadoop Hive
Databricks	Databricks
DataStax	DataStax Enterprise, DataStax Community
Exasolution	EXASOL
Google	Google BigQuery
Hortonworks	Hadoop Distrubted File System (HDFS)
	Hadoop Hive
HP	Vertica
IBM	IBM DB2
	IBM Netezza/Pure Data Systems
MapR	Hadoop Distrubted FIle System (HDFS)
	Hadoop Hive
Microsoft	Microsoft Azure SQL Data Warehouse
	Microsoft SQL Server 2009, 2012, 2014, 2016
MySQL	MySQL
Netsuite	Netsuite Suite Analytics
Oracle	Oracle
Pivotal	Pivotal Greenplum
PostgreSQL	PostgreSQL
SAP	SAP Hana
	Sybase Adaptive Server Enterprise
	Sybase SQL Anywhere 10
Teradata	Teradata
	Teradata Aster

Summary

Optimizing your workflow is a key component of building your workflow. There will be workflows with not so many tools utilized, and some with an infinite number of tools to analyze your data. In both cases, opportunities will arise where resource optimization will come in handy by adjusting the system, user, or workflow level memory to either increase or decrease the amount of memory used. We learned about processing data faster by using the Select tool to limit the number of fields and the Filter tool to limit the number of rows. We also looked at using the **Auto Field** tool to automatically assign the lowest possible size and type to your data. Keep in mind that any data that is irrelevant to your analysis will inhibit speed processing. If everything we saw is applied and performance is still not at the optimal level, then enable Performance Profiling to determine which tools or computer may be slowing performance.

You can connect to data in Alteryx through the **Input Data**, **Text Input**, **Map Input**, and **Connect-In DB** tools. Whether you are connecting to an existing file, manually creating a data file or spatial file, or connecting to a database table, these tools are widely used to kick-start workflow. You are now prepared to connect to a bundle of file types and databases, and Alteryx makes it accessible to construct a workflow from a magnitude of data sources. The next chapter you will learn about data preparation and data blending to slice and dice your data to provide meaningful insights. You will also dive into creating efficient workflows that will guide you to self-service analytics.

3
Data Preparation and Blending

The processes of data preparation, blending, and joining are the most powerful capabilities of Alteryx. Data analysts have found themselves struggling to get the best results from their data using Microsoft Excel or other legacy tools. With Alteryx, you'll embark on a journey of self-service data analytics, and build quick and reliable datasets for business decision-making. In this chapter, you will prep and cleanse data from spreadsheets, cloud applications, and other sources. This will be the foundation for an analytic dataset.

The journey will continue in this chapter; you'll tailor data to your needs by filtering and combining data with other sources and joining them together. This chapter will cover the following topics:

- Data preparation
- Data cleansing
- Filtering
- Join and union

Data preparation

The ability to retrieve an analytic dataset and turn it into actionable insights all begins with preparing the data to meet customer intelligence. A repeatable workflow to ensure errors are eliminated and automation is fully controlled will enrich data quality, all through drag-and-drop tools. These streamlined data preparation methods are the building blocks for analyzing future outcomes with predictive analytics. It all begins with data preparation. In this section, we will use the Florida Local Data for Better Health workflow, along with the resources located in the data folder. Let's begin by building a workflow with some of the most common data preparation tools within Alteryx:

Step 1: Using the **Input Data** tool, connect to the `Florida Local Data for Better Health.csv` file located in the `\Learn Alteryx\Chapter` directory. The following image is the same file you connected to in `Chapter 2`, *Workflow Optimization*.

Step 2: Select the **Auto Field** tool from the Preparation tool palette and drag it onto the canvas. Connect the **Auto Field** tool to the Input Data tool:

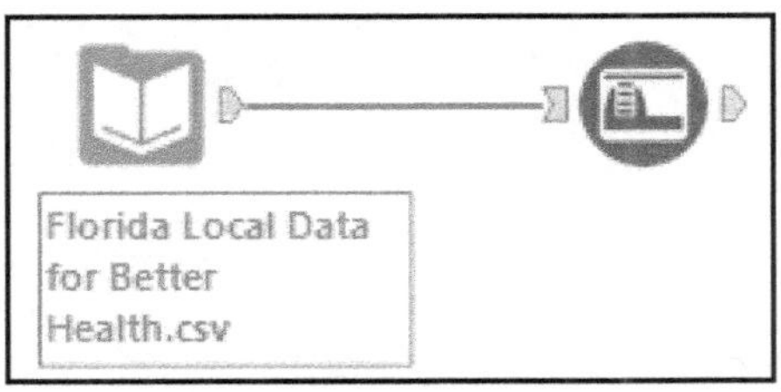

The **Auto field** tool will automatically assign each string field to the smallest field type and size. Let's look at the metadata before and after using the **Auto Field** tool.

Before using the **Auto Field** tool:

Record #	Name	Type	Size
1	Year	V_String	254
2	StateAbbr	V_String	254
3	StateDesc	V_String	254
4	CityName	V_String	254
5	GeographicLevel	V_String	254
6	DataSource	V_String	254
7	Category	V_String	254
8	UniqueID	V_String	254
9	Measure	V_String	254
10	Data_Value_Unit	V_String	254
11	DataValueTypeID	V_String	254
12	Data_Value_Type	V_String	254
13	Data_Value	V_String	254
14	Low_Confidence_Limit	V_String	254
15	High_Confidence_Limit	V_String	254
16	Data_Value_Footnote_Symbol	V_String	254
17	Data_Value_Footnote	V_String	254
18	PopulationCount	V_String	254
19	GeoLocation	V_String	254
20	CategoryID	V_String	254
21	MeasureId	V_String	254
22	CityFIPS	V_String	254
23	TractFIPS	V_String	254
24	Short_Question_Text	V_String	254

After using the **Auto Field** tool:

Record #	Name	Type	Size
1	Year	Int16	2
2	StateAbbr	String	2
3	StateDesc	String	7
4	CityName	V_String	15
5	GeographicLevel	String	12
6	DataSource	String	5
7	Category	V_String	19
8	UniqueID	String	19
9	Measure	V_String	190
10	Data_Value_Unit	String	1
11	DataValueTypeID	String	9
12	Data_Value_Type	V_String	23
13	Data_Value	Double	8
14	Low_Confidence_Limit	Double	8
15	High_Confidence_Limit	Double	8
16	Data_Value_Footnote_Symbol	String	1
17	Data_Value_Footnote	String	48
18	PopulationCount	Int32	4
19	GeoLocation	String	31
20	CategoryID	String	7
21	MeasureId	V_String	12
22	CityFIPS	Int32	4
23	TractFIPS	Int64	8
24	Short_Question_Text	V_String	40

You will notice the file size has decreased significantly in all fields after using the **Auto Field** tool, and furthermore the data types have been assigned to what will accommodate the data in each field.

TIP: The **Auto Field** tool will optimize performance by reducing file size. Use this tool often, especially when working with very large datasets, as millions of records can run faster when the file size is reduced substantially.

Next, we'll review the Random % Sample tool to get a sample of our data. Randomization is a gold standard for eliminating individual testimony in data research. Ever watch an infomercial claiming, I got ripped abs in 30 days from this new ab roller? This individual testimony is not evidence it works for most people; it could work for the guy in the infomercial, but what about others? Taking a random sample of the data would give us more confidence as to whether the new ab roller does do the trick or not. Another example is healthcare survey data: a random sample of patient satisfaction scores will provide a better focus on improvement areas than taking one individual survey.

Step 3: Select the Random % Sample tool from the Preparation tool palette and drag it onto the canvas. Connect the Random % Sample tool to the Auto Field tool:

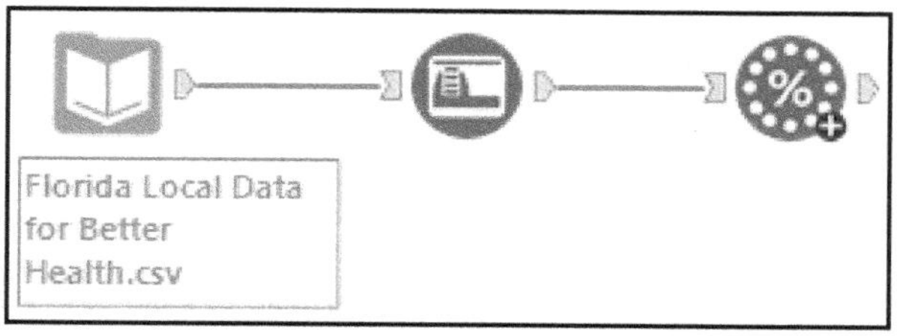

There are three configuration options contained in the Random % Sample tool. Let's look at these options and their benefits when attempting a random sample:

- **Random N Records**: A random number of records specified will be returned
- **Random N% of Records**: A random percentage specified will be returned
- **Deterministic Output**: A random seed is specified and will return the same set of random results

Let's select the Random N% of Records option in the configuration and enter **10** for Percent of Records. We'll analyze a random 10% of records. This is a good sample size for reviewing data from multiple cities in Florida.

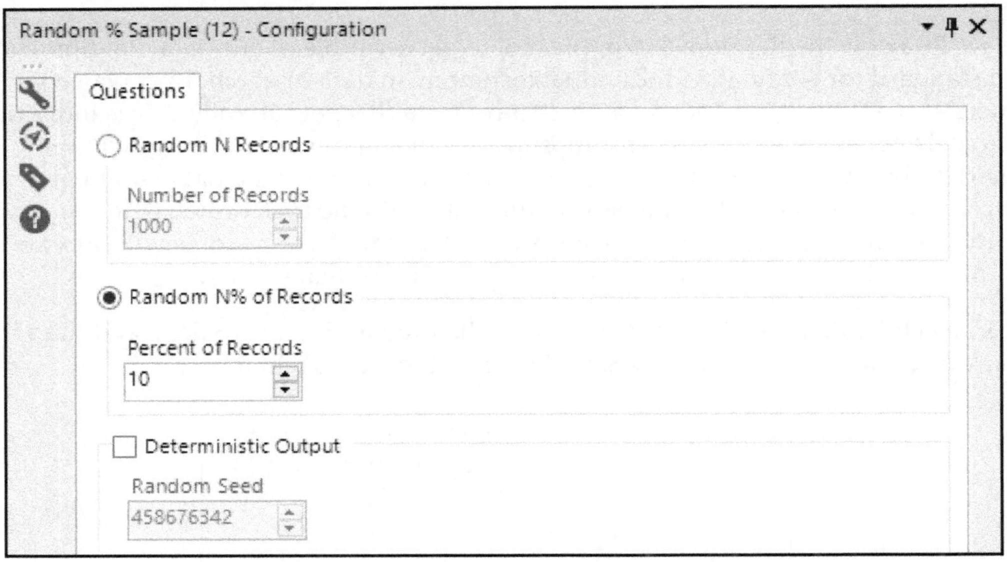

Step 4: Select the Unique tool from the Preparation tool palette and drag it onto the canvas. Connect the Unique tool to the Random % Sample tool:

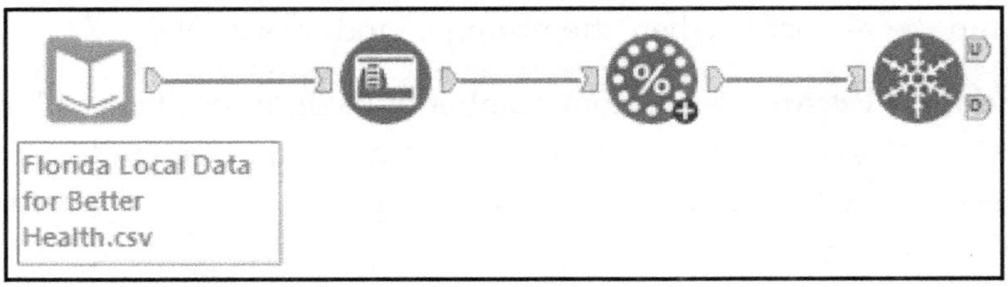

The Unique tool is used to separate data from unique and duplicate records. This is helpful for determining distinct records and when we only want to analyze these records downstream. Let's review the two output streams U and D from the Unique tool:

- **U**: U stands for Unique and contains the first rows that have a unique set of values for the fields selected
- **D**: D stands for Duplicate and contains matching values from the U output

In this instance, the goal is to analyze all records by category that come through the Random % Sample tool, only obtain the first row of the unique records and remove any duplicates. In the configuration settings, under Unique Fields, select only the `UniqueID` field and run the workflow. You will notice for `CityName = Clearwater` there are 35 unique records. This only supplies the records that come through the Random % Sample tool just once for `Clearwater` regardless of Category. We want to review all records by category, only get the first row of the set of unique values, and remove the other rows if the same category exists per record. In order to accomplish this, multiple unique groupings will need to be selected. Let's select the `Category` and `UniqueID` fields and run the workflow. Notice there are now 74 unique records in the U output stream. What this is telling us is that there are unique records per category and if they are repeated for the same category they come through the D output stream:

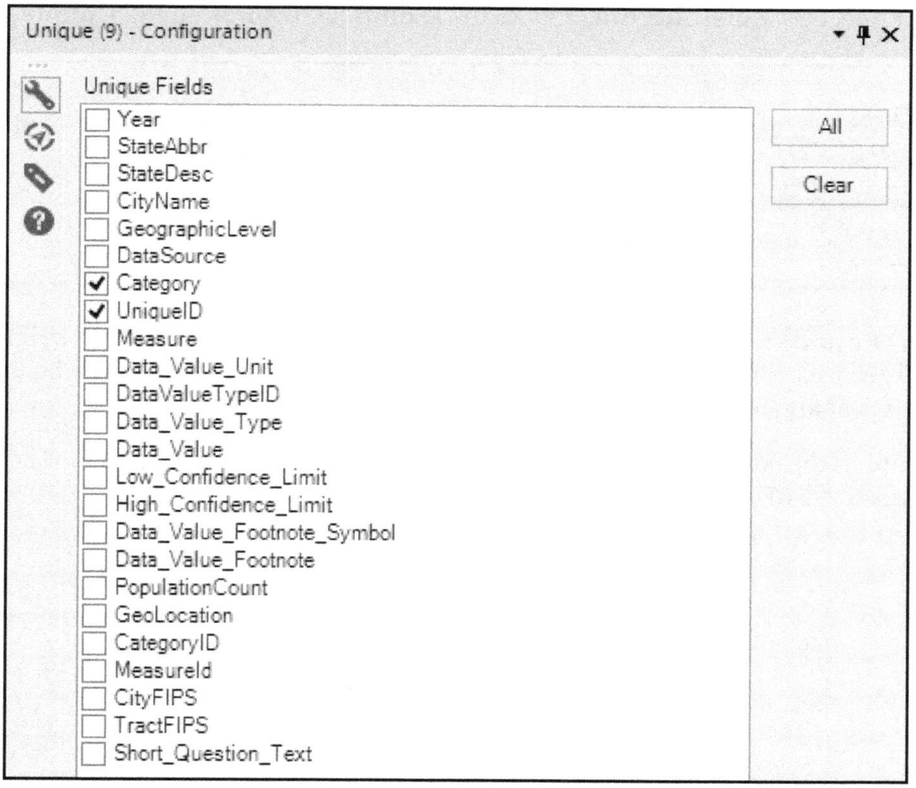

`UniqueID 1212875` is an example of this result. It has five records from the Random % Sample output. After making **Category** and **UniqueID** selections in the **Unique** tool, the first three rows of data highlighted in the following screenshot are our result from the **U** output stream, with a unique record per category. The **Unhealthy Behaviors** and **Prevention** category values are excluded as they are duplicated categories.

Record #	Category	UniqueID	Measure
1	Prevention	1212875	Taking medicine for high blood pressure control among adults aged >=18 Years with high blood pressure
2	Unhealthy Behaviors	1212875	Current smoking among adults aged >=18 Years
3	Health Outcomes	1212875	Mental health not good for >=14 days among adults aged >=18 Years
4	Unhealthy Behaviors	1212875	Obesity among adults aged >=18 Years
5	Prevention	1212875	Papanicolaou smear use among adult women aged 21â“65 Years

Step 5: Select the **Select Records** tool from the **Preparation** tool palette and drag it onto the canvas. Connect the **Select Records** tool to the **U** output stream from the **Unique** tool:

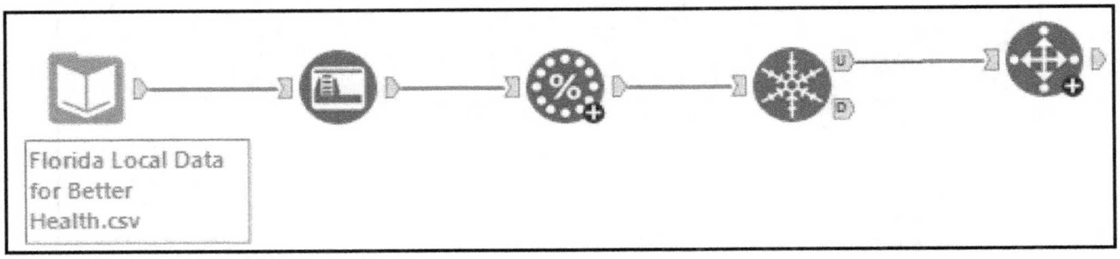

The **Select Records** tool allows for a subset of input records to be selected. A single record, a range of records, all records after a certain row, and multiple selections can be made. This is flexible for analyzing data in a specific area within the dataset.

Let's specify in the configuration for the **Select Record** tool the ranges `1-650`. The hyphen is used between the first row and last row specified:

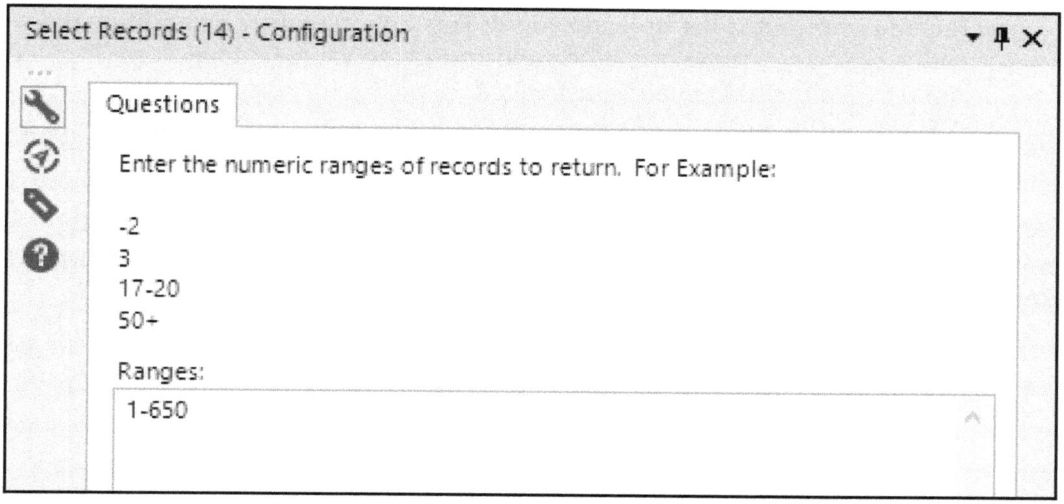

The output now contains data from rows 1 through 650. Selecting specific ranges is useful for sampling and troubleshooting.

Step 6: Select the Imputation tool from the **Preparation** tool palette and drag it onto the canvas. Connect the **Imputation** tool to the **Select Records** tool:

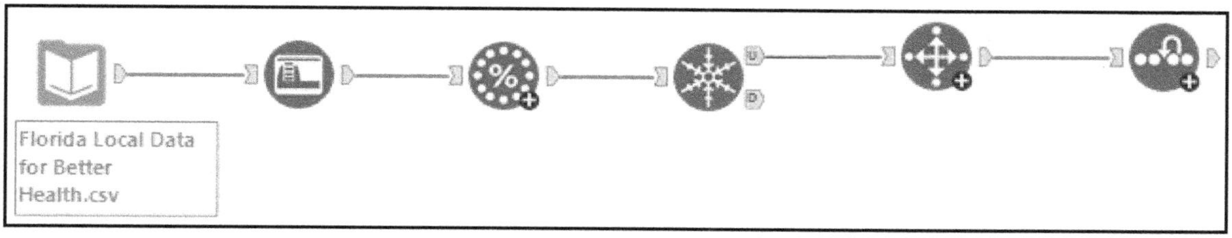

The **Imputation** tool is best utilized when numeric values are to be replaced with another number, which is especially useful for nulls. Let's review the **Imputation** Options within the **Imputation** configuration:

- **Fields to impute**: Contains fields to impute with an option to select All or None
- **Incoming value to replace**: Contains `Null()` to replace null values or a user, specified value with a specific value
- **Replace with value**: Contains Average, Median, Mode, or a user specified value to select from

- **Include imputed value indicator field**: This option will create additional fields with `suffix _Indicator`, with 1 indicating the value that has been imputed and 0 the value that remains unchanged
- **Output imputed values as a separate field**: This option will create new fields with the `suffix _ImputedValue` and leaving the original fields as it is

We will focus on nulls in the data for the `TractFIPS` field and replace nulls with the **Average** value for all values within the `TractFIPS` field. Apply the following selections in the **Imputation** configuration:

- Fields to impute: `TractFIPS`
- Incoming value to replace: `Null()`
- Replace with value: `Average`

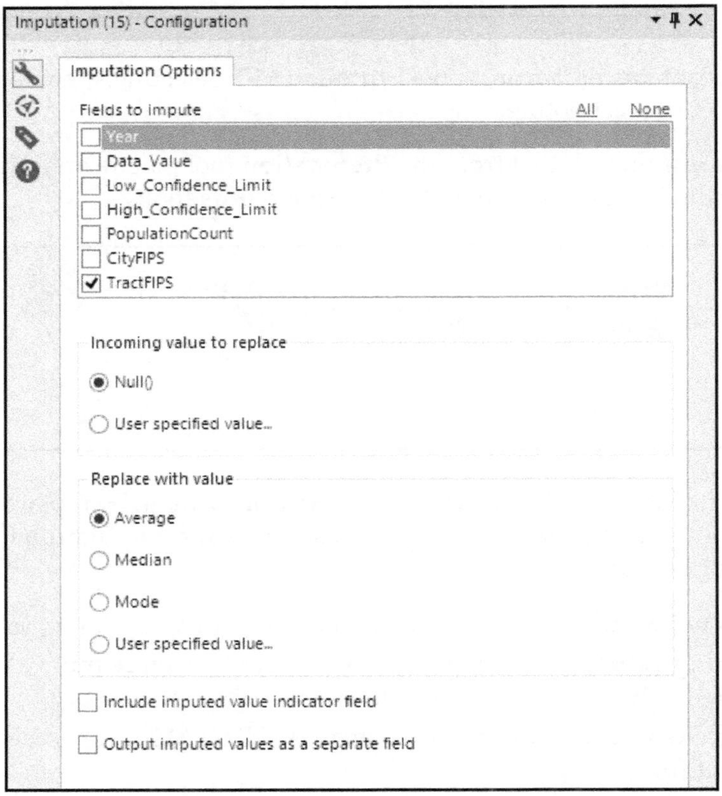

Note that for the UniqueID 1214400 (Record #97) and UniqueID 1216475 (Record #115), before the Imputation tool is added, there are null values for both these UniqueIDs. There are other null values as well, but for simplicity let's focus on these two and how the null values change after applying the **Imputation** selections. The value to replace in this case is null and we want to replace that with the Average value. Let's review the output from the Imputation tool. Notice that all null values for the `TractFIPS` field have been replaced with the average value `12071010405`.

Step 7: Select the **Multi-Field Binning** tool from the **Preparation** tool palette and drag it onto the canvas. Connect the **Multi-Field Binning** tool to the **Imputation** tool:

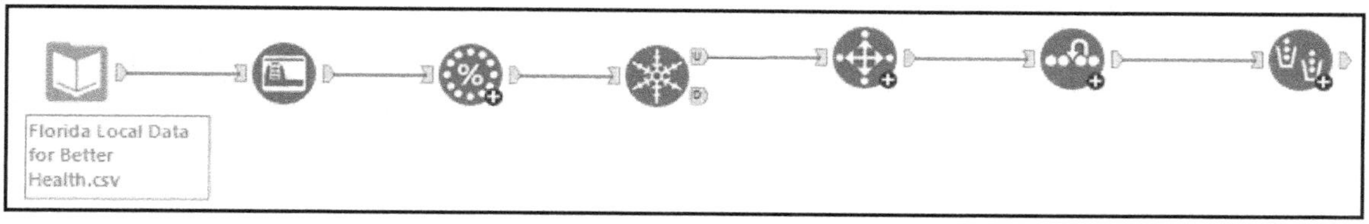

The ability to group numerical values is useful when the goal is to divide records into equal-sized ranges. This can be accomplished by using the **Multi-Field Binning** tool to group multiple numeric values into bins. This is helpful for predictive analysis and to identify where the distribution of values falls between a minimum and maximum value. The binning can be applied using equal records or equal intervals. Let's review the tile options available for this tool:

- **Select fields for binning (only numeric fields are shown)**: Select one or more numeric fields to group the data in bins. The All or None option is available to expedite selecting multiple numeric fields or deselecting multiple numeric fields.
- **Equal Records (Number of Tiles)**: Records are assigned equally into the specific value entered in the Number of Tiles box. The maximum number of tiles is 1,000. Note: Not all bins will have the same number of records. For example, if there are 40 records and the number of tiles is set to 3, since 40 divided by 3 does not provide an equal distribution not all bins will have the same number of records.
- **Equal Intervals**: The intervals are selected by subtracting the minimum from the maximum and dividing by the number of intervals. Records are divided into equally sized ranges dependent on values in the selected field.

The `Data_Value` field is the primary metric we are focused on grouping into equal records to get a better understanding of which numeric group the values fall under. Let's apply the following selections to the **Multi-Field Binning** tool:

- Select fields for binning (only numeric fields are shown): `Data_Value`
- Equal Records (Number of Tiles): `10`

The following screenshot shows how the screen looks when fields are selected for binning:

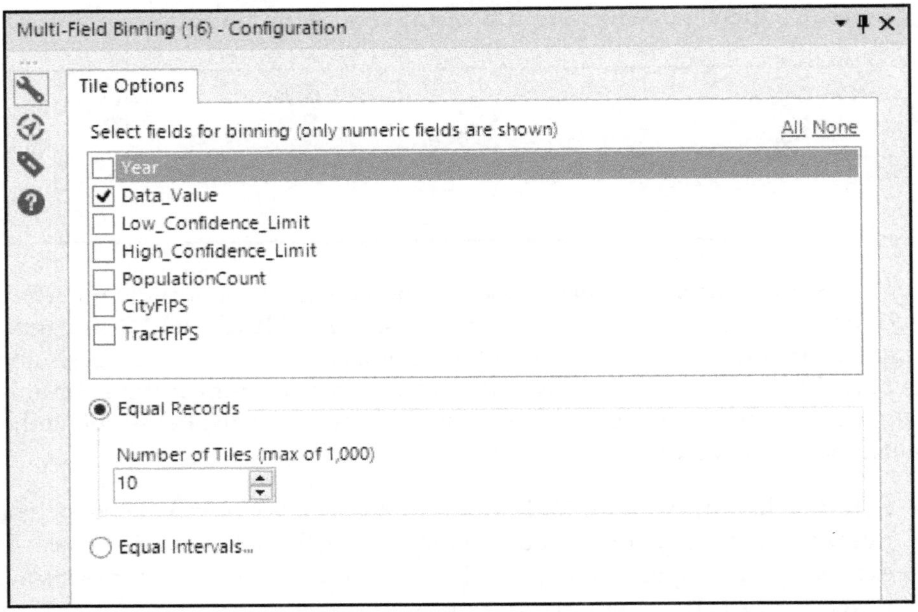

All the values from the `Data_Value` field are now equally binned to `10` bins located in the `Data_Value_Time_Num` field.

Step 8: Select the **Sort** tool from the **Preparation** tool palette and drag it onto the canvas. Connect the **Sort** tool to the **Multi-Field Binning** tool:

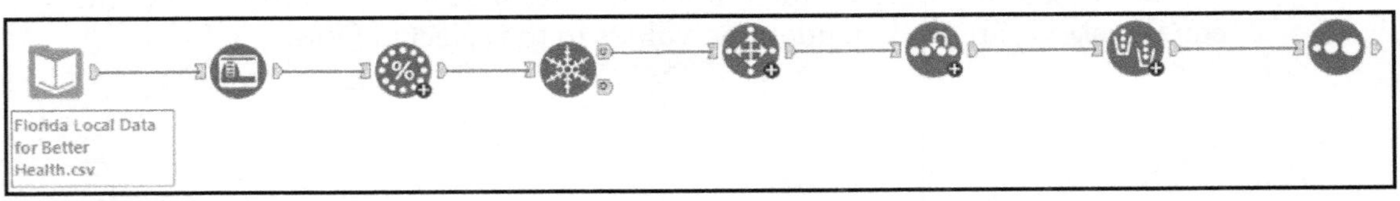

The **Sort** tool will sort records in ascending or descending order in one or more fields. Sorting is useful when troubleshooting and as the last tool when completing the workflow, so the outputted data is sorted in a fashion that meets the needs of the customer. Apply the following selections within the **Sort** tool:

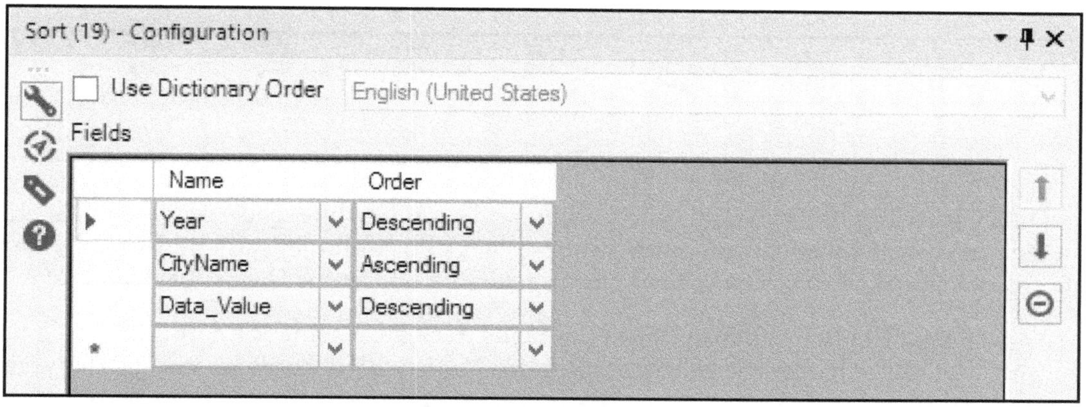

This sorts the data first by `Year`, in descending order from the highest year to the lowest year. Next, it sorts the data by `CityName` in ascending order from cities starting A to Z. Last, the `Data_Value` field is sorted from the highest value to lowest value.

Let's review the first 19 records as these records all fall under `Boca Raton`, the `CityName` value that is used within this sorting. The Year values are displaying most recent years at the top and oldest years at the bottom, starting with 2014. The `CityName` starts with `Boca Raton` as this is the first value in ascending order, while the `Data_Value` ranges from `34.5` at the highest value to `2.4` at the lowest value.

Data cleansing

Imagine a world where data cleansing had to be done manually. Countless hours would be spent fixing data to get the desired output. This would delay business decisions. Fortunately, with Alteryx less time can be spent cleaning your data and more time focused on analyzing your data. There is a very popular tool located in the Preparation tool palette called, you guessed it, Data Cleansing. It would only be fitting to start this section with the Data Cleansing tool.

In this section, we will continue to use the `Florida Local Data for Better Health` workflow from the **Data Preparation** section.

Step 1: Select the **Data Cleansing** tool from the Preparation tool palette and drag it onto the canvas. Connect the **Data Cleansing** tool to the Sort tool:

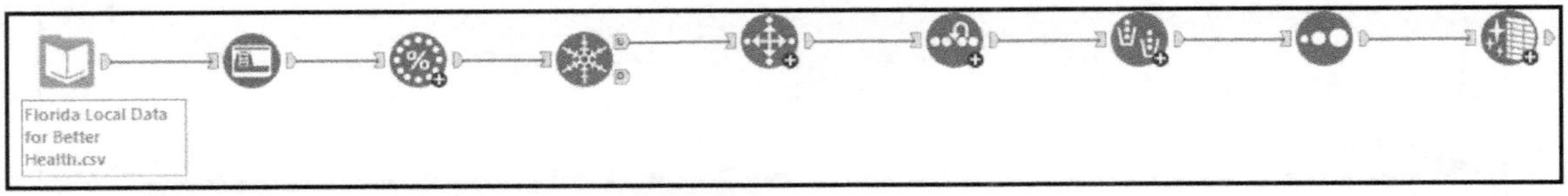

The **Data Cleansing** tool can eliminate leading and trailing whitespace, remove nulls, clear numbers from a string entry, and with a simple check box automatically perform common data cleansing tasks. Let's review the options available within the Data Cleansing tool:

- **Select fields to cleanse**: Select the fields to cleanse using the configuration options. All options, except for Replace Nulls with 0, apply to string data types. To specify different options for different fields, use multiple Data Cleansing tools in your workflow.
- **Replace nulls**: Replace nulls with blanks in string data types. Replace nulls with 0 in numeric data types. Both options are selected by default. To replace nulls with values other than blanks or 0, use the Imputation tool.
- **Remove unwanted characters**:
    - Leading and Trailing Whitespace is selected by default.
    - Tabs, Line Breaks, and Duplicate Whitespace replaces any occurrence of whitespace with a single space, including line endings, tabs, multiple spaces, and other consecutive whitespace.
    - All Whitespace removes any occurrence of whitespace.
    - Letters removes all letters. This includes letters outside the Latin alphabet.
    - Numbers removes all numbers.
    - Punctuation removes the following characters:
      ! " # $ % & ' ( ) * + , \ - . / : ; < = > ? @ [/] ^ _ ` { | } ~

The goal for the `Data_Value`, `Low_Confidence_Limit`, and `High_Confidence_Limit` numeric fields needs to be replaced with `0` instead of nulls and the string field `Data_Value_Footnote` displaying null data needs to be displayed with blanks instead. Apply the following selections in the configuration options:

- Select fields to cleanse: **Data_Value, Low_Confidence_Limit, High_Confidence_Limit**, and **Data_Value_Footnote**
- Replace nulls: **Replace with Blanks (String Fields)** and **Replace with 0 (Numeric Fields)**

The following screenshot gives a better idea of the selections to be made in the configuration options:

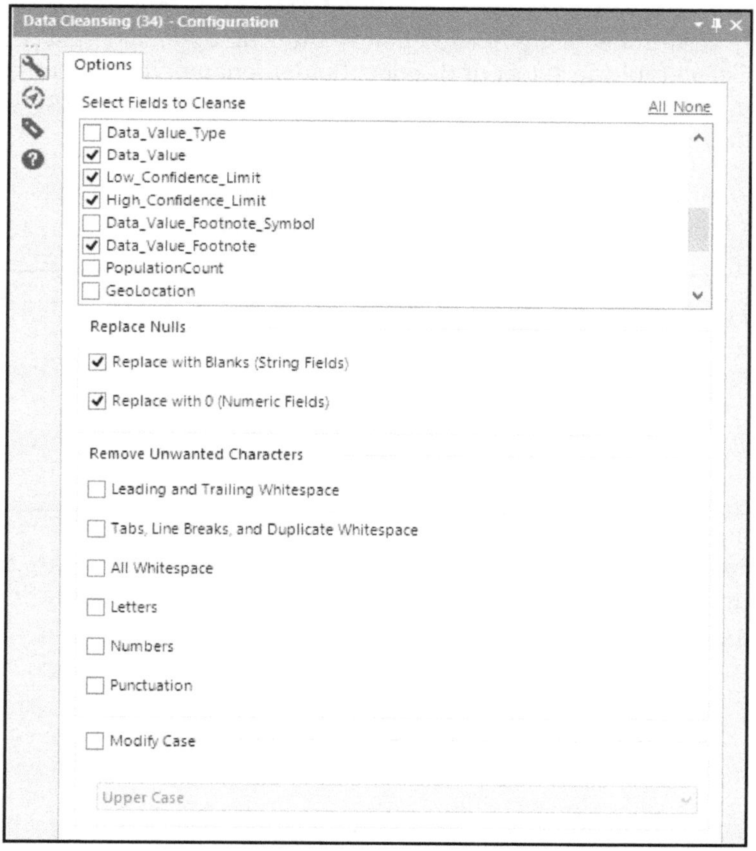

Notice that the numeric fields that have null values - `Data_Value`, `Low_Confidence_Limit`, and `High_Confidence_Limit` - have been replaced with 0, and the string field `Data_Value_Footnote` has been replaced with blanks instead of nulls. Beauty lies in the eye of the Data Cleansing tool!

Filtering

There are instances where data should be limited to only where to focus the analysis on. For example, instead of viewing all the cities in your analysis you may want to view only a couple cities. The ability to filter data is useful for limiting data to the desired output and not all data coming through the workflow downstream. It's also helpful for troubleshooting by filtering down to a specific area or row in the dataset to narrow down where a problem may exist. If only certain fields are needed before filtering data, it's good practice to use the Select tool. The Select tool can select or deselect fields, rename fields, change data types and sizes, add a description for the fields, and save/load field types. Let's add the Select tool to the canvas, continuing from the Data Cleansing section:

Step 1: Select the **Select** tool from the **Preparation** tool palette and drag it onto the canvas. Connect the **Select** tool to the **Data Cleansing** tool:

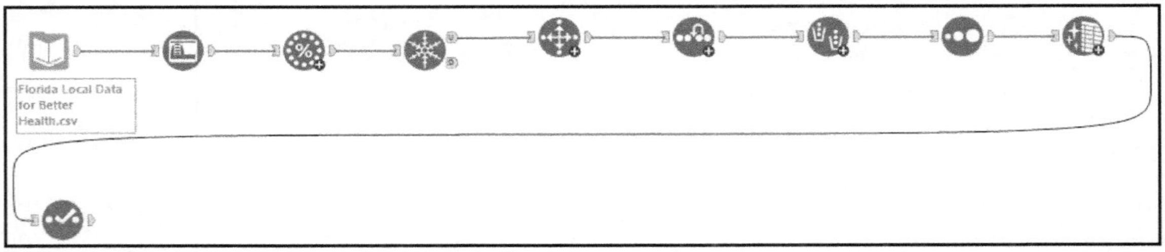

The **Select** tool includes, excludes, and reorders columns of data that pass through a workflow. Excluding columns can limit the data passing through a workflow and improve performance. Apply the following field selections:

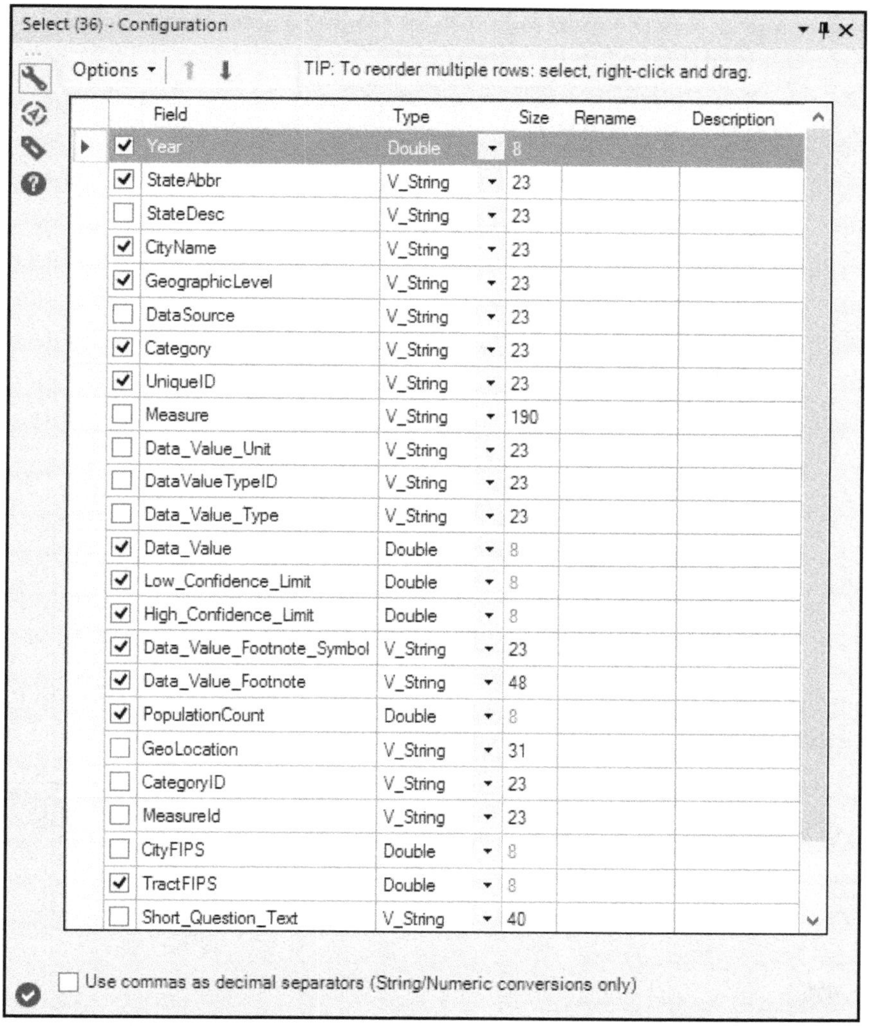

Select (36) - Configuration
Options
TIP: To reorder multiple rows: select, right-click and drag.
Field
Type
Size
Rename
Description
Year Double 8
StateAbbr V_String 23
StateDesc V_String 23
CityName V_String 23
GeographicLevel V_String 23
DataSource V_String 23
Category V_String 23
UniqueID V_String 23
Measure V_String 190
Data_Value_Unit V_String 23
DataValueTypeID V_String 23
Data_Value_Type V_String 23
Data_Value Double 8
Low_Confidence_Limit Double 8
High_Confidence_Limit Double 8
Data_Value_Footnote_Symbol V_String 23
Data_Value_Footnote V_String 48
PopulationCount Double 8
GeoLocation V_String 31
CategoryID V_String 23
MeasureId V_String 23
CityFIPS Double 8
TractFIPS Double 8
Short_Question_Text V_String 40
Use commas as decimal separators (String/Numeric conversions only)

The output from the **Select** tool will only contain those fields selected. This is beneficial to avoid bringing any fields that aren't of interest for analyzing. The next step will involve limiting data using the **Basic Filter** and **Custom Filter** options within the **Filter** tool.

The following image shows the metadata output from the Select tool. Note that all the fields selected are the fields displayed in the output:

Results - Select (36) - Output

13 of 13 Fields | Metadata

Record #	Name	Type	Size
1	Year	Double	8
2	StateAbbr	V_String	23
3	CityName	V_String	23
4	GeographicLevel	V_String	23
5	Category	V_String	23
6	UniqueID	V_String	23
7	Data_Value	Double	8
8	Low_Confidence_Limit	Double	8
9	High_Confidence_Limit	Double	8
10	Data_Value_Footnote_Symbol	V_String	23
11	Data_Value_Footnote	V_String	48
12	PopulationCount	Double	8
13	TractFIPS	Double	8

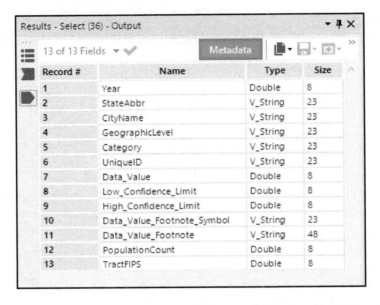

Step 2: Select the **Filter** tool from the **Preparation** tool palette and drag it onto the canvas. Connect the **Filter** tool to the Select tool:

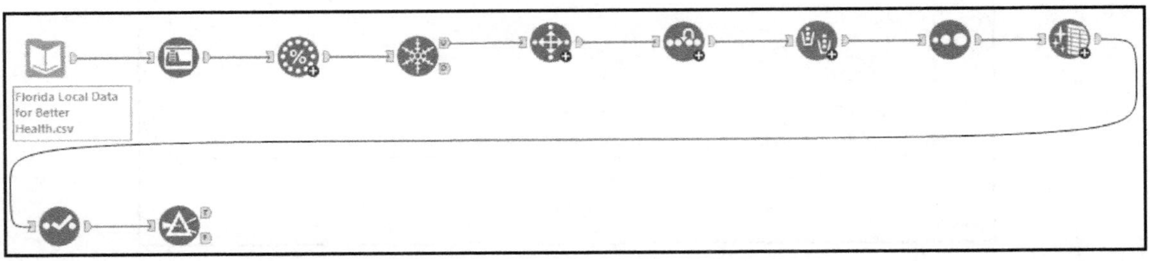

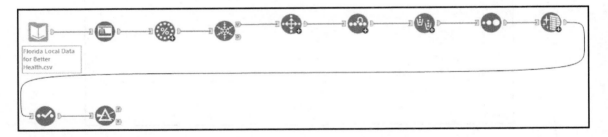

The **Filter** tool queries records by using an expression and splits data into two outputs: True, where the data meets the specified criteria, and False, where the data does not meet the specified criteria. Use this tool to identify records in your data that meet a specified criterion. You may choose to handle records that come from the True output differently from the False output by connecting additional tools to the workflow on either side.

Basic Filter: There are multiple cities located in the dataset. The objective is to filter to where `CityName` is `Clearwater`. The **Basic Filter** allows a filter on one field. The drop-down selections vary if a field is a numeric or a string. In this case it's a string. Select `CityName` from the field drop down, Equals, and enter `Clearwater` in the text box. In the True Output, only data for `Clearwater` will show and all other cities will come through the False Output.

Custom Filter: Custom Filter will allow querying one or more fields. The objective is to filter to where the Year is 2014 and the `CityName` is either `Clearwater` or `Fort Lauderdale`. Select **Custom Filter** on the radio button selection and add the following to the **Expression** window:

```
[Year] = 2014
 &&
 ([CityName] = "Clearwater"
 OR [CityName] = "Fort Lauderdale")
```

The result is as follows:

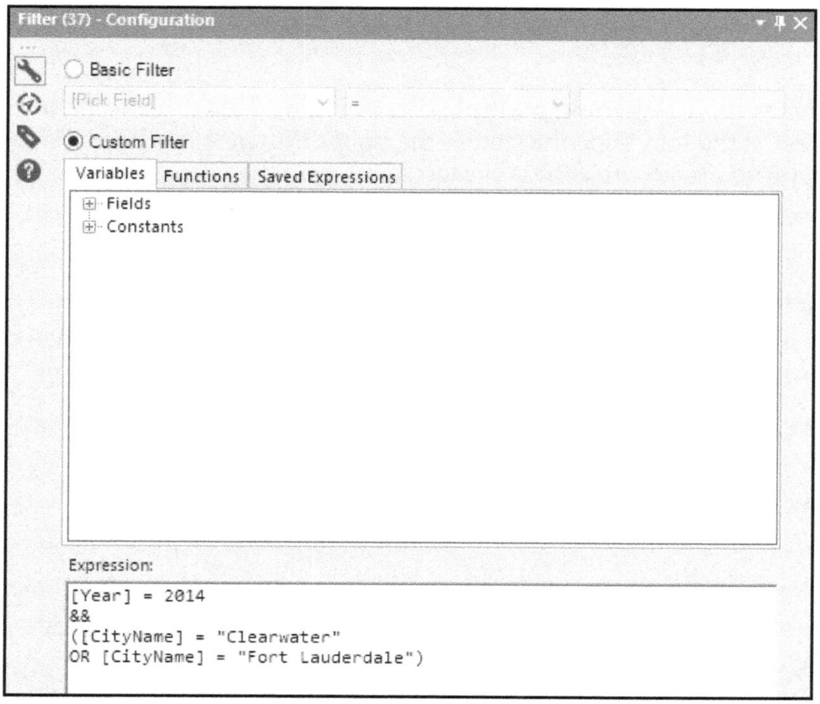

The True output will contain data for 2014 with data for both `Clearwater` and `Fort Lauderdale`. The False Output will contain 2014 data for all cities except `Clearwater` and `Fort Lauderdale` and all data for 2013 with all cities contained in the output. Note that `Fort Lauderdale` displays in the False Output since it has data for 2013; the expression only states data for the year 2014, which is in the True Output.

Join and union

The ability to enable vital decisions with a few tools across multiple data tables is taking self-service analytics to the next level. The tools that we will review in this section include Join, Join Multiple, and Union. These core tools allow joining two inputs together using the Join tool, joining more than two inputs together using the Join Multiple tool, and combining two or more data streams together. Volumes of data can be streamlined within minutes using these helpful, powerful tools. Let's continue using the same workflow from the last section.

Join

We'll begin this section by joining multiple files together. This can also be done using database tables, as the Join logic the same - the only difference is where the data comes from. The purpose is to identify the Average Age for all the cities in the `Florida Local Data for Better Health.csv` file. Let's go through how the Join tool can be applied in a workflow.

Step 1: Using an **Input Data** tool, connect to the file `Florida Better Health Age.xlsx`, located in the `\Learn Alteryx\Chapter` directory, and add it to the canvas below the **Select** tool. This file contains the Average Age for all the cities located in Florida Local Data for `Health.csv`.

Step 2: Select the **Join** tool from the **Join** tool palette and drag it onto the canvas. Connect the **Select** tool to the Left input (L) of the **Join** tool. Connect the `Florida Better Health Age.xlsx` file to the Right input (R) of the **Join** tool:

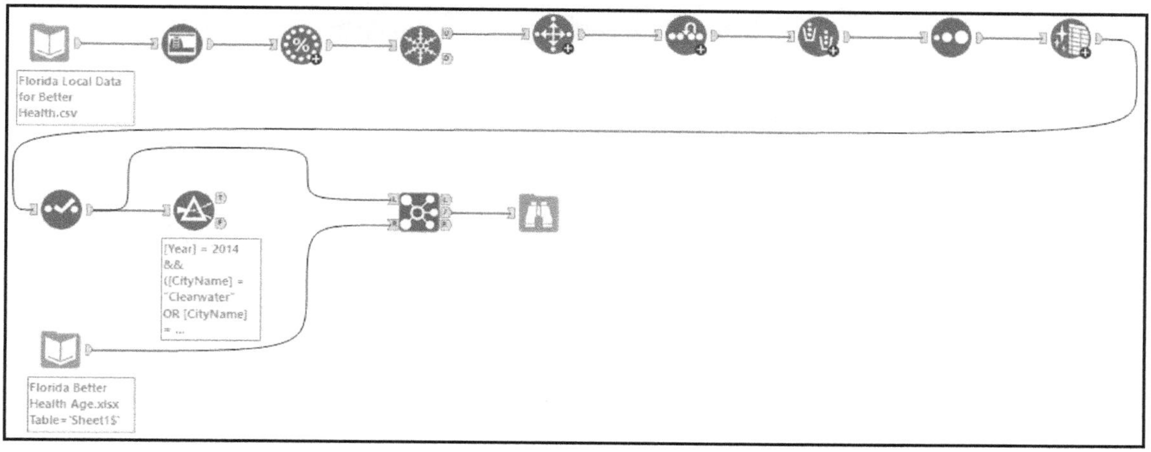

Step 3: In the Join tool configuration, select **Join by Specific Fields**. Select `CityName` from both the Left and Right dropdowns.

Step 4: Deselect from the Right input the following fields: `StateAbbr`, `StateDesc`, and `CityName`. These are deselected since they are duplicate fields that already exist in the Left input.

Step 5: Add the **Browse** tool to the canvas and connect the **J** output from the **Join** tool to the **Browse** tool. The **J** output contains records that joined the **L** input to those records in the **R** input. This is the result of an **Inner Join**:

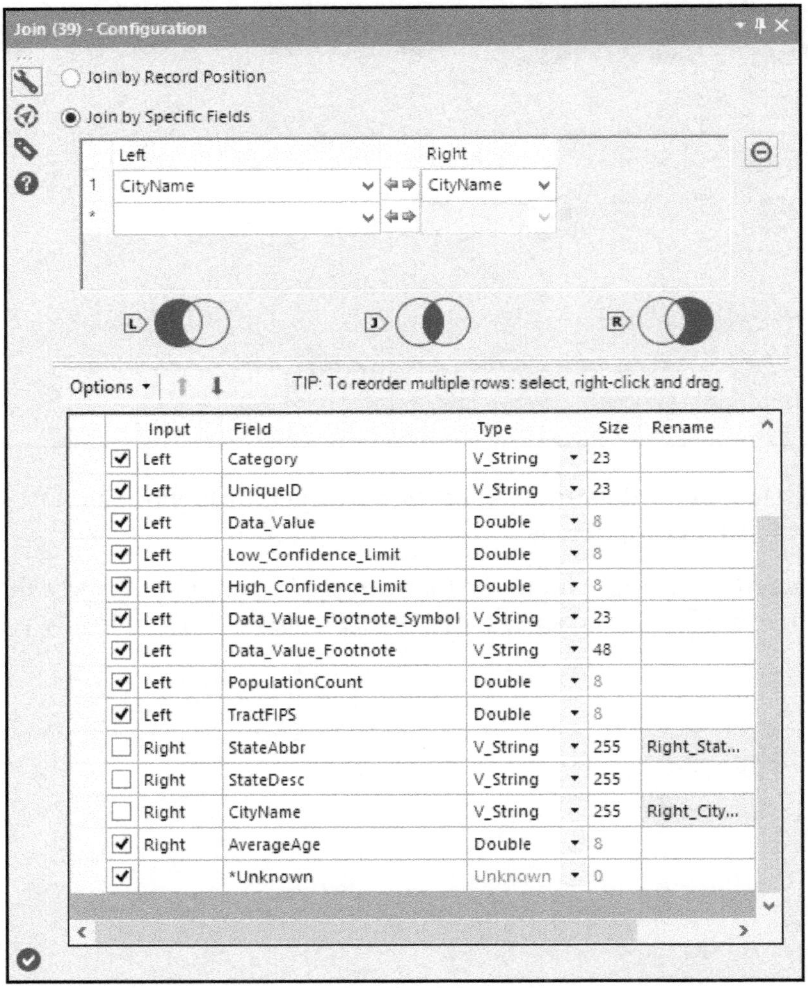

Notice after running the workflow that the J output contains the `AverageAge` field. An Inner Join worked out great in this case, since all the cities are in both files. The output now contains the Average Age for all the cities and further analysis can quickly be accomplished.

Join multiple

Having reviewed the **Join** tool, we'll now focus in on the **Join Multiple** tool, which is quite like the **Join** tool. The **Join Multiple** tool allows for two or more inputs to be joined together and all records to be joined without using a **Union** tool. Rather than connecting the Left (L) output, J (J) output, and the Right (R) from the Join outputs to the **Union** tool, the **Join Multiple** tool can be used to provide an all records output. The objective is to determine which cities have a population greater than 90,000 and an average age between 51-69, the generation known as the baby boomers. This will help to analyze the health outcomes for baby boomers. Three input files will be used to obtain this information. Let's see the benefits of the **Join Multiple** tool:

Step 1: Using an **Input Data** tool connect to the file **Florida Large Populations.xlsx**, located in the `\Learn Alteryx\Chapter` directory, and add it to the canvas. This file contains the Populations and if they are greater than or less than 90,000 for all the cities located in the `Florida Local Data for Health.csv.`

Step 2: Connect the **Select** tool, the `Florida Better Health Age.xlsx` input, and the `Florida Large Populations.xlsx` input to the **Join Multiple** tool. The input streams are numbered **#1**, **#2**, and **#3**:

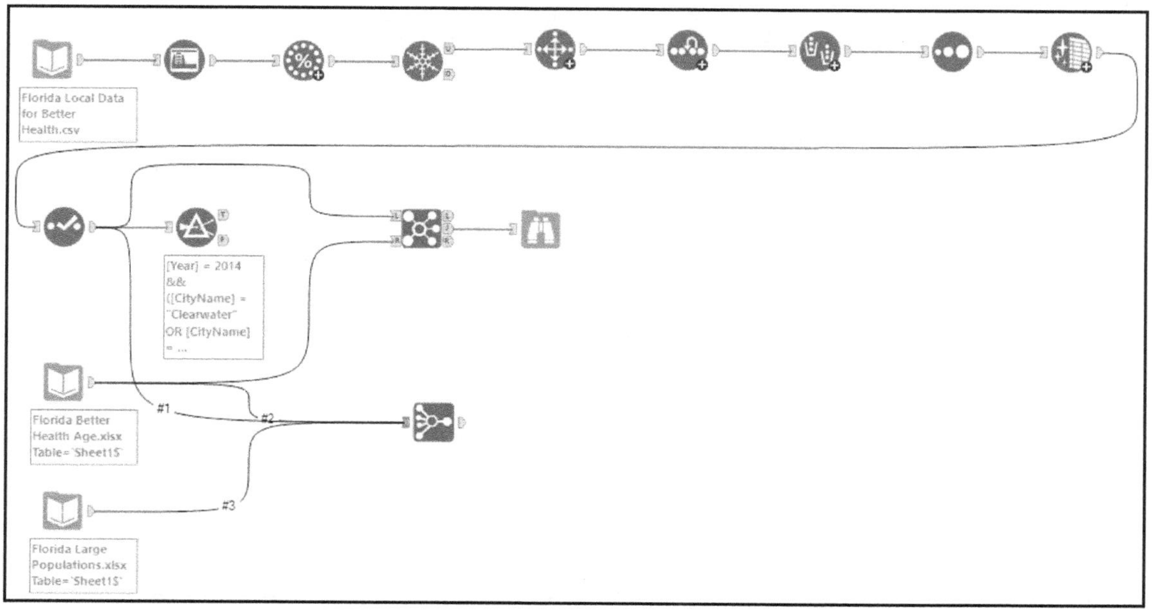

Step 3: In the **Join** tool configuration, select **Join by Specific Fields**. Select `CityName` from all three drop downs.

Step 4: Deselect the following fields from Input_#2: `StateAbbr`, `StateDesc`, and `CityName`. Deselect the following fields from Input_#3: `Year`, `StateAbbr`, `StateDesc`, `CityName`, and `PopulationCount`. These fields either already exist in Input_#1 or are not needed for this analysis:

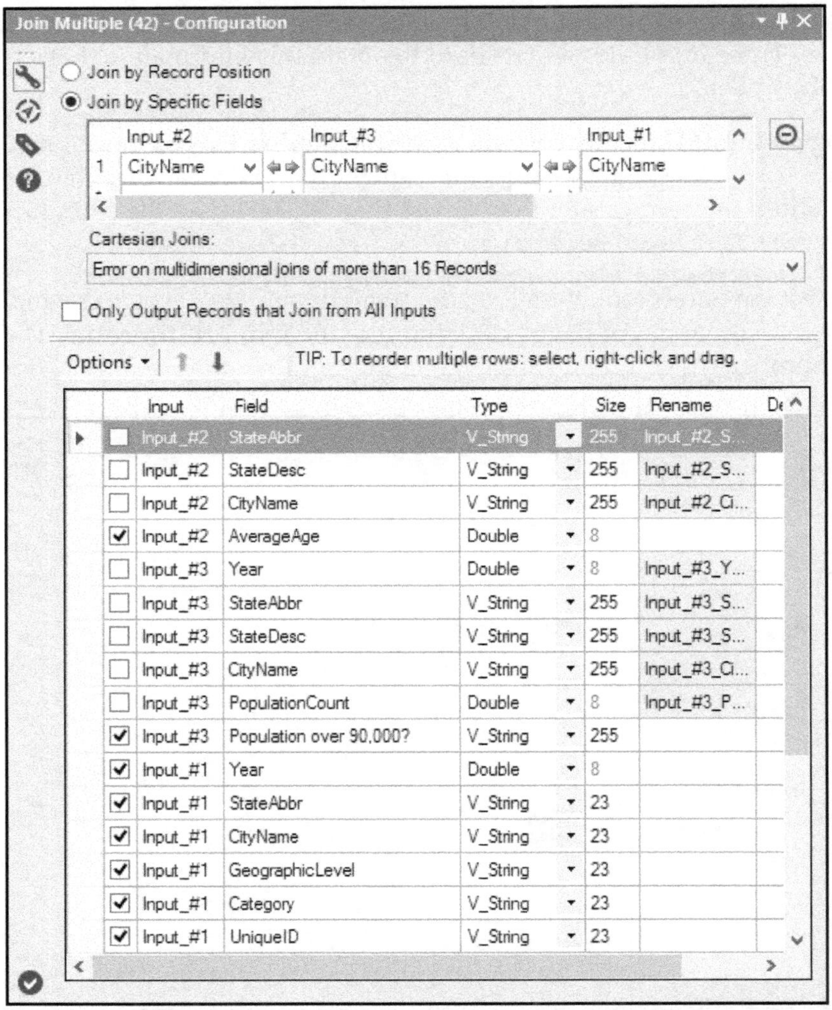

Step 5: Add the **Browse** tool to the **Join Multiple** tool and run the workflow.

> Record #'s 651 through 661 will contain nulls where cities are not located in the output of the **Select** tool that contains data from the `Florida Local Data for Better Health.csv` file. The cities are in both of the other files.

Step 6: Connect the **Filter** tool to the output of the **Join Multiple** tool.

Step 7: Select **Custom Filter** on the radio button selection, and add the following to the **Expression** window:

```
!IsNull([Year])
 &&
 [Population over 90,000?] = 'YES'
 &&([AverageAge] >= 51 && [AverageAge] <= 69)
```

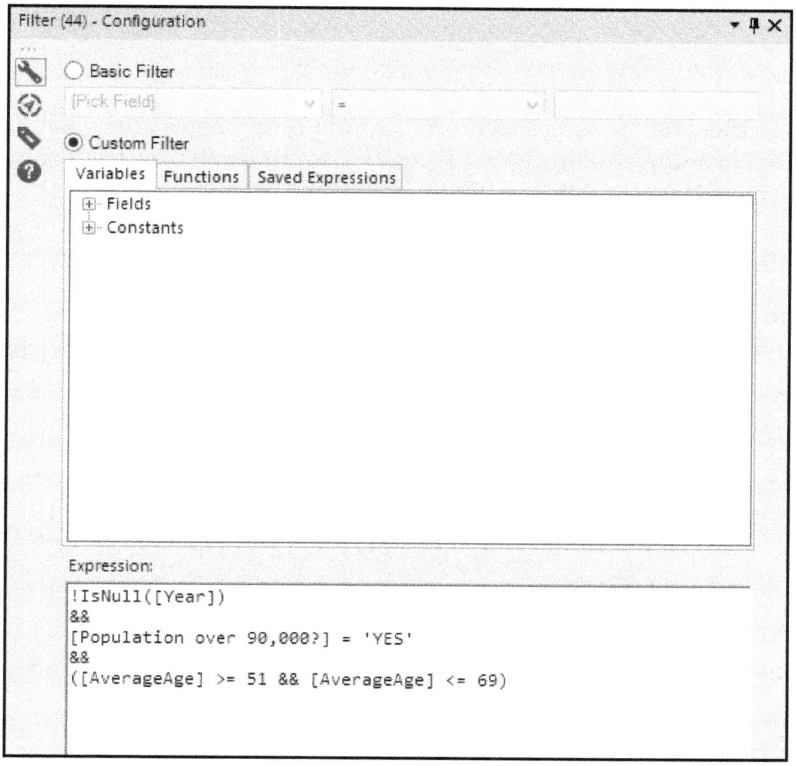

The first expression, `!IsNull([Year])`, will remove the nulls where cities are not located in the output of the **Select** tool containing data from `Florida Local Data for Better Health.csv`. The second expression, `[Population over 90,000?] = 'YES'`, identifies populations over 90,000. The third expression, `([AverageAge] >= 51 && [AverageAge] <= 69)`, identifies the baby boomers, ages `51` to `69`.

Step 8: Add **All Browses** to show for the True and False outputs.

Notice the True output contains only information relative to the expression from the Filter tool. The data has been joined from three different inputs on an identical field. The Filter tool is used to isolate the data needed for analysis by using a **Custom Filter** to provide more than the field to be included in the expression. The key is the **Join Multiple** tool, which allows three different inputs to be joined together. Many database tables contain information that needs to be joined together to get those fields needed for analysis and using the **Join Multiple** tool will help streamline this process.

Union

Combining multiple data streams based on common field names and positions, which leads to rows from two or more streams being placed on top of each other, is a function of the Union tool. We have data for 2013 and 2014 from the `Florida Local Data for Better Health.csv` file and have just received a new file for partial 2015 data. The goal is to combine all three years together in one dataset.

Step 1: Using the Input Data tool, connect to the file 2015 `Florida Local Data for Better Health.csv` located in the `\Learn Alteryx\Chapter` directory and add it to the canvas. This file contains the same data structure as the `Florida Local Data for Better Health.csv` file, which includes the 2013 and 2014 data.

Step 2: Connect the **Select** tool and the **Input Data** tool 2015 `Florida Local Data for Better Health.csv` to the **Union** tool. The input streams are numbered #1 and #2:

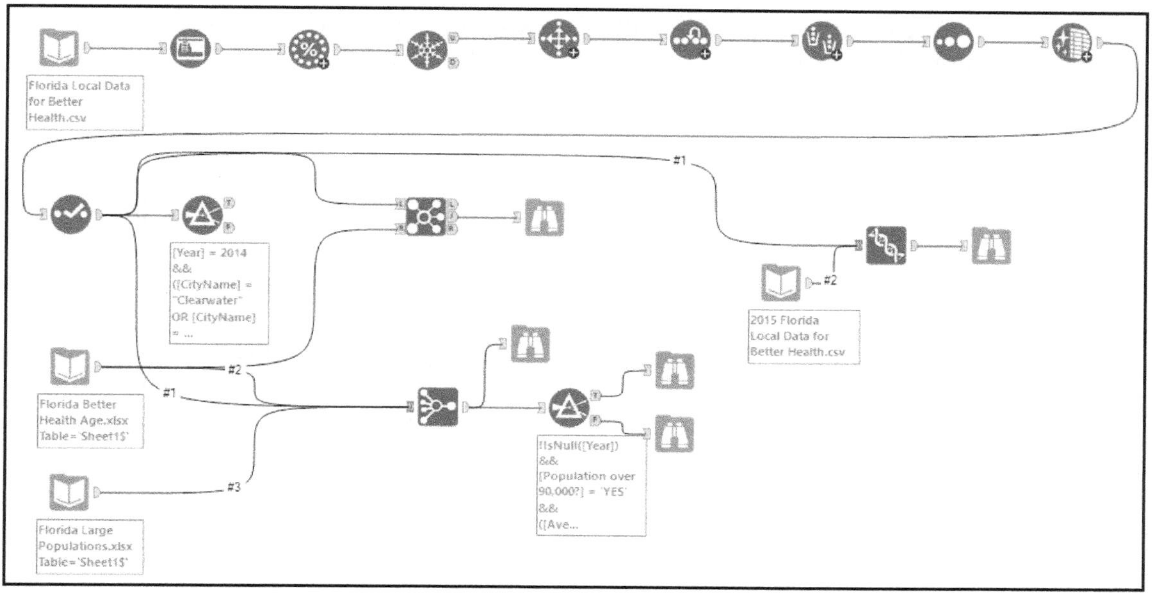

Step 3: Leave the **Union** tool configuration as-is with the drop down selection set to **Auto Config by Name**. When the inputs are not in the same order, the **Auto Config by Name** option aligns them correctly.

Step 4: Add the **Browse** tool to the **Union** tool.

Step 5: Select the **Input Data** tool, **Union** tool, and **Browse** tool by holding down the left-click and selecting all three tools at once. Right-click on any of the three tools and select **Add To New Container**. **Tool Container** is a tool that is located under the **Documentation** tool palette and is very helpful for organizing tools so they can be collapsed or disabled in a single box.

There are various formatting options available within the **Tool Container**, such as **Text Color**, **Fill Color**, **Border Color**, **Transparency**, and **Margin**:

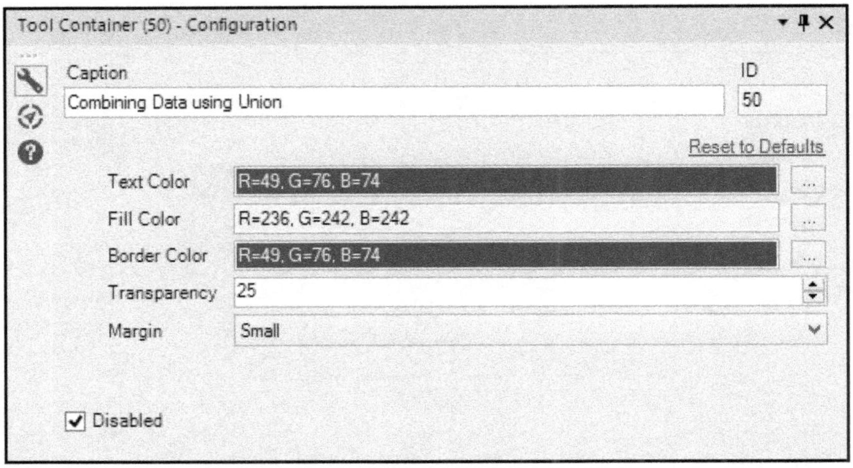

Step 6: Rename the Container the `Combining Data using Union`.

Step 7: Select the Disabled checkbox and click on **Tool Container**. The tool has now been disabled; when the workflow is running it will not do so through the tools in the **Tool Container**. Notice the **Tool Container** has now been collapsed and disabled. Note: clicking anywhere on the canvas will enable or disable the Tool Container.

Step 8: Select the Combining data using the **Union Tool Container** tool and deselect the Disabled box in the configuration options.

Step 9: Run the workflow:

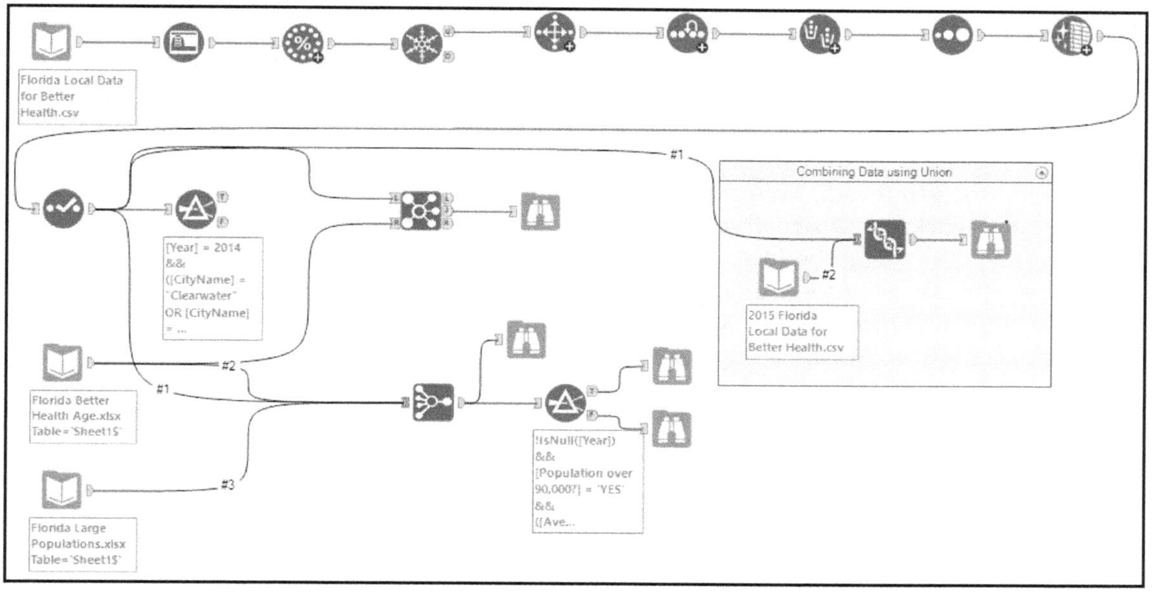

The Browse tool contains a total of 683 records, 650 coming from the Select tool and 33 coming from the 2015 `Florida Local Data for Better Health.csv` file. The output now contains 2013, 2014, and 2015 data combined using the **Union** tool. The ability to utilize the **Join**, **Join Multiple**, and **Union** tools is a major component of building intuitive workflows that equate to a faster slicing and dicing method for data investigation and analysis.

Summary

In this chapter, we reviewed how important data preparation is for quickly blending and organizing data. The data preparation tools used in this chapter are used in every day analytics to develop efficient workflows. The **Data Cleansing** tool is a one-stop shop for cleaning data and handling those nulls that are always bound to exist in input files. Once all the data has been prepared and cleansed, it's time to discover what data needs to be limited by utilizing the **Filter** tool. This can be used to limit data to what the customer needs or to optimize the workflow downstream. The next part included how to join multiple inputs and combine data using the **Join**, **Join Multiple**, and **Union** tools. The **Join** and **Union** tools are a powerful combination for creating inner and outer joins for analysis. The tools utilized in this chapter will provide you with the fundamentals to develop optimal workflows and allow for accurate and quicker business decisions.

In the upcoming chapter, you will learn about the Formula, Multi-Row Formula, and Multi-Field Formula tools. These tools will help in creating robust expressions to update one or more fields.

4
Writing Fast and Accurate Expressions

There are various tools in Alteryx that allow for a broad variety of calculations. You will utilize multiple expressions to create new data columns, update existing columns, and reference data to qualifying rows. You will use more rigorous expressions to maximize the potential of the Formula, Multi-Row Formula, and Multi-Field Formula tools. The goal is to gain a solid foundation in the different types of Formula tools so you can write powerful expressions.

This chapter will cover the following topics:

- Formula
- Multi-Row Formula
- Multi-Field Formula

Formula

The **Formula** tool is where you can write a variety of calculations and operations. The ability to perform calculations, such as if/else conditional formulas, can be quickly used to create a new column or modify an existing column. More than one calculation can be written within the Formula tool rather than creating a formula for each tool. This is quite helpful when creating a calculation for a new column and finding out you want to modify the new column immediately after creating it. The best part of it all is that after writing the expressions they can be saved!

This is great when the same calculation, or one similar to it, needs to be written in the same workflow downstream, or in a different workflow. Alteryx will save the expression, saving you time from writing it out again, and providing a reminding thought on how it was created. We will go through 15 expressions that will provide you with a solid foundation in writing expressions all in one tool, the Formula tool.

In this section, we will use the `U.S. Chronic Disease Indicators` workflow, along with the resources located in the data folder. Let's begin by building out a workflow with some popular expressions within the Formula tool.

Expression #1: Create a data source field to indicate the source where data is coming from.

Step 1: Using an Input Data tool, connect to the file `U.S. Chronic Disease Indicators.csv` located in the `\Learn Alteryx\Chapter` directory.

Step 2: Select the Auto Field tool from the Preparation tool palette and drag it onto the canvas. Connect the Auto Field tool to the Input Data tool. Each string field has now been automatically updated to the smallest field type and size.

Step 3: Select the Formula tool from the Preparation tool palette and drag it onto the canvas. Connect the Formula tool to the Auto Field tool:

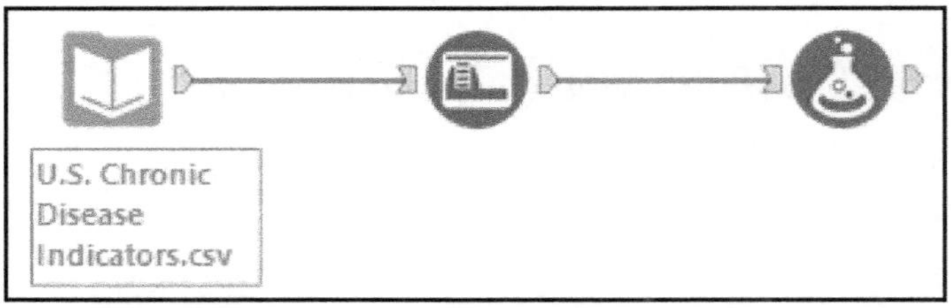

Before writing valuable expressions, let's review the options available within the Formula configuration:

- **Output Column**: + Add Column to create a new column, or select an existing column to modify the column
- **Data Preview**: This provides a preview of what the output of the expression will be
- **Date type**: Select a data type
- **Size**: Change the size of the data
- **Functions**: Search a variety of functions

- **Columns & Constants**: Search existing columns or newly created columns
- **Recent & Saved Expressions**: Search recently created and saved expressions
- **Save Expression**: Save an expression so that it can be used later
- **Add Expression**: Add an expression
- **Expand or Collapse Expression**: Select this option to expand an expression to view the written expression, or collapse an expression to hide the written expression
- **Delete Expression**: Select this to delete an expression

Step 4: Select the **Select Column** option under **Output Column**. Select + Add Column.

Step 5: Enter Data Source in the Expression window.

Step 6: Write the following expression:

```
U.S. CDI
```

Leave the data type and size options as is.

Step 7: Add the Browse tool to the Formula tool.

Step 8: Run the workflow.

The following screenshot shows how the screen looks after running the workflow:

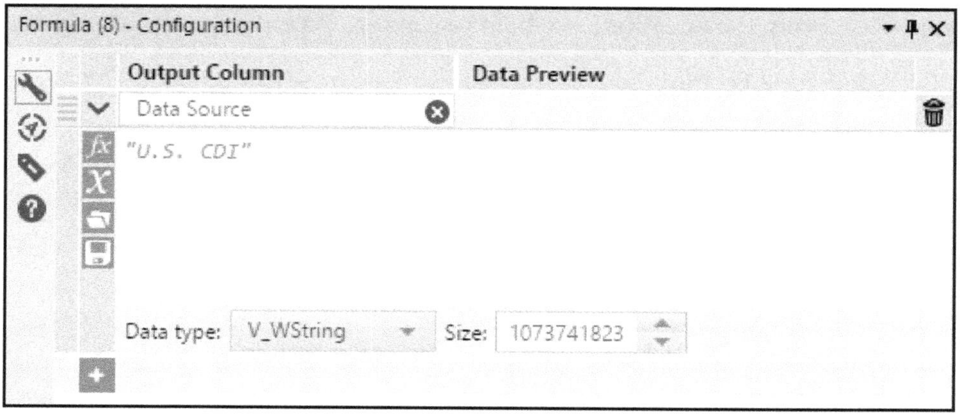

This is a manually created string formula. You will notice that in the Browse tool output the new field Data Source has been added, with each row containing the value `U.S. CDI`.

The following snapshot shows the newly created field Data Source and U.S. CDI value showing for every row:

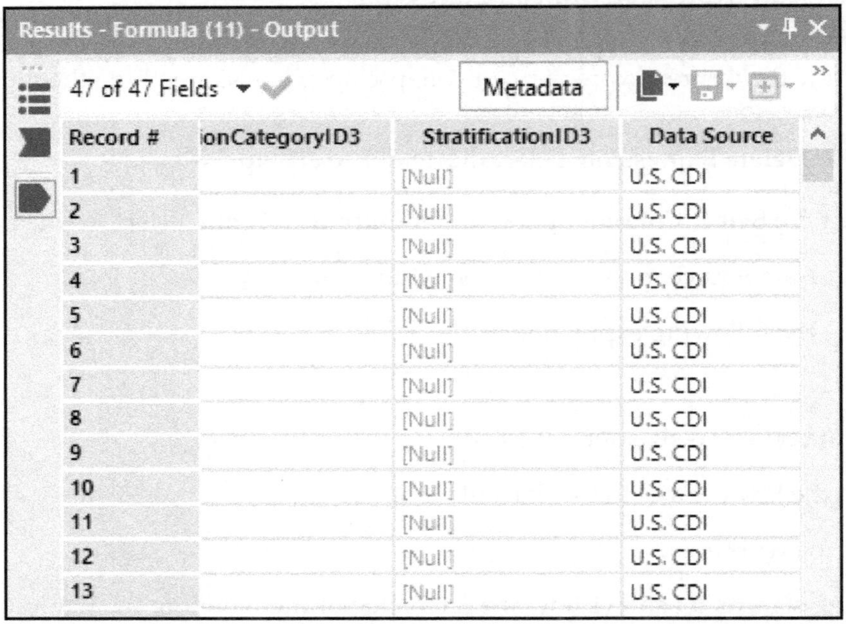

Record #	ionCategoryID3	StratificationID3	Data Source
1		[Null]	U.S. CDI
2		[Null]	U.S. CDI
3		[Null]	U.S. CDI
4		[Null]	U.S. CDI
5		[Null]	U.S. CDI
6		[Null]	U.S. CDI
7		[Null]	U.S. CDI
8		[Null]	U.S. CDI
9		[Null]	U.S. CDI
10		[Null]	U.S. CDI
11		[Null]	U.S. CDI
12		[Null]	U.S. CDI
13		[Null]	U.S. CDI

Expression #2: Modify the LocationDesc field to convert the entire string to uppercase.

Step 1: Using the same Formula tool as the last expression, select the Add Expression icon .

Step 2: Select `LocationDesc` from the Select Column dropdown.

Step 3: Write the following expression:

```
Uppercase([LocationDesc])
```

Notice that Data preview gives a preview of what the output will be. In this case, Alaska has been modified to `ALASKA` based on the expression written.

Step 4: Collapse the Data Source column created in the last expression by selecting the Expand or Collapse Expression icon >.

Step 5: The following screenshot shows how the screen looks after we run the workflow:

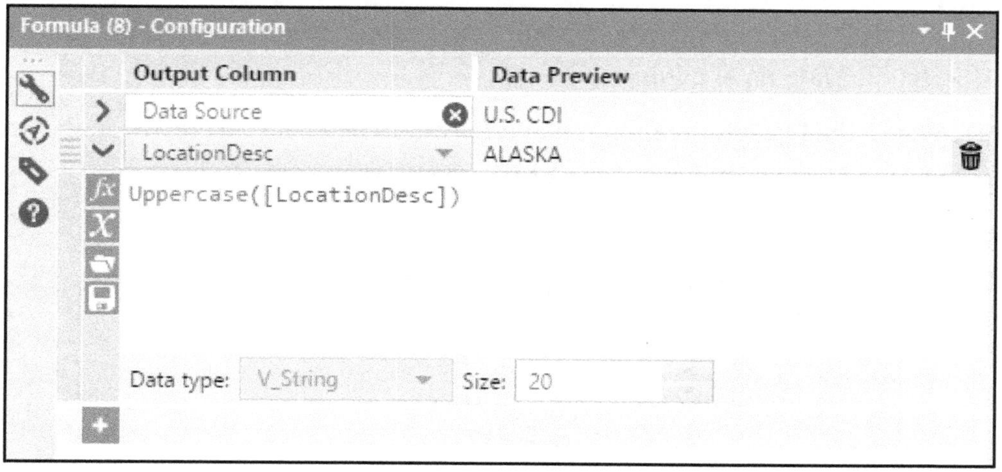

This is a string-related formula to update all values in the field to uppercase. All the values in the existing `LocationDesc` field have now been modified to uppercase. There is also a Lowercase function, which will update the values to all lowercase.

Expression #3: Create a new field to identify if the Topic field contains Diabetes.

Step 1: Using the same Formula tool as the last expression, select the Add Expression icon .

Step 2: In the Select Column dropdown, select + Add Column and enter: Contains Diabetes?

Step 3: Write the following expression:

```
Contains([Topic],'Diabetes')
```

> **TIP**: While writing an expression, add an open bracket after the first parenthesis `Contains([` that will display all available columns to quickly select from in the dropdown rather than manually typing out the field.

Step 4: Select the **Data type: Bool**.

Step 5: Collapse the **Data Source** column and **LocationDesc** column created in the previous expressions by selecting the Expand or Collapse Expression icon .

Step 6: Run the workflow:

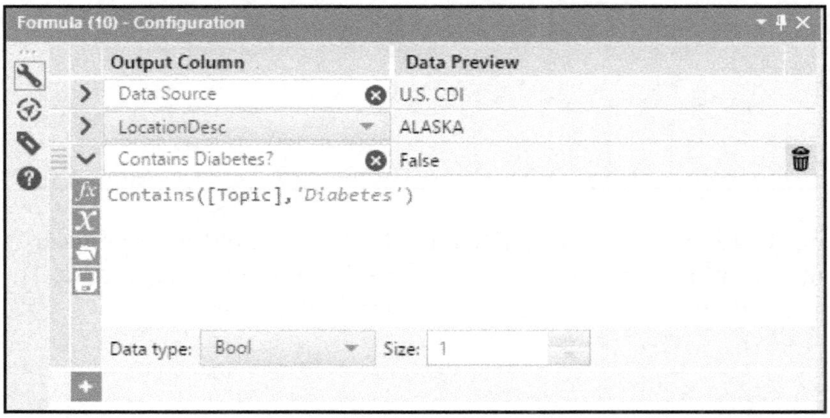

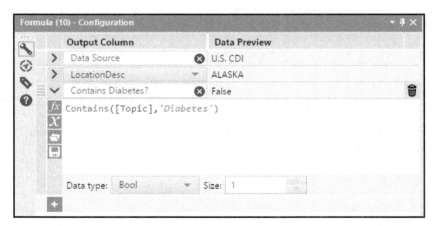

This is a string-related formula to identify whether a field contains a specific string. You will notice the output in the Browse tool contains a new field called Contains Diabetes? with the values True or False based on the **Bool** data type selected. The True value will conclude that the Topic field contains Diabetes, whereas False contains everything but Diabetes. This rapidly identifies where in a large dataset the Diabetes topic is, and can be limited to just this topic by using the Filter tool as you explored in the previous chapter.

Expression #4: Create a new field to identify the length of the Question field.

Step 1: Using the same Formula tool as the last expression, select the Add Expression icon +.

Step 2: In the **Select Column** dropdown, Select + Add Column and enter: `Length Diabetes`.

Step 3: Write the following expression:

```
Length([Question])
```

Leave the **Data type** and **Size** options as is.

Step 4: Collapse all the previous expressions by selecting the Expand or Collapse Expression icon >.

Step 5: Run the workflow:

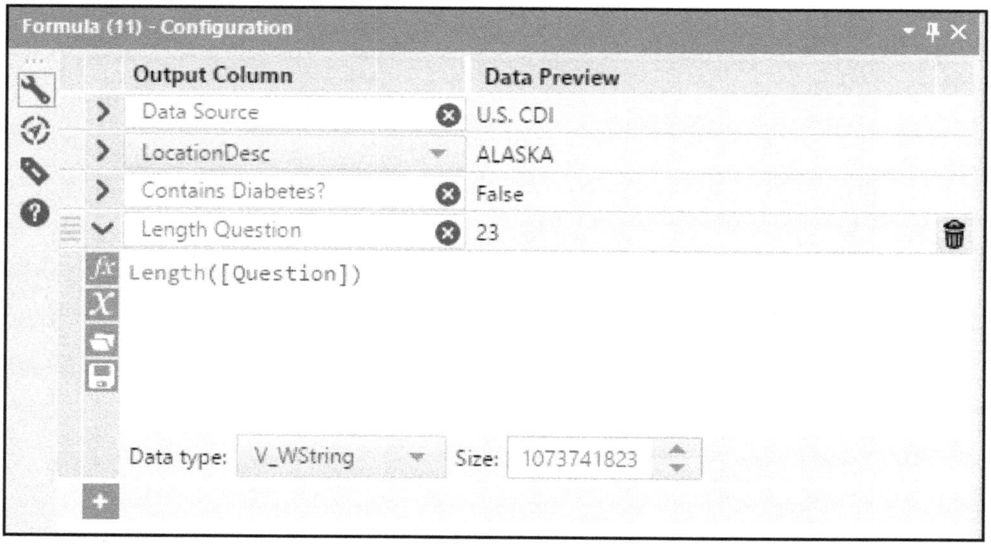

This is a string-related formula to identify the length of the values for a given field. The new field, Length Question, returns the length of the question. This is great to identify whether you want the length of a field to be a minimum length or a maximum length.

Expression #5: Create a new field to identify if the StratificationCategory1 is Overall. If it's Overall, then identify the values under Main Category; if not then identify the values under the Non-Main Category.

Step 1: Using the same Formula tool as the last expression, select the Add Expression icon +.

Step 2: In the **Select Column** dropdown, select + Add Column and enter: `Category Type`

Step 3: Write the following expression:

```
IF [StratificationCategory1] = 'Overall' THEN 'Main Category'
 ELSE 'Non-Main Category'
 ENDIF
```

Leave the **Data type** and **Size** options as is.

Step 4: Collapse all the previous expressions by selecting the Expand or Collapse Expression icon >.

Step 5: Run the workflow:

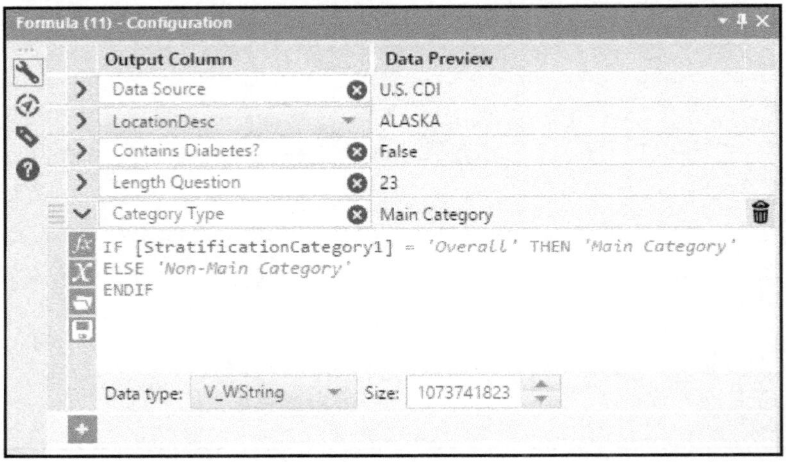

This formula uses a basic IF/ELSE conditional formula. The output now contains a new field, Category Type, with the values `Main Category` where (`StratificationCategory1` is `Overall`) and `Non-Main Category` (where `StratificationCategory1` is anything but `Overall`).

Expression #6: Create a new field to add the % sign after the values under the DataValue field only if the DataValueUnit contains %. If the DataValueUnit doesn't contain %, return the original value under the DataValue field.

Step 1: Using the same Formula tool as the last expression, select the Add Expression icon .

Step 2: In the **Select Column** dropdown, select + Add Column and enter: `DataValue %`

Step 3: Write the following expression:

```
IF Contains([DataValueUnit],'%') &&
 !IsNull([DataValue]) THEN [DataValue] + '%'
 ELSE [DataValue]
 ENDIF
```

Leave the **Data type** and **Size** options as is.

Step 4: Collapse all the previous expressions by selecting the Expand or Collapse Expression icon .

Step 5: Run the workflow:

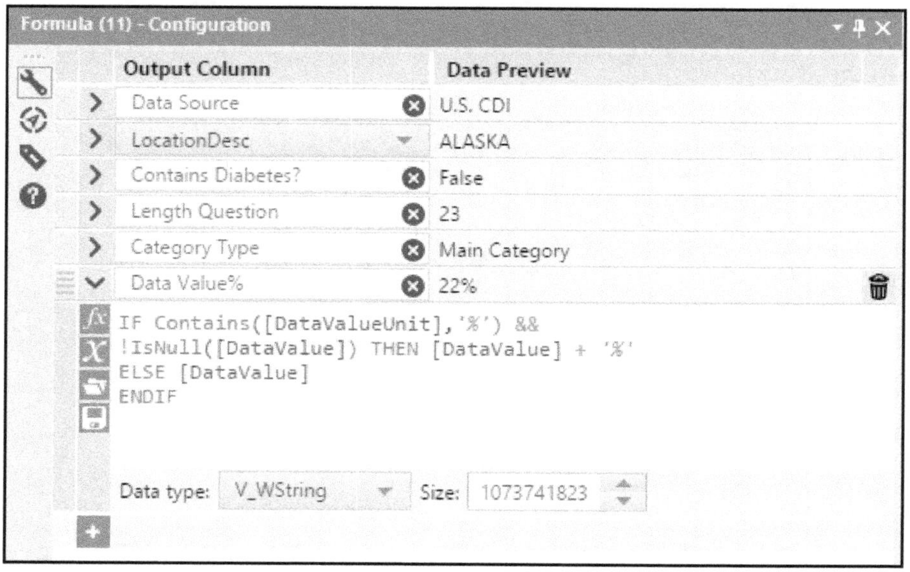

This IF/ELSE conditional formula specifies more than one criterion to give the desired output. This is a useful solution for a reporting format if the desired output needs to have a `%` sign for a certain value to clarify the format, rather than a number. The new field `DataValue %` contains the `%` sign concatenated with the `DataValue` field only if the `DataValueUnit` field contains the `%` sign and the `DataValue` field is not null. If this is not true then the original `DataValue` field will be returned.

Expression #7: Modify the existing field DataValueTypeID to replace the value Nmbr with Number. All other values will remain the same.

Step 1: Using the same Formula tool as the last expression, select the Add Expression icon .

Step 2: Select `DataValueTypeID` from the **Select Column** dropdown.

Step 3: Write the following expression:

```
Replace([DataValueTypeID], 'Nmbr', 'Number')
```

Leave the **Data type** and **Size** options as is.

Step 4: Collapse all the previous expressions by selecting the Expand or Collapse Expression icon .

Step 5: Run the workflow:

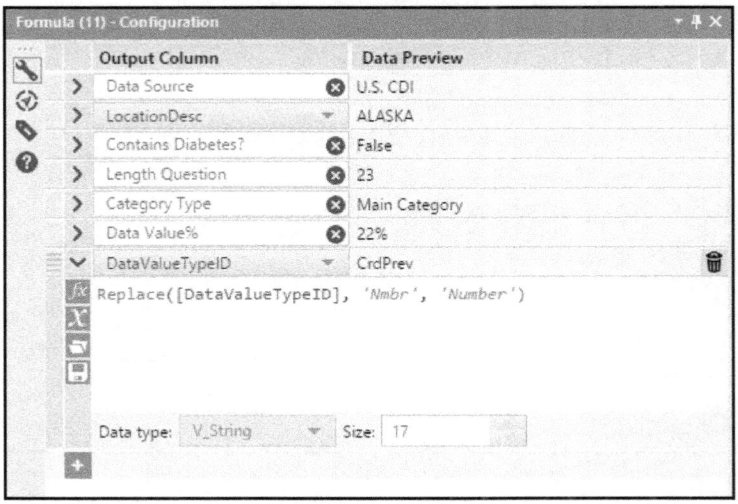

This is a string-related formula. Notice that all the values that were `Nmbr` are replaced with `Number` within the existing `DataValueTypeId` field. The `Replace` function is a handy solution to quickly handle replacement values in your data.

Expression #8: Create a new field that identifies the LocationDesc that start with N.

Step 1: Using the same Formula tool as the last expression, select the Add Expression icon ＋.

Step 2: In the **Select Column** dropdown, select + Add Column and enter: `N Locations`

Step 3: Write the following expression:

```
StartsWith([LocationDesc], 'N')
```

Step 4: Select the Data type: **Bool**. The Data Type Bool is known for Boolean giving a True or False result.

Step 5: Collapse all the previous expressions by selecting the Expand or Collapse Expression icon >.

Step 6: Run the workflow:

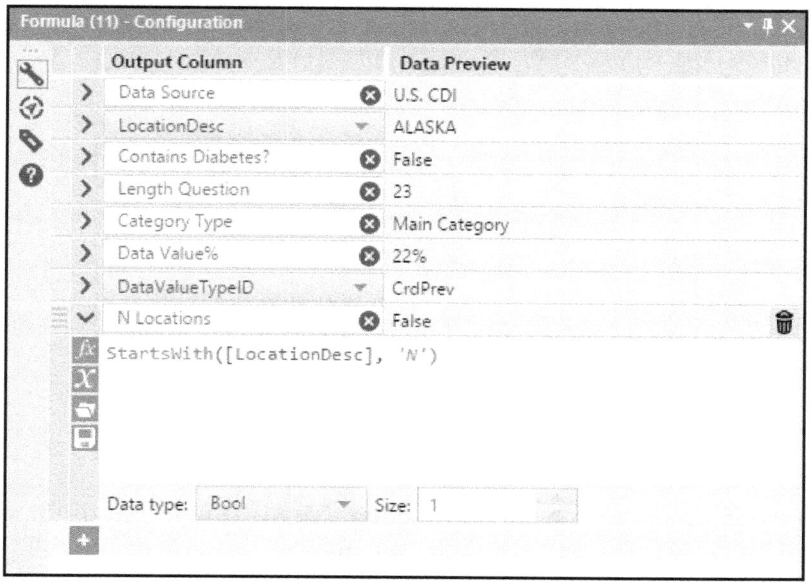

This is a string-related formula that identifies the first letter of the field and returns `True` if the target `N` is met. All `LocationDesc` that start with `N` will be `True`, and all other `LocationDesc` that do not start with `N` will be `False`.

Expression #9: Create a new field that returns the largest integer less than or equal to the LowConfidenceLimit field.

Step 1: Using the same Formula tool as the last expression, select the Add Expression icon .

Step 2: In the **Select Column** dropdown, select + Add Column and enter: `New_LCL`

Step 3: Write the following expression:

```
FLOOR([LowConfidenceLimit])
```

Leave the **Data type** and **Size** options as is.

Step 4: Collapse all the previous expressions by selecting the Expand or Collapse Expression icon .

Step 5: Run the workflow:

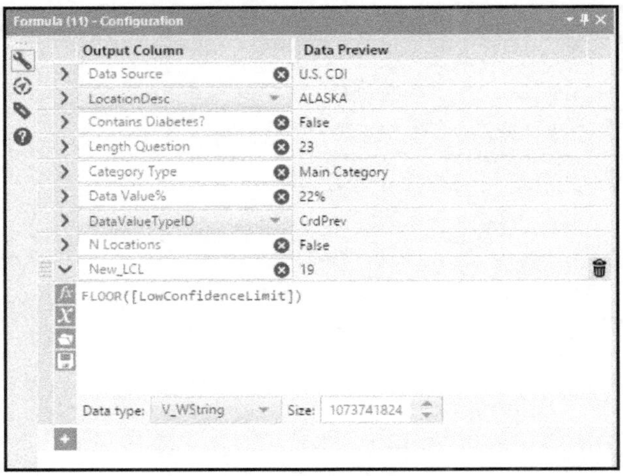

This is math-related function. The `FLOOR` function will identify the largest integer less than or equal to the `LowConfidenceLimit` field. The inverse of this is the `CEIL` function, which will return the smallest integer greater than or equal to the defined value.

In most cases, the `ROUND` function will be used to round the data values, however there are instances where, if the goal is not met, rounding down is necessary using the `FLOOR` function, or if rounding up is desired then the `CEIL` function can be used.

Expression #10: Create a new field that returns the Square Root of the DataValue field and rounds to two decimal places.

Step 1: Using the same Formula tool as the last expression, select the Add Expression icon.

Step 2: In the **Select Column** dropdown, select + Add Column and enter: `SQRT_DataValue`

Step 3: Write the following expression:

```
ROUND(SQRT(tonumber([DataValue])),0.01)
```

Leave the **Data type** and **Size** options as is.

Step 4: Select the Save Expression icon. Name the saved expression: `Rounded Square Root`

Step 5: Collapse all the previous expressions by selecting the Expand or Collapse Expression icon.

Step 6: Run the workflow:

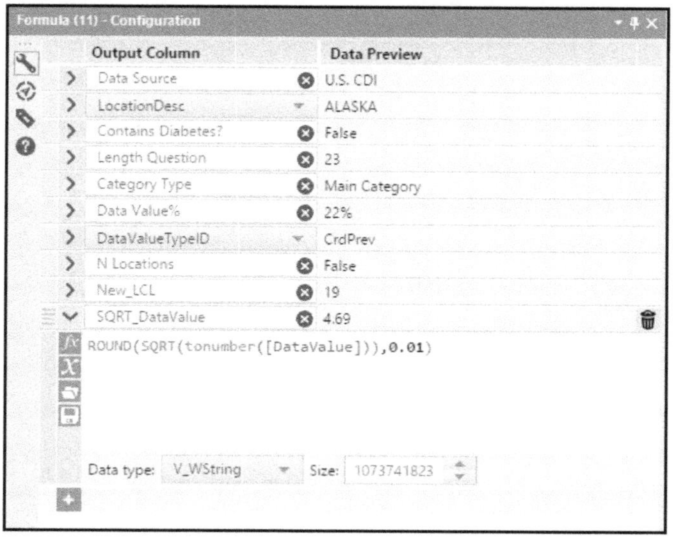

This is a math-related formula. The `DataValue` field is a string to begin with, and needs to be converted to a number first before finding the Square Root. By wrapping the `DataValue` field with a `tonumber` function, it converts the field within the expression as a number. The `SQRT` function will determine the Square Root of the `DataValue` field. The final step is to wrap the entire expression with a `ROUND` function, and note the 0.01 to specify a round to two decimal places. Success! This is a great way of altering data types within an expression and getting the value rounded to meet the desired output. You saved the expression Rounded Square Root, which can quickly be referenced if the same or a similar calculation needs to be used.

Expression #11: Create a new field that returns only the third word from the Question field.

Step 1: Using the same Formula tool as the last expression, select the Add Expression icon .

Step 2: In the **Select Column** dropdown, select + Add Column and enter: `3rd_Question_Word`

Step 3: Write the following expression:

```
GetWord([Question],2)
```

Leave the **Data type** and **Size** options as is.

Step 4: Collapse all the previous expressions by selecting the Expand or Collapse Expression icon .

Step 5: Run the workflow:

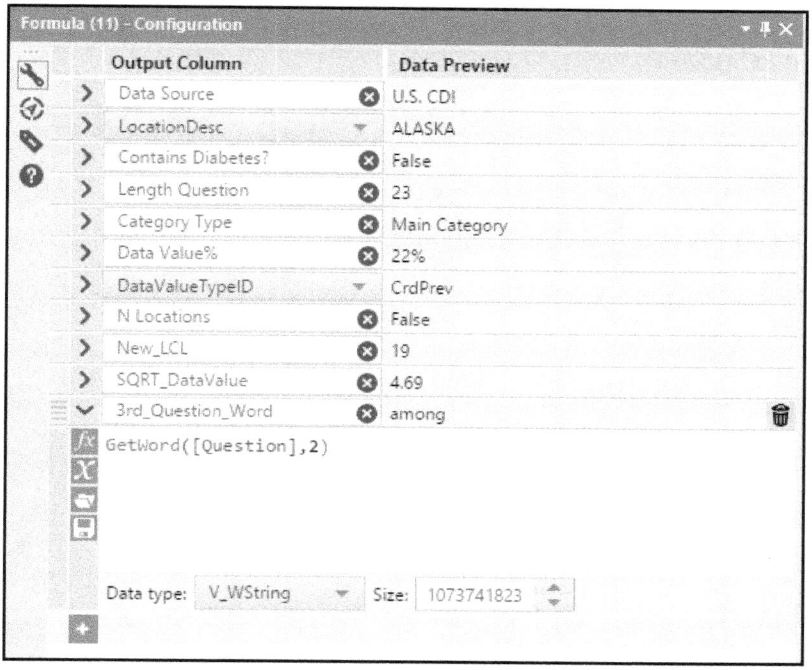

This is a string-related function. The `GetWord` function will return the Nth word in the string. The first word starts at 0, so you are looking to identify the third word where you use 2 as the specified Nth word. This is great to identify which words are included in the question.

Expression #12: Create a new field that pads 1-digit characters in LocationID with 0, so that all values for this field have two characters.

Step 1: Using the same Formula tool as the last expression, select the Add Expression icon .

Step 2: In the **Select Column** dropdown, select + Add Column and enter: `Pad_LocationID`

Step 3: Write the following expression:

```
PadLeft(ToString([LocationID]),2,'0')
```

Leave the **Data type** and **Size** options as is.

Step 4: Collapse all the previous expressions by selecting the Expand or Collapse Expression icon.

Step 5: Run the workflow:

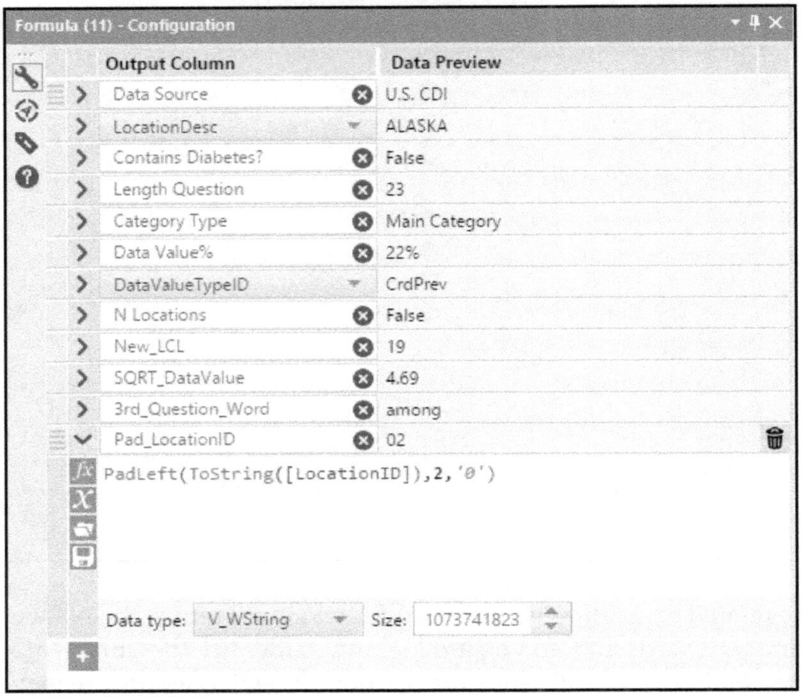

This is a string-related formula. The `LocationID` field is not a string, so you will first convert it to a string by using the `ToString` function. `PadLeft` will pad the left side of the `LocationID` field with a `0`, as specified in the expression. The `2` indicates the length. Notice in the new field, `Pad_LocationId`, the 1-value characters have now been transformed to 2-value characters. The `LocationID` has `2` by specifying the `LocationID` length. This is a valuable string function if leading or trailing zeros need to be added. `PadRight` is the same as `PadLeft`, except it pads the specified character to the right of the string.

Expression #13: Create a new field that identifies how many words are contained in the Question field.

Step 1: Using the same Formula tool as the last expression, select the Add Expression icon.

Step 2: In the **Select Column** dropdown, select + Add Column and enter: `Question_Word_Count`

Step 3: Write the following expression:

```
CountWords([Question])
```

Leave the **Data type** and **Size** options as is.

Step 4: Collapse all the previous expressions by selecting the Expand or Collapse Expression icon >.

Step 5: Run the workflow:

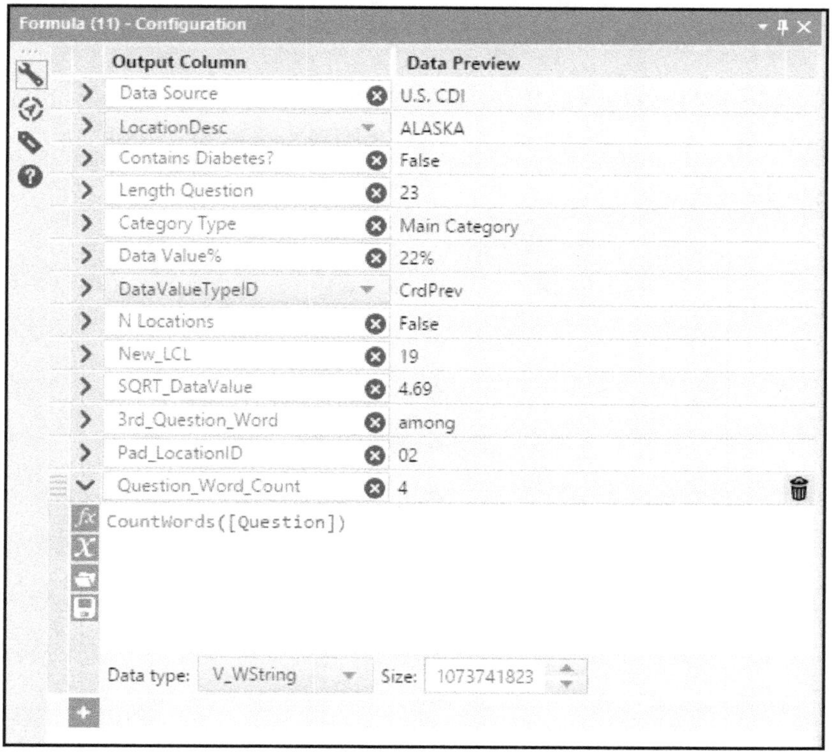

This is a string-related formula. The `CountWords` function will identify the number of words within the Question field, which is great for identifying if a specific word count has been met.

Expression #14: Create a new field that identifies the 4th character in the QuestionID field for values that start with TOB, and all other values as NA.

Step 1: Using the same Formula tool as the last expression, select the Add Expression icon .

Step 2: In the **Select Column** dropdown, select + Add Column and enter: `TOB_SEQUENCE`

Step 3: Write the following expression:

```
IF LEFT([QuestionID],3) = 'TOB' THEN
 Substring([QuestionID],3,1)
 ELSE "NA"
 ENDIF
```

Leave the **Data type** and **Size** options as is.

Step 4: Collapse all the previous expressions by selecting the Expand or Collapse Expression icon .

Step 5: Run the workflow:

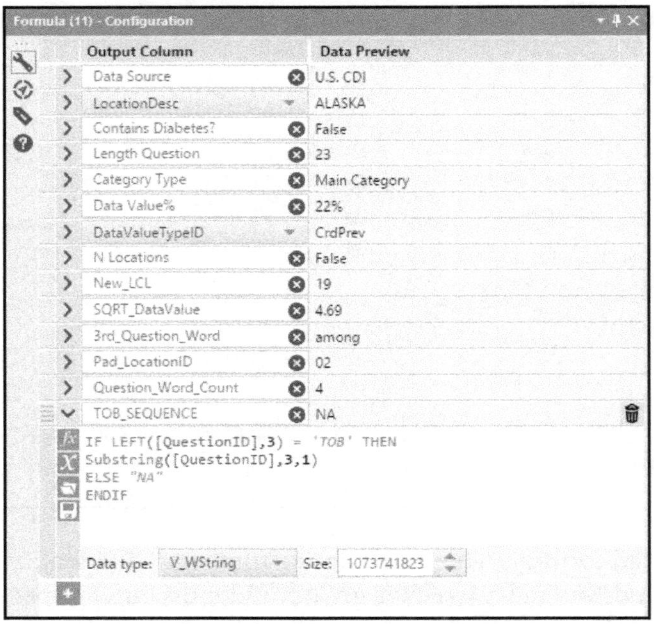

Expression #15: Create a new field that identifies the Date and Time the workflow is run.

Step 1: Using the same Formula tool as the last expression, select the Add Expression icon .

Step 2: In the **Select Column** dropdown, select + Add Column and enter: `UPDATE_DATETIME`

Step 3: Write the following expression:

```
DateTimeNow()
```

Leave the **Data type** and **Size** options as is.

Step 4: Select the **Data type**: `DateTime`.

Step 5: Collapse all the previous expressions by selecting the Expand or Collapse Expression icon .

Step 6: Run the workflow:

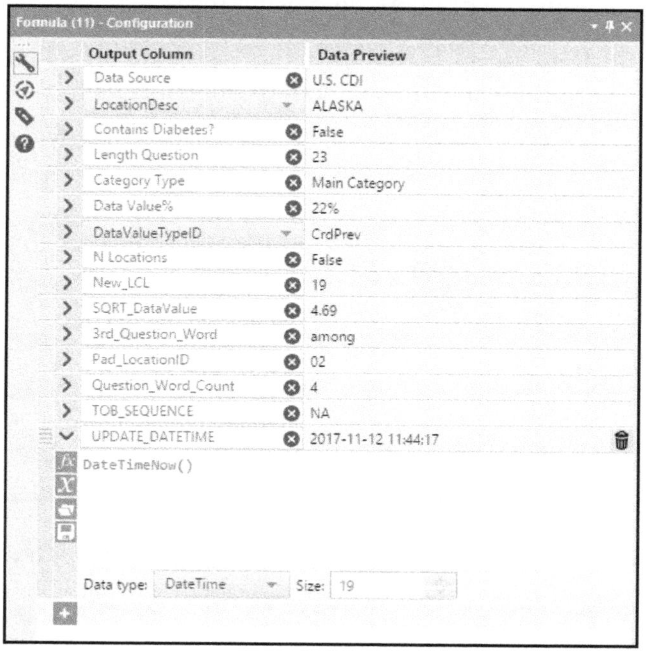

This is a DateTime-related formula. `DateTimeNow()` will provide the date and time the workflow is run, which is great for creating an updated date and time when outputting data, and a quick reference to the date and time when the data was last updated. The `DateTimeToday()` function is similar in that it only provides the date, and removes the time component.

Multi-Row Formula

You went through some great use cases for the Formula tool, and are now probably wondering how you can update multiple rows based on an expression. The Multi-Row Formula tool accomplishes just that by writing expressions to references preceding and/or following rows. This can be done by creating a new field or modifying existing fields.

In this section, we will use the same workflow from the last section; the U.S. Chronic Disease Indicators workflow. Let's go through a couple of expressions to understand how helpful the Multi-Row Formula is.

Expression #1: Update the existing field DatavalueFootnote where, if the current row is null, then fill in the null with the previous row using the same field.

Step 1: Select the Multi-Row Formula tool from the Preparation tool palette and drag it onto the canvas. Connect the Multi-Row Formula tool to the Formula tool.

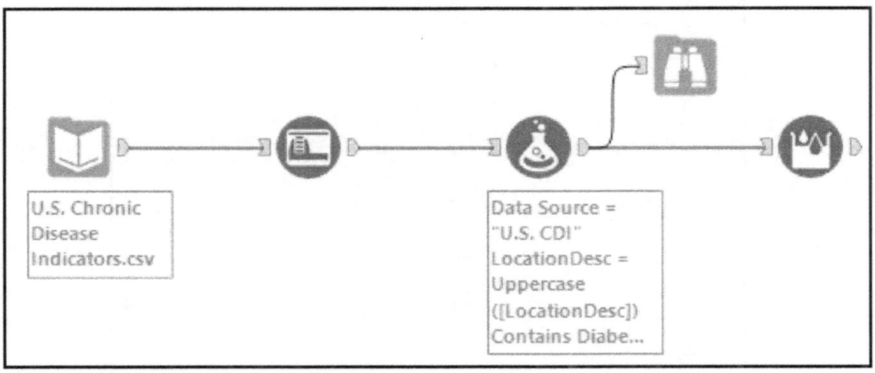

Step 2: Select Update Existing Field, and from the dropdown select `DatavalueFootnote`.

Step 3: Write the following expression:

```
IF IsNull([DatavalueFootnote])
 THEN [Row-1:DatavalueFootnote]
 ELSE [DatavalueFootnote]
 ENDIF
```

Step 4: Add the Browse tool to the Multi-Row Formula tool.

Step 5: Run the workflow:

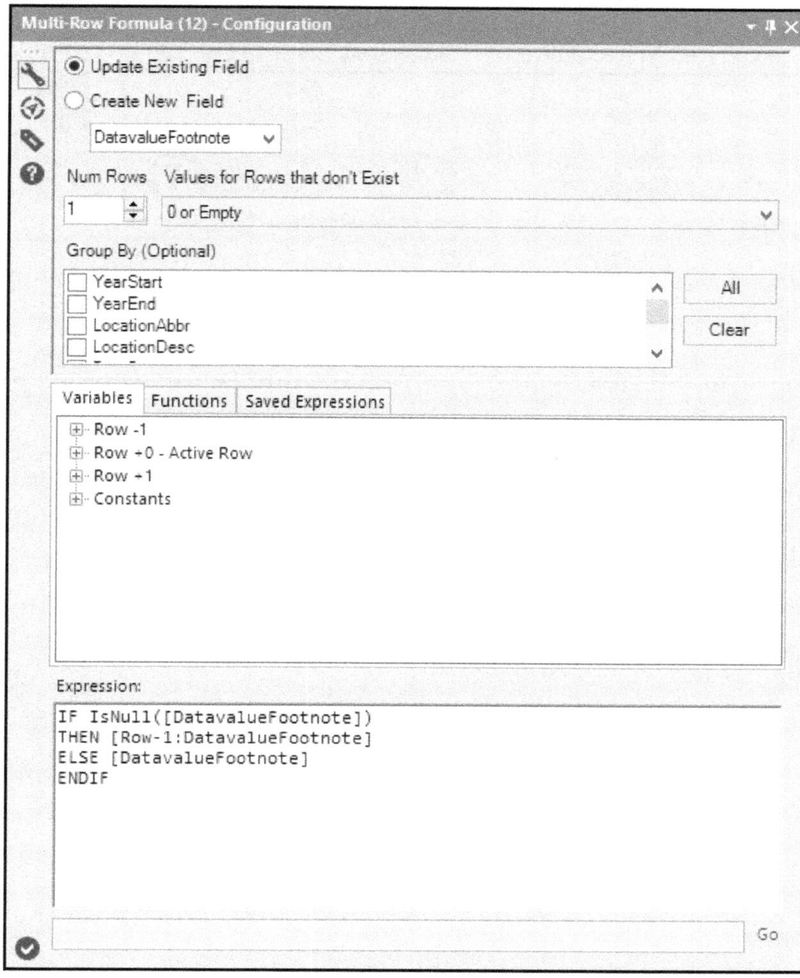

Notice, each row in the existing `DatavalueFootnote` field has now been updated with the previous row data, where the current row, which is identified in the **Row +0 - Active Row** variables, is null. If that is not the case, then leave the current row as is for the `DatavalueFootnote` field.

Expression #2: Create a new field that provides a new Record ID for every YearEnd field.

Step 1: Select the Multi-Row Formula tool from the Preparation tool palette and drag it onto the canvas. Connect the Multi-Row Formula tool to the existing Multi-Row Formula tool from the last expression. You will now have two Multi-Row Formula tools connected to each other.

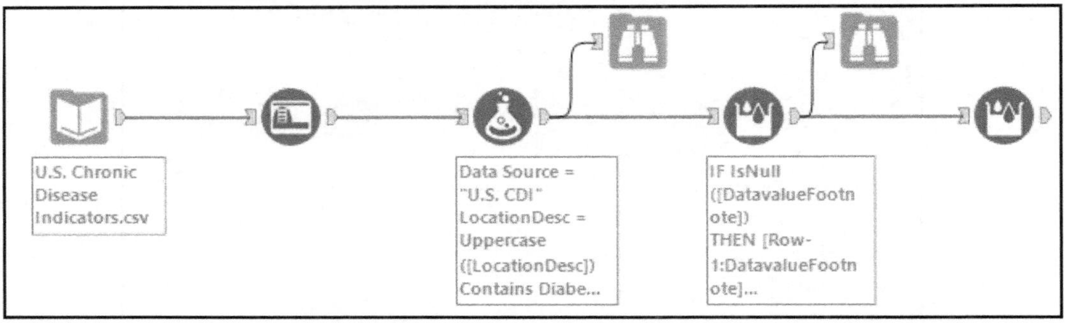

Step 2: Select Create New Field, and enter this in the text box: `RecordID`.

Step 3: Select `YearEnd` from the Group By (Optional) options.

Step 4: Write the following expression:

```
[Row-1:RecordID]+1
```

Step 5: Add the Browse tool to the Multi-Row Formula tool.

Step 6: Run the workflow:

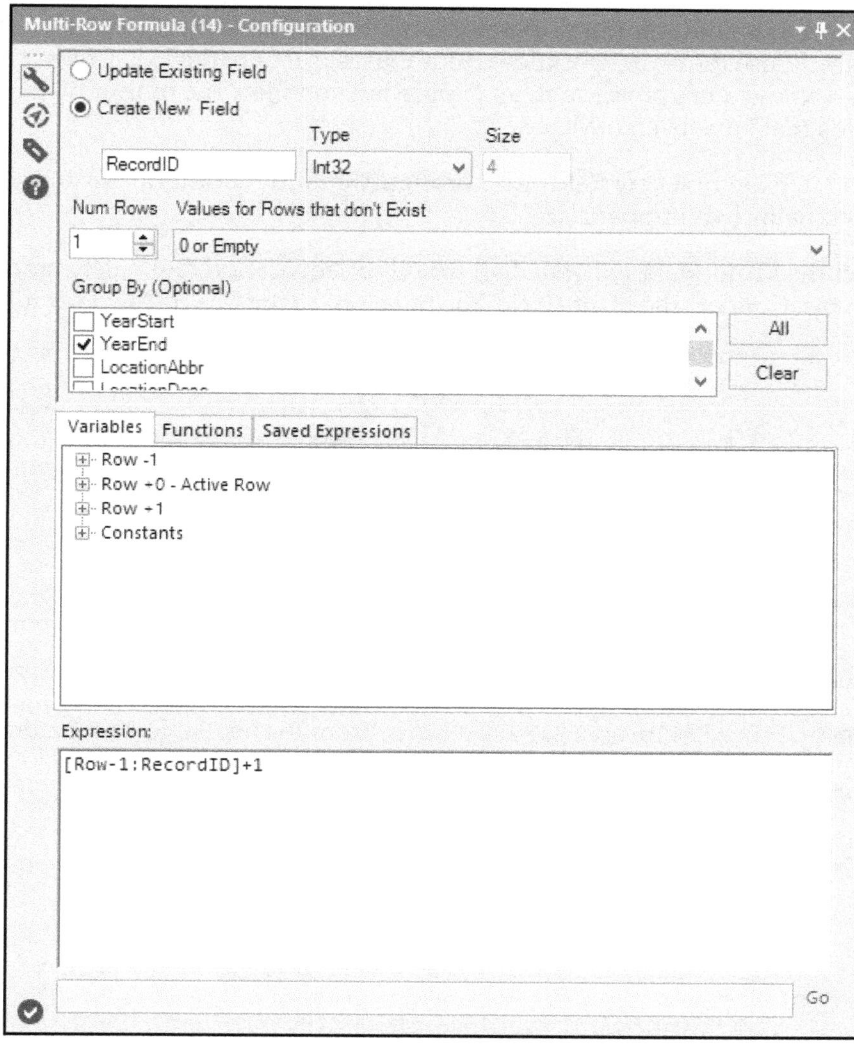

`RecordID` field takes the previous row value and adds 1 for each `YearEnd` noted by the `YearEnd` Group By selection. As soon as a new `YearEnd` is identified `[Row-1:RecordID]+1` will start a new count. This is great for identifying records by a group. More than one group can be identified by selecting more than one Group By option.

Multi-Field Formula

Multi-Field Formula allows for multiple fields to be updated at once through a single function. We will use the same workflow from the last section, the U.S. Chronic Disease Indicators workflow. Let's go through an expression and view the output displaying multiple fields that have been updated.

Expression #1: Create two new fields for LocationAbbr and LocationDesc to update the values in both fields to all uppercase.

Step 1: Select the Multi-Field Formula tool from the Preparation tool palette and drag it onto the canvas. Connect the Multi-Field Formula tool to the Multi-Row Formula tool.

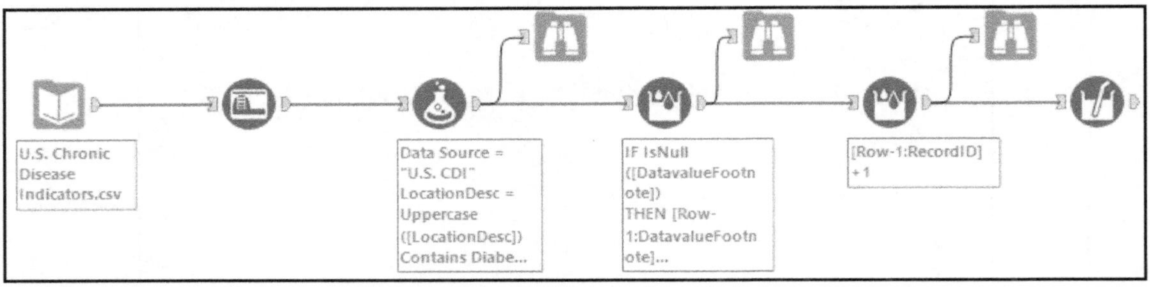

Step 2: Select Text from the dropdown field options.

Step 3: Select `LocationAbbr` and `LocationDesc` from the available Text fields.

Step 4: Select **Copy Output Fields Add** and enter `Uppercase_ as` a Prefix.

Step 5: Write the following expression:

```
UPPERCASE([_CurrentField_])
```

Step 6: Add the Browse tool to the Multi-Field Formula tool.

Step 7: Run the workflow:

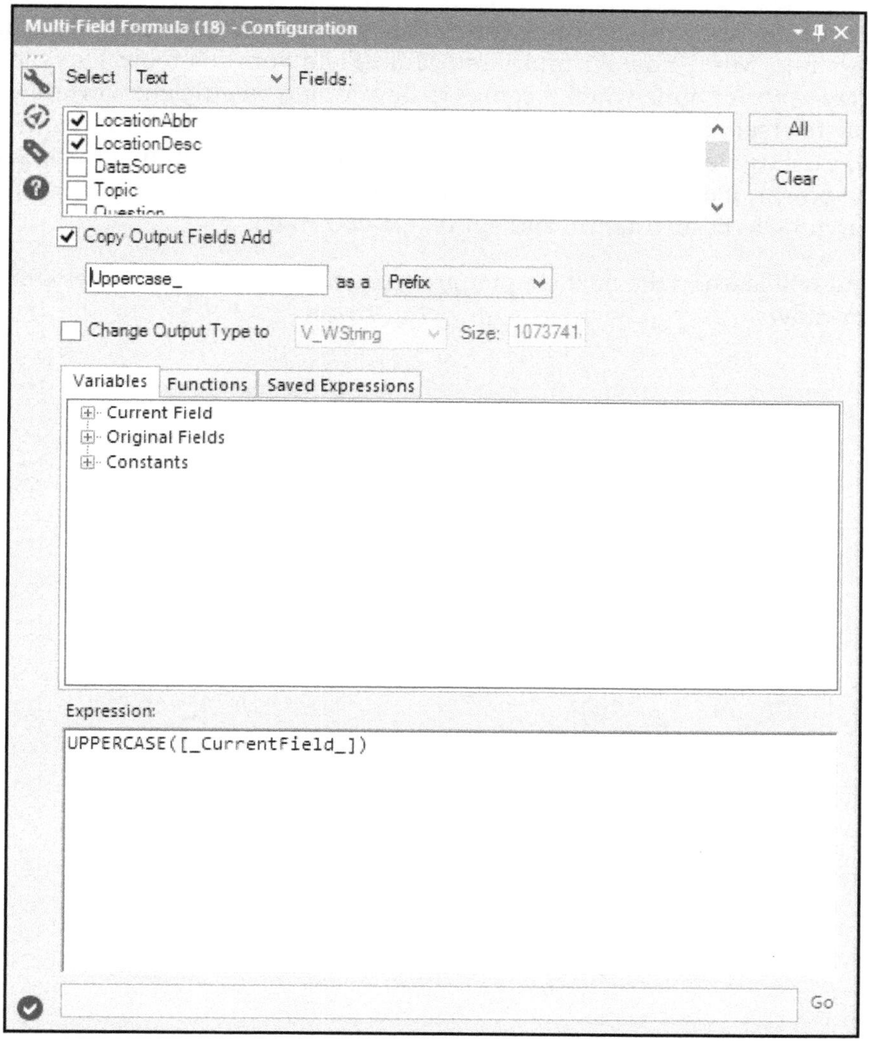

Notice the two new fields now contain `Uppercase_LocationAbbr` and `Uppercase_LocationDesc`, with all the values updated to uppercase. This is a handy solution for updating more than one field in one instance.

Summary

The ability to create fast and accurate expressions can be accomplished and optimized by using the Formula, Multi-Row Formula, and Multi-Field Formula tools. Flexible and dynamic, they save you time when it comes to developing an efficient workflow. Alteryx makes it easy to create these formulas by providing helpful options for them. Whether it's updating an existing field, or creating a new field using a variety of functions, you have explored the power of creating calculations to meet customer needs. The next chapter you will dive into how to best structure and aggregate your data.

The tools you will learn in the next chapter are frequently used when developing your efficient workflows.

5
Transforming Data

Transforming data in Alteryx can ensure that the dataset best fits the needs of how the output data should be analyzed. In this chapter, you'll learn the pivot orientations of the Transpose and Crosstab tools and how they help to guide the pathway to a visual representation of your data. Once your data has been aligned to meet business needs, you will dive into summarizing and aggregating your data to perform various numeric and string actions.

This chapter will cover the following topics:

- Transforming data
- Summarizing and aggregating data
- Running total
- Weighted average

Transforming data

The way we see data and visualize trends begins with the data structure. The data structure is key when creating data visualizations. Knowing how it's structured and why it's structured in a specific orientation leads to a smoother workflow build and design that turns into a successful output table to create brilliant data visualizations. We'll cover two tools that transform data in this section: the **Transpose** tool and the **Crosstab** tool.

The Transpose tool will pivot a wide dataset to a narrow dataset. This is the tall and skinny dataset that will put the fields in rows, and the values in rows as well. More rows will be created when data is transposed to a narrower dataset. This is great for trying to get one field that contains all the field names and the values associated with those field names alongside each other in rows. A calculation can be referenced on one field, rather than an individual calculation referencing each field if they were in their own columns. Transposing data is also known as unpivoting data, converting it from a crosstab format to a tabular format.

In this section, we will use the `U.S. Chronic Disease Indicators` workflow, along with the resources located in the data folder. Let's begin by building out a workflow that leads to an opportunity to transpose the data.

Let's first review how the data structure changes once transposed. This is an example from the `U.S. Chronic Disease Indicators` dataset. Notice that there are seven fields presented; the fields with the values are the data fields to transpose. We want to change the data structure from a wider dataset to a narrow dataset. The other fields are known as key fields and they are to remain as their own fields.

Key Fields: `YearEnd`, `LocationAbbr`, `Topic`, and `Question`.

Data Fields: `DataValue`, `LowConfidenceLimit`, and `HighConfidenceLimit`.

YearEnd	LocationAbbr	Topic	Question	DataValue	LowConfidenceLimit	HighConfidenceLimit
2015	FL	Arthritis	Arthritis among adults aged >= 18 years who have diabetes	22.1	14	33.1

The goal is to unpivot the data, so that the three data fields are now under one field, identified as Name, with their associated values under the Value field. Notice that, before transposing the data there was one row of data with a wider data structure and that, after transposing the data, there are three rows of data with a narrow data structure.

`YearEnd`	`LocationAbbr`	`Topic`	`Question`	`Name`	`Value`
2015	FL	Arthritis	Arthritis among adults aged >= 18 years who have diabetes	DataValue	22.1
2015	FL	Arthritis	Arthritis among adults aged >= 18 years who have diabetes	LowConfidenceLimit	14
2015	FL	Arthritis	Arthritis among adults aged >= 18 years who have diabetes	HighConfidenceLimit	33.1

Let's begin by building out this type of transposing example in a workflow, so you can see how helpful structuring data can be.

Transposing Example #1: Filter data to only 2015. Create a narrow dataset using `DataValue`, `LowConfidenceLimit`, and `HighConfidenceLimit` as the data fields.

Step 1: Using an Input Data tool, connect to the file `U.S. Chronic Disease Indicators.csv`, located in the `\Learn Alteryx\Chapter` directory.

Step 2: Select the Auto Field tool from the Preparation tool palette and drag it onto the canvas. Connect the Auto Field tool to the Input Data tool. Each string field has now been automatically updated to the smallest field type and size.

Step 3: Select the Select tool from the Preparation tool palette and drag it onto the canvas. Connect the Select tool to the Auto Field tool.

Step 4: Select the following fields in the Select tool:

`YearEnd`, `LocationAbbr`, `Topic`, `Question`, `DataValue`, `LowConfidenceLimit`, and `HighConfidenceLimit`

Step 5: Select the Filter tool from the Preparation tool palette and drag it onto the canvas. Connect the Filter tool to the Select tool.

Step 6: Select the Basic Filter option in the Filter tool configuration. From the dropdown, select the field `YearEnd` and `=`. In the text box, enter: `2015`.

Step 7: Select the Transpose tool from the Transform tool palette and drag it onto the canvas. Connect the Transpose tool to the True output from the Filter tool:

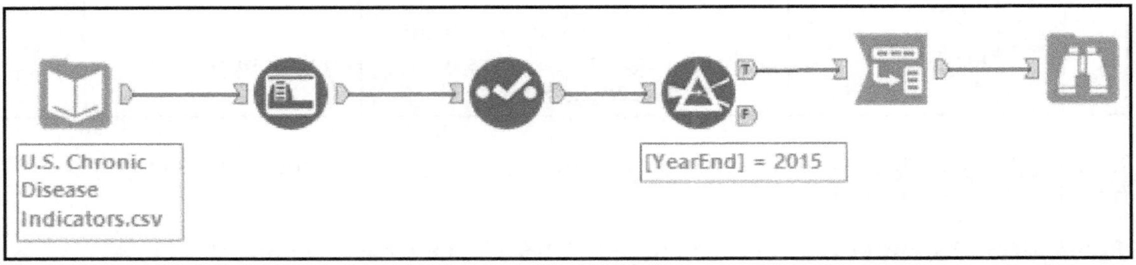

Step 8: Select the following Key Fields in the Transpose tool configuration:

`YearEnd`, `LocationAbbr`, `Topic`, and `Question`

Step 9: Select the `DataValue`, `LowConfidenceLimit`, and `HighConfidenceLimit`

Data Fields in the Transpose tool configuration:

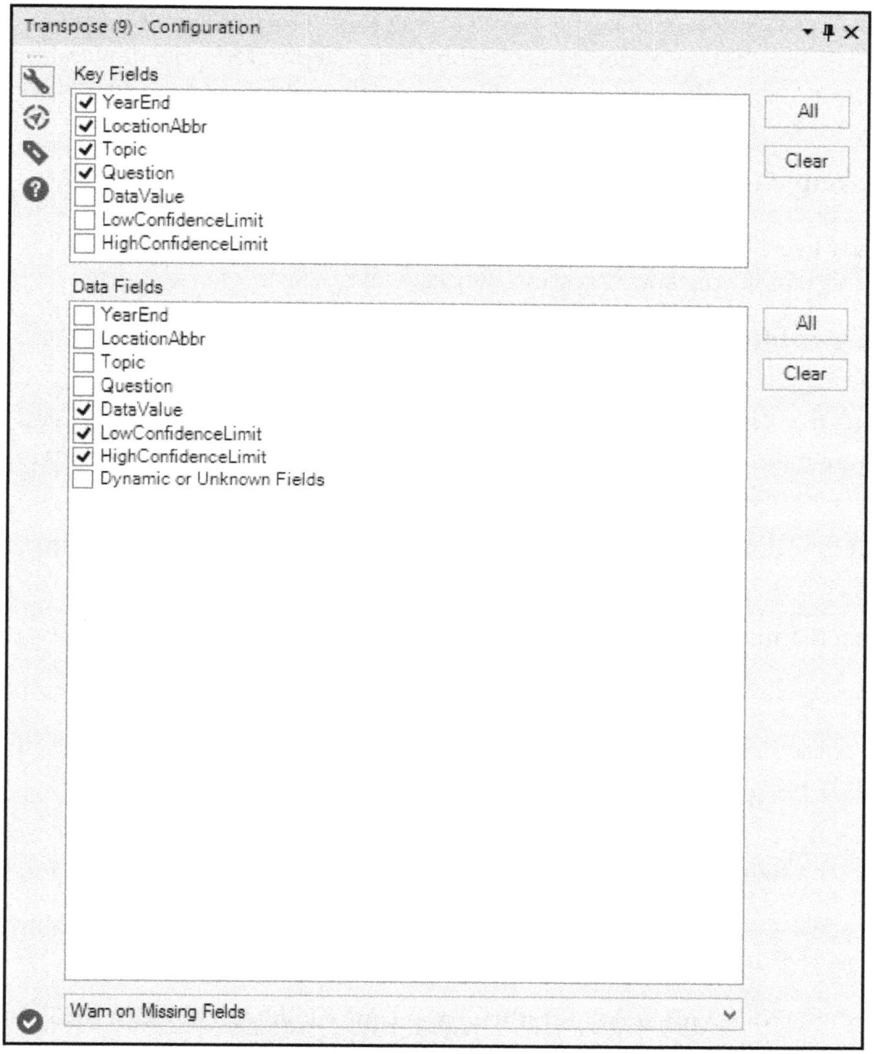

Step 10: Run the workflow.

Notice that the data fields selected are under the Name field and their respective values are under the Value field. The transposing reduced the number of fields from a wide dataset down to a narrow dataset. The Name and Value fields can be renamed to something more intuitive, but the key here is the transformation of data all within one tool, a great way to unpivot data to structure it the way it fits best for your analysis.

The opposite of the Transpose tool is the Crosstab tool. The Crosstab tool pivots the data from a narrow dataset to a wider dataset. The data gets pivoted, so a new column is created for each unique value. The goal is to get the values in an existing field to convert to their own field. Let's go through a pivoting orientation using the Crosstab tool.

Crosstab Example #1: Filter data to Florida. Create a wide dataset using the `StratisfactionCategory1` field by transforming the values for this field into their own fields for each Topic and Question. Find only the first values for the `DataValue` field and group them by Topic and Question. Replace all null values with zero.

Step 1: Using an Input Data tool, connect to the file `U.S. Chronic Disease Indicators.csv`, located in the `\Learn Alteryx\Chapter` directory.

Step 2: Select the Auto Field tool from the Preparation tool palette and drag it onto the canvas. Connect the Auto Field tool to the Input Data tool. Each string field has now been automatically updated to the smallest field type and size.

Step 3: Select the Select tool from the Preparation tool palette and drag it onto the canvas. Connect the Select tool to the Auto Field tool.

Step 4: Select the following fields in the Select tool:

`LocationAbbr`, `Topic`, `Question`, `DataValue`, and `StratisfactionCategory1`

Step 5: Select the Filter tool from the Preparation tool palette and drag it onto the canvas. Connect the Filter tool to the Select tool.

Step 6: Select the Basic Filter option in the Filter tool configuration. From the drop-down menu, select the field `LocationAbbr` and `Equals`. In the textbox, enter: `FL`.

Step 7: Select the Crosstab tool from the Transform tool palette and drag it onto the canvas. Connect the Crosstab tool to the True output from the Filter tool.

Step 8: Select the following fields for the Group Data by these Values in the Crosstab tool configuration:

```
Topic and Question
```

Step 9: Select the `StratisfactionCategory1` field for New Column Headers in the Crosstab tool configuration:

```
DataValue
```

Step 10: Select First for Method for Aggregating Values in the Crosstab tool configuration.

The following screenshot is a snapshot of the configuration:

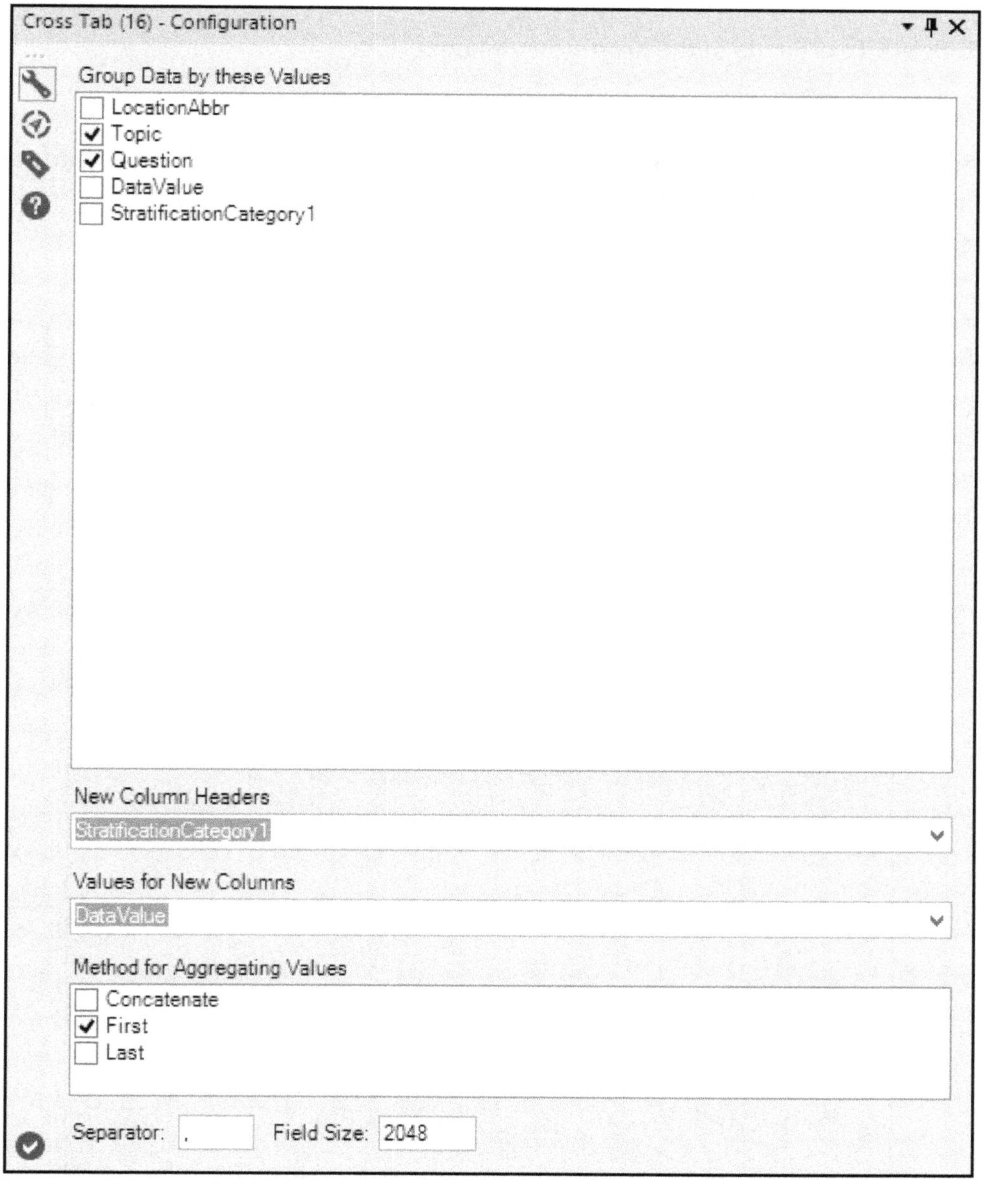

Step 11: Select the Multi-Formula tool from the Preparation tool palette and drag it onto the canvas. Connect the Multi-Field Formula tool to the output from the Crosstab tool.

Step 12: Select Text Fields in the drop-down menu.

Step 13: Select `Gender`, `Overall`, and `Race_Ethnicity` from the field options.

Step 14: Deselect **Copy Output Fields Add** and select **Change Output Type to** and select **String** from the drop-down options.

Step 15: Write the following expression in the Multi-Field Formula tool:

```
IIF(IsNull([_CurrentField_]),0,[_CurrentField_])
```

The following is the snapshot for the Multi-Field Formula Configuration:

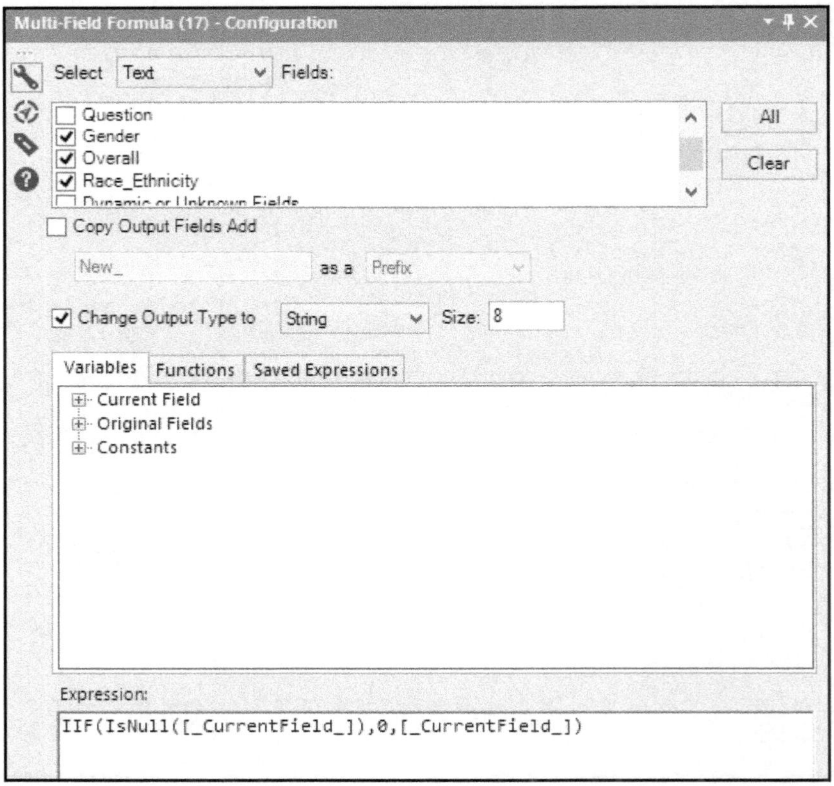

Step 16: Run the workflow.

The Crosstab tool identifies the field that will be pivoted, which is the `StratisfactionCategory1` field, and the respective values for this field are identified by the `DataValue` field. Selecting first for Method for Aggregating Values will provide only the first value for the `DataValue` field for each Topic and Question, which is identified by selecting these fields from the Group Data by the values option. The final step is to replace null values for all fields with a zero. Let's walk through the Multi-Field Formula tool used to update this. The text fields are selected where the calculation should refer to the current fields. An Inline If statement is used for the first part, where if the current field is null, then give a zero, and if that's not true, then give the current field value. Notice that, in the output all nulls have been replaced by zero.

The following snapshot shows the final workflow:

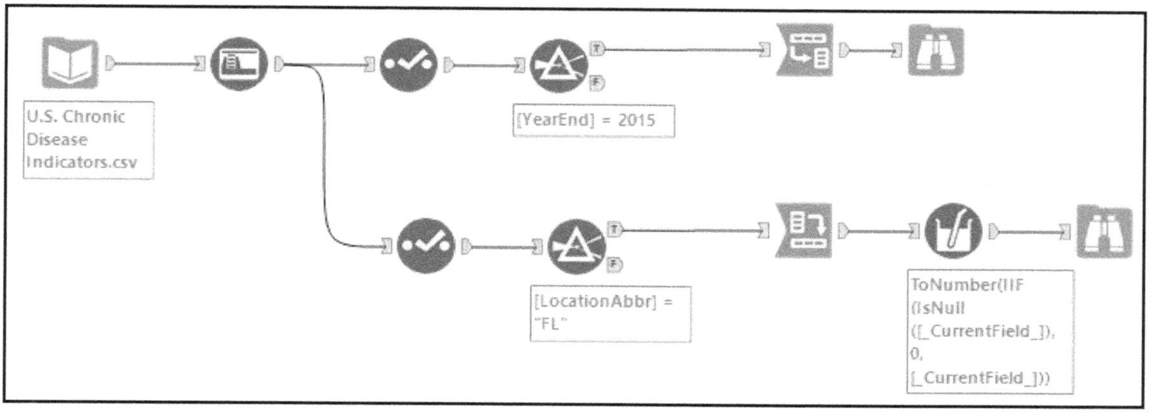

The workflow build will look like this when complete, with the top stream using the Transpose tool to unpivot data by changing a wider dataset to a narrow dataset. The inverse of the Transpose tool, which you went through in the bottom stream, pivoted data by changing a narrow dataset to a wider dataset. These two tools are very popular for transforming data, and the way you shape your data will lead to easier and faster analysis.

Summarizing and aggregating data

Summary calculations and aggregating data at various levels using group by functions are available through the Summarize tool. This is a popular tool that performs a variety of summation calculations, including: summing, math, min/max, string concatenation, grouping, and much more.

We will go through seven various calculations using the summary tool, and why these calculations are beneficial. Let's begin by looking through these examples using the same workflow as the previous section.

Summarize Example #1: Find the `Min` and `Max` DataValue by `YearEnd`, `LocationAbbr`, `Topic`, and `Question`.

Step 1: Select the Summarize tool from the Transform tool palette and drag it onto the canvas. Connect the Auto Field tool to the Summarize tool.

Step 2: Select the following fields and select Add from the dropdown to select their respective actions:

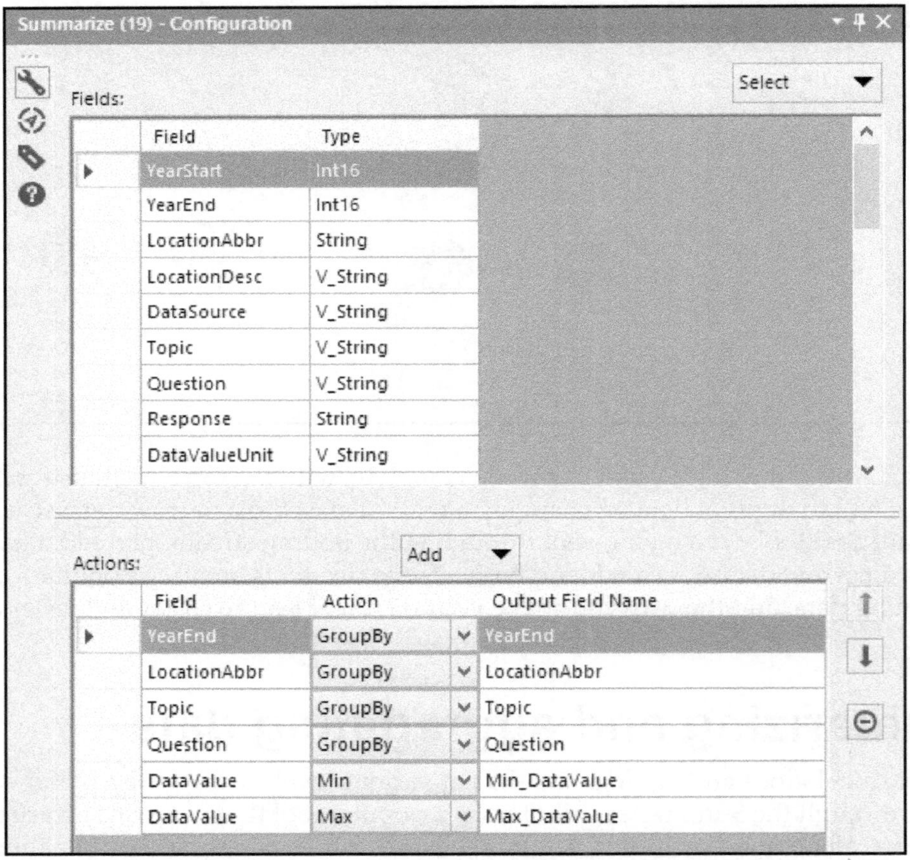

Step 3: Add a Browse tool to the Summarize tool.

Step 4: Run the workflow.

Notice that in the Browse tool, the min and max data values have been identified by `YearEnd`, `LocationAbbr`, `Topic`, and `Question`. This is a quick way to identify the **Min** and **Max** values in a dataset. If you are interested in finding the min and max values for the entire dataset without any groupings, then remove all the Group By actions, and this will give you the desired result.

Summarize Example #2: Find the longest and shortest question for each Topic.

Step 1: Select the Summarize tool from the Transform tool palette and drag it onto the canvas. Connect the Auto Field tool to the Summarize tool.

Step 2: Select the following fields and select Add from the dropdown to select their respective actions:

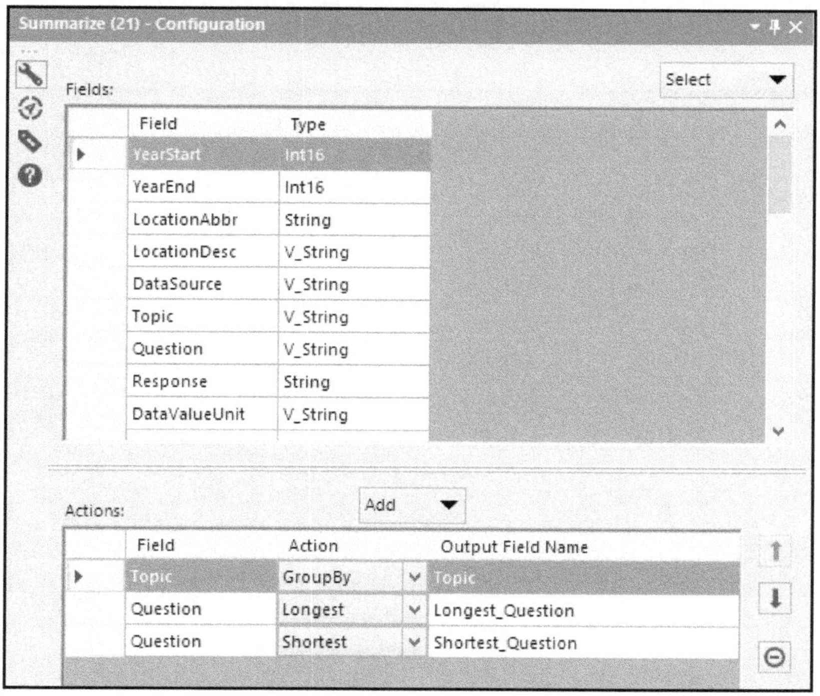

Step 3: Add a Browse tool to the Summarize tool.

Step 4: Run the workflow.

This is a great way of determining the longest and shortest values within a field, and is very useful for survey data and identifying if they need to meet a certain threshold. In this instance, the longest and shortest values are found for each Topic.

Summarize Example #3: Find the median value for the `HighConfidenceLimit` field by `YearEnd` and `LocationAbbr`.

Step 1: Select the Summarize tool from the Transform tool palette and drag it onto the canvas. Connect the Auto Field tool to the Summarize tool.

Step 2: Select the following fields and select Add from the dropdown to select their respective actions:

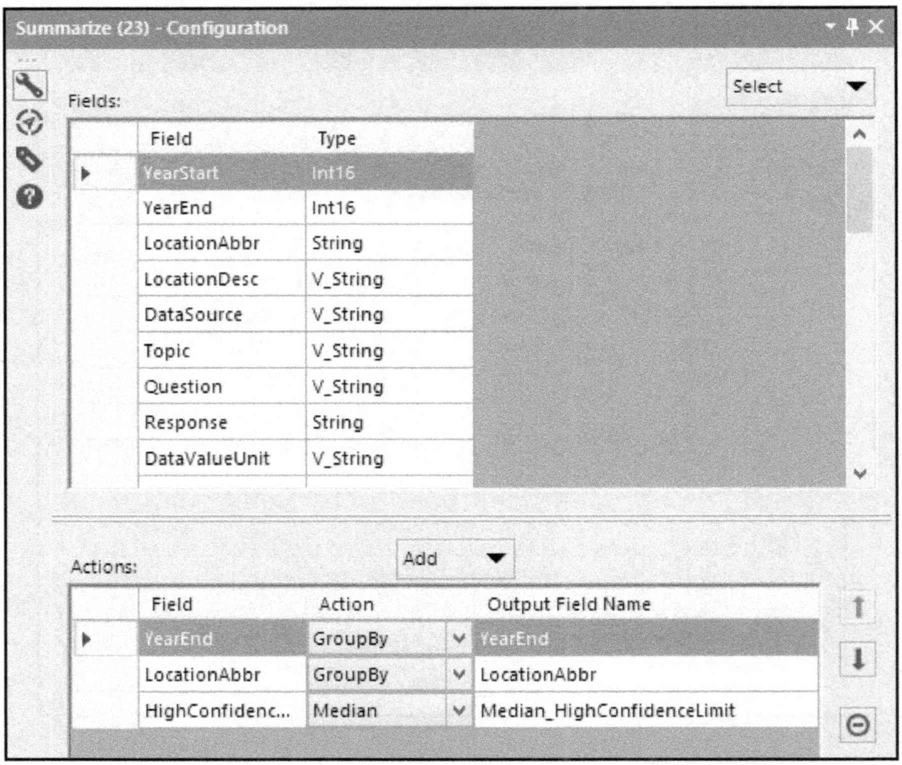

Step 3: Add a Browse tool to the Summarize tool.

Step 4: Run the workflow.

You may have noticed by now the variety of aggregations within the Summarize tool. Determining the median value for a field is possible, and in this case the median value is identified by `YearEnd` and `LocationAbbr`.

Summarize Example #4: Count the distinct data values for the DataValue field that are non-nulls only by `YearEnd`, `LocationAbbr`, and `Topic`.

Step 1: Select the Summarize tool from the Transform tool palette and drag it onto the canvas. Connect the Auto Field tool to the Summarize tool.

Step 2: Select the following fields and select Add from the dropdown to select their respective actions:

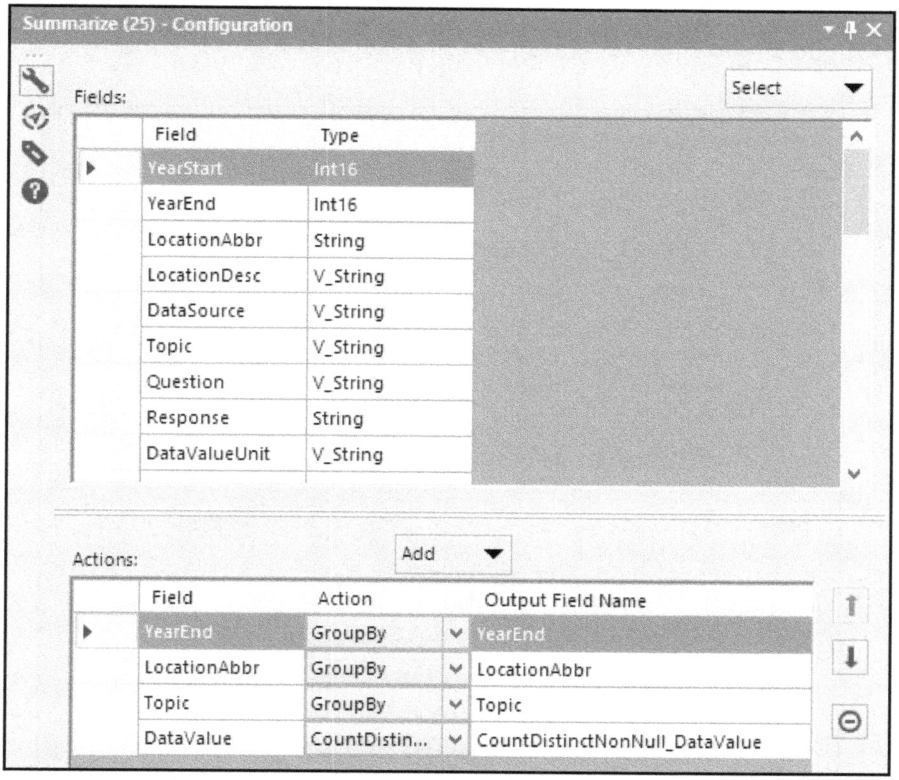

Step 3: Add a Browse tool to the Summarize tool.

Step 4: Run the workflow.

I really enjoy the aggregations that don't include nulls. Nulls just sound bad! And are they ever in our data sets? Thankfully, there are built-in aggregations within the Summarize tool. The goal here is to count the distinct values that are not null. If you were to use CountDistinct rather than CountDistinctNonNull, this would increase the count as nulls would be included. By using the `CountDistinctNonNull` action grouped by `YearEnd`, `LocationAbbr` and `Topic` will grant the desired result.

Summarize Example #5: Find the sum of the `LowConfidenceLimit` by `YearEnd` and `Topic`.

Step 1: Select the Summarize tool from the Transform tool palette and drag it onto the canvas. Connect the Auto Field tool to the Summarize tool.

Step 2: Select the following fields and select Add from the dropdown to select their respective actions:

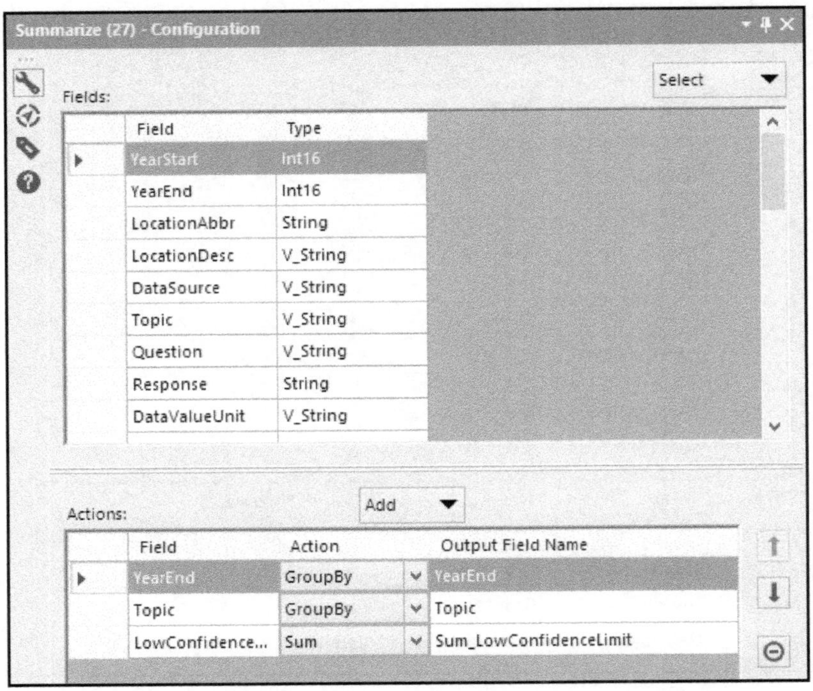

Step 3: Add a Browse tool to the Summarize tool.

Step 4: Run the workflow.

Sum is a very popular aggregation. In this example, the goal is to find the sum of all the values contained within the `LowConfidenceLimit` field by `YearEnd` and `Topic`. The `Sum` action is readily available within the Summarize tool.

Summarize Example #6: Find the distinct `StratisfactionCategoryID1` values for each `Topic`.

Step 1: Select the Summarize tool from the Transform tool palette and drag it onto the canvas. Connect the Auto Field tool to the Summarize tool.

Step 2: Select the following fields and select Add from the dropdown to select their respective actions:

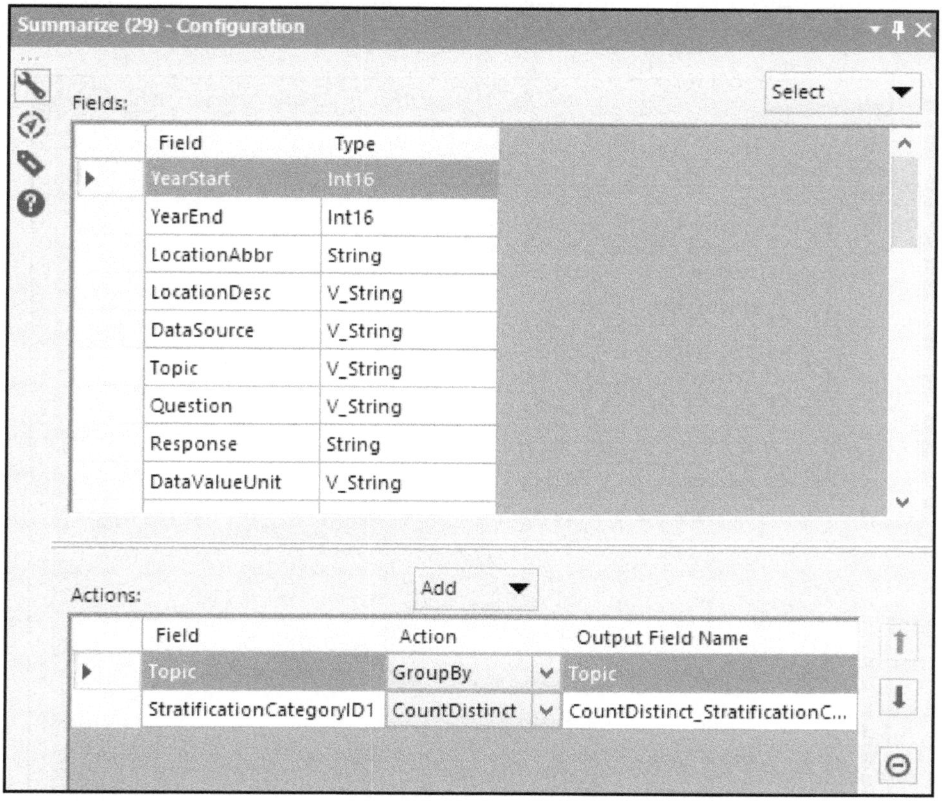

Step 3: Add a Browse tool to the Summarize tool.

Step 4: Run the workflow.

The distinct count of `StratificationCategoryID1` values can be found by using the `CountDistinct` action. Notice that the more Group By actions there are, the more rows there will be, as it will keep grouping the data to a more granular level. In this case, only the Topic is used for `Group By`, and the output is `17` records, since there are `17` different Topics. Each Topic will have a distinct count of `StratificationCategoryID1` values.

Summarize Example #7: Find the average and the average ignoring zeros using the `DataValueAlt` field by `Topic` and `TopicID`.

Step 1: Select the Summarize tool from the Transform tool palette and drag it onto the canvas. Connect the Auto Field tool to the Summarize tool.

Step 2: Select the following fields and select Add from the dropdown to select their respective actions:

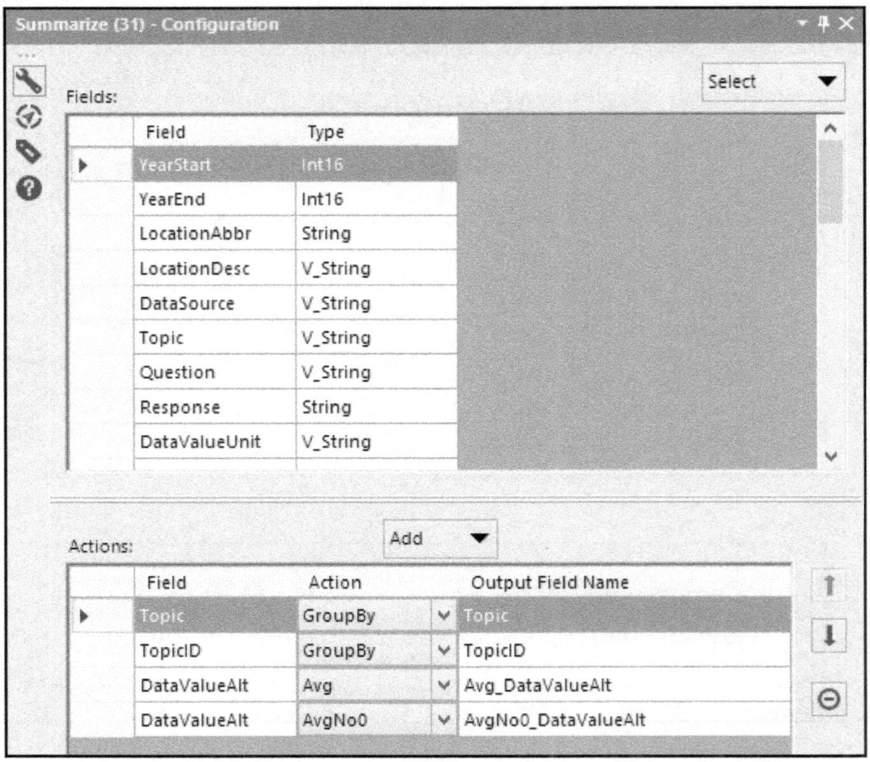

Step 3: Add a Browse tool to the Summarize tool.

Step 4: Run the workflow.

Another great example of ignoring zeros is when an average of all the values for a field, in this case `DataValueAlt`, needs to be averaged without considering the zeros in the dataset. This is possible by using the AvgNo0 action. The AvgNo0 action is used to average the values without including zeros in the averaged result. The output contains the variance between using the Avg compared to AvgNo0 actions.

Running total

A running total is a great way of obtaining a cumulative sum per record. The Running Total tool can be used to create a running total, and like the Summarize tool, there are Group By options available to include if you want to group the data by the available fields. Running Totals are useful for getting a total for a group; in this case, a running total of `DataValueAlt` by `YearEnd` and `Topic`. The cumulative sum will be continuing to aggregate until a new `YearEnd` and `Topic` appears in the data set. Once this occurs, the running total will start the cumulative sum again. Let's look at how to apply running totals using the same workflow from the previous section.

Running Total Example #1: Find the running total for `DataValueAlt` by `YearEnd` and `Topic`.

Step 1: Select the Running Total tool from the Transform tool palette and drag it onto the canvas. Connect the Auto Field tool to the Running Total tool.

Step 2: Select the following fields under the **Group By (Optional)** selections: `YearEnd` and `Topic`.

Step 3: Select the following field under the Create Running Total selections: **DataValueAlt**:

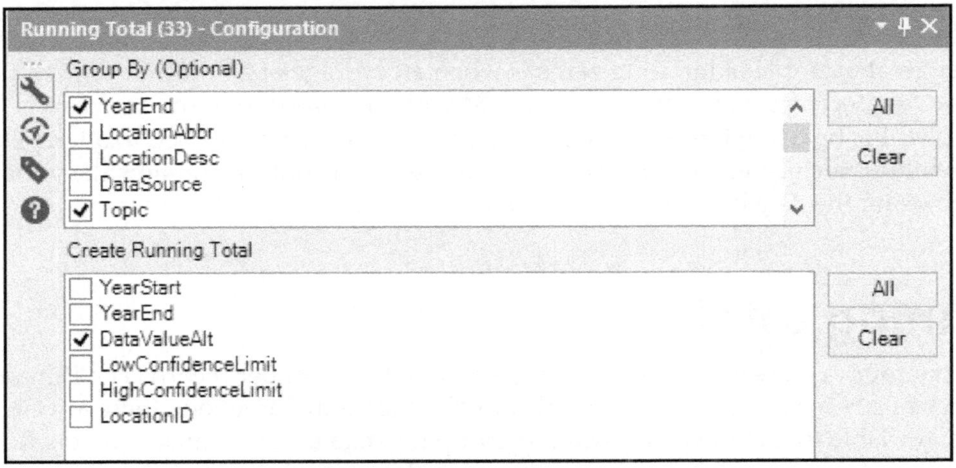

Step 4: Add a Browse tool to the Summarize tool.

Step 5: Run the workflow.

Notice that the row count stays the same from the input and output of the Running Total tool. This is due to the cumulative sum coming into action. It sums all the data for the given group by options, since `YearEnd` and `Topic` is defined as the point when the cumulative sum should reach a certain level and start over again.

The following image shows the new field created `RunTot_DataValueAlt`, containing the cumulative sum per record:

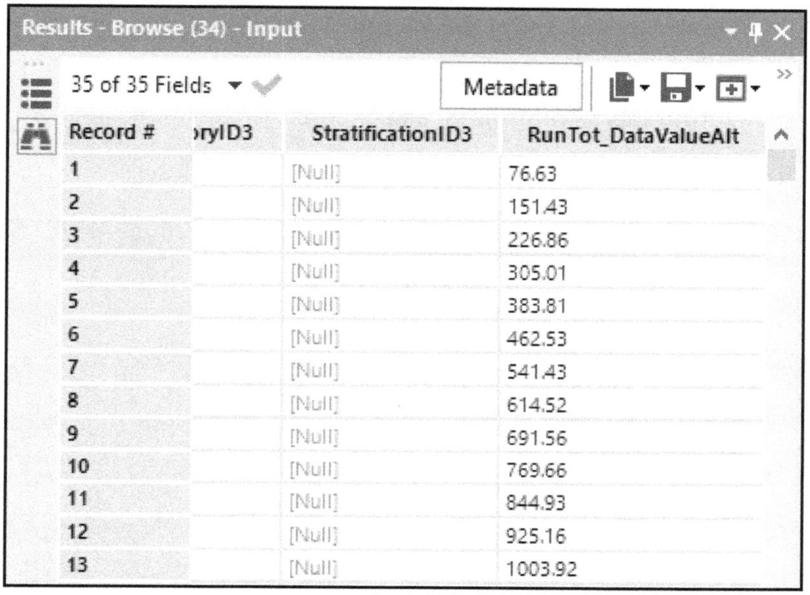

Record #	›ryID3	StratificationID3	RunTot_DataValueAlt
1		[Null]	76.63
2		[Null]	151.43
3		[Null]	226.86
4		[Null]	305.01
5		[Null]	383.81
6		[Null]	462.53
7		[Null]	541.43
8		[Null]	614.52
9		[Null]	691.56
10		[Null]	769.66
11		[Null]	844.93
12		[Null]	925.16
13		[Null]	1003.92

Weighted average

The contribution amount to a set of values is defined as weighting, where some records are configured to contribute more than others. The Weighted Average tool located within the Transform tool palette contains questions that will help identify how the weighting should be computed. Let's look at an example of using the Weighted Average tool using the same workflow as the previous section.

Weighted Average Example #1: Find the running total for `DataValueAlt` by `YearEnd` and `Topic`.

Step 1: Select the Weighted Average tool from the Transform tool palette and drag it onto the canvas. Connect the Auto Field tool to the Weighted Average tool.

Step 2: Select the following field under the **Value Field (Numeric)** dropdown: `DataValueAlt`.

Step 3: Select the following field under the **Weight Field (Numeric)** dropdown: `HighConfidenceLimit`.

Step 4: Leave the Output Field Name as is, `WeightedAverage`.

The snapshot for the Weighted Average Configuration is as follows:

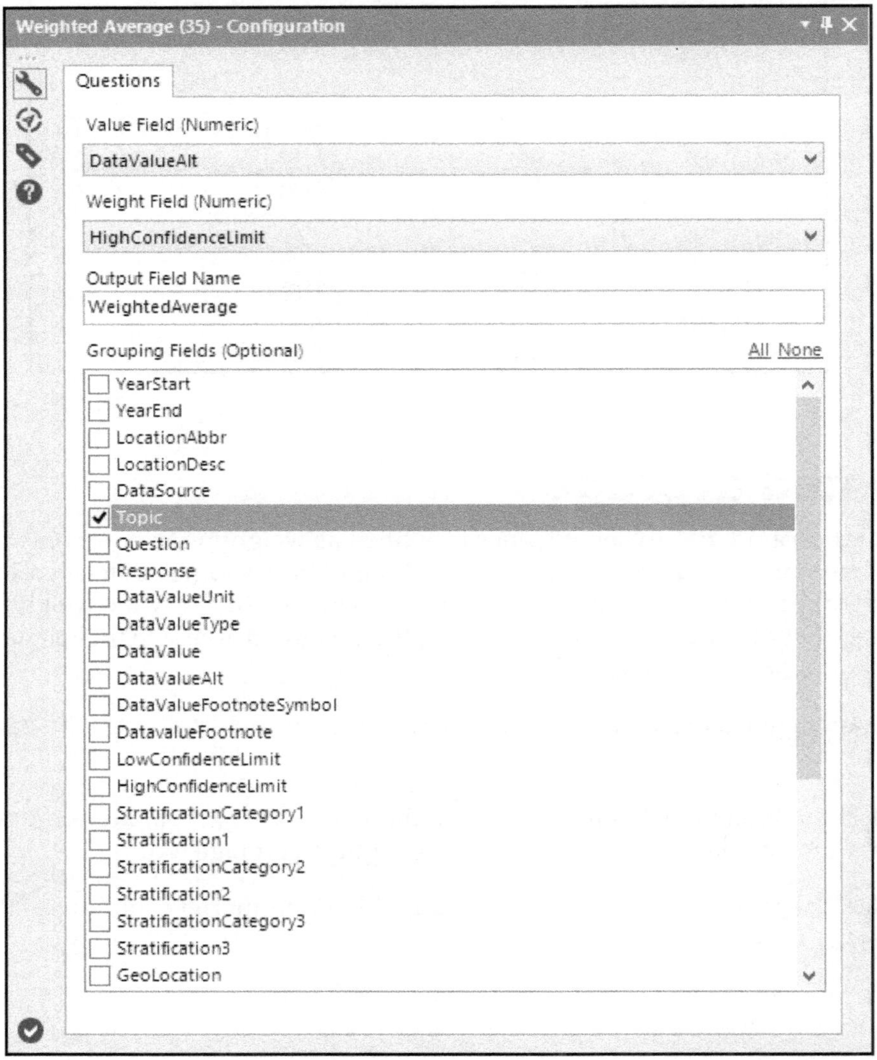

Step 5: Add a Browse tool to the Summarize tool.

Step 6: Run the workflow.

A weighted average has been computed by using `DataValueAlt` as the data field and the `HighConfidenceLimit` is the weighting contribution for each Topic. This will have the 17 individual Topics supplying a weighted average. It's quite helpful to have a tool handy to compute the weighted average, rather than using multiple tools to sum and average data to compute the outputted field.

This is the final workflow layout containing all sections you reviewed in this chapter. All the main tools reviewed are located under the Transform section:

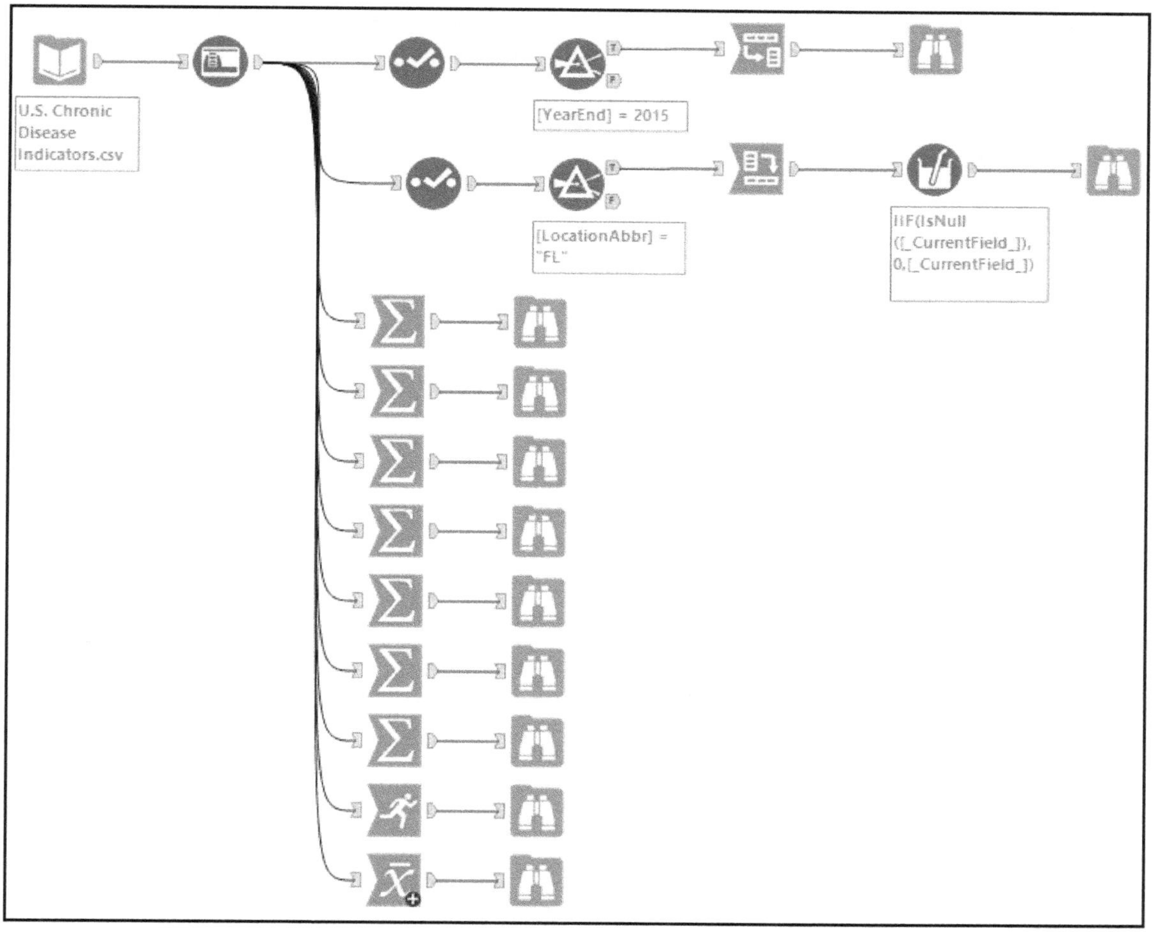

Summary

The ideal way to structure your data depends on how the result is defined. You may notice within a workflow that data needs to be transformed in a certain way, and the two ways this can be done are by using the Transpose tool to unpivot data, changing data from a wide dataset to a narrow dataset, and by using the Crosstab tool to pivot data, changing data from a narrow dataset to wider dataset. In this chapter, we reviewed many aggregation types available within the Summarize tool. The granularity of data can be defined within the Group By actions and the aggregation types are an action selection away to achieve the desired result. The Running Total is a great option for obtaining a cumulative sum of your data up to a certain point, defined by the Group By options, and the Weighted Average is used for applying a contribution amount for more records than others. This tool also contains the Group By option, specifying how data needs to be grouped together. These tools, available within the Transform tool palette, are always handy, and will allow you to achieve faster analytic results in no time.

The next chapter will cover parsing techniques to split data into columns and rows, converting date/time data type formats, and creating regular expressions to take parsing to the next level.

6
Data Parsing Techniques

The Parse Tool palette offers parsing options that will save you time by having the tools that do it all for you, such as the Text to Columns tool, which allows you to split text from one field into multiple columns or rows. Don't forget the numerous times a file comes in with a string formatted field when it should be a date formatted field. This complexity is all solved by utilizing the DateTime tool. The opportunities for parsing are limitless with **regular expressions**, where you will dive into more advanced features of parsing your data.

This chapter will cover the following topics:

- Text to columns
- Converting string to dates and dates to strings
- Regular expressions

Text to columns

Text to columns is a great way to split data apart based on delimiters. This parsing technique will split data into columns or rows based on specified delimiters. You may have used text to columns before in legacy platforms, such as Excel, where the data is split on specified delimiters into multiple columns. This is similar to Alteryx and it is all located in one tool called Text to Columns. Who would have thought? The Text to Columns tool splits the text from one field into separate columns or rows. There are advanced options that can ignore certain delimiters or skip empty fields. We'll explore a few examples on how simple, yet powerful the Text to Columns tool is.

In this section, we will use the `U.S. Chronic Disease Indicators.csv` file to build out the workflow, along with the resources located in the data folder. Let's go through a few helpful examples using the Text to Columns tool.

Text to Columns Example #1: Split the field, `QuestionID` into two columns using the underscore _ delimiter.

Step 1: Using an Input Data tool connect to the `U.S. Chronic Disease Indicators.csv` file located in the `\Learn Alteryx\Chapter` directory.

Step 2: Select the Auto Field tool from the Preparation tool palette and drag it onto the canvas. Connect the Auto Field tool to the Input Data tool. Each string field has now been automatically updated to the smallest field type and size.

Step 3: Select the Select tool from the Preparation tool palette and drag it onto the canvas. Connect the Select tool to the Auto Field tool.

Step 4: Select the following fields in the Select tool:

`YearEnd`, `LocationAbbr`, `Topic`, `Question`, `Response`, `DataValueAlt`, `GeoLocation`, and `QuestionID`.

Step 5: Select the Text to Columns tool from the Parse tool palette and drag it onto the canvas. Connect the Text to Columns tool to the Select tool.

Step 6: Select `QuestionID` from the **Field to Split** drop down and add _ in the text box under **Delimiters**.

Step 7: Select the radio button, **Split to Columns** and enter `2` in the text box next to **# of Columns**. The following screenshot will give you a better idea:

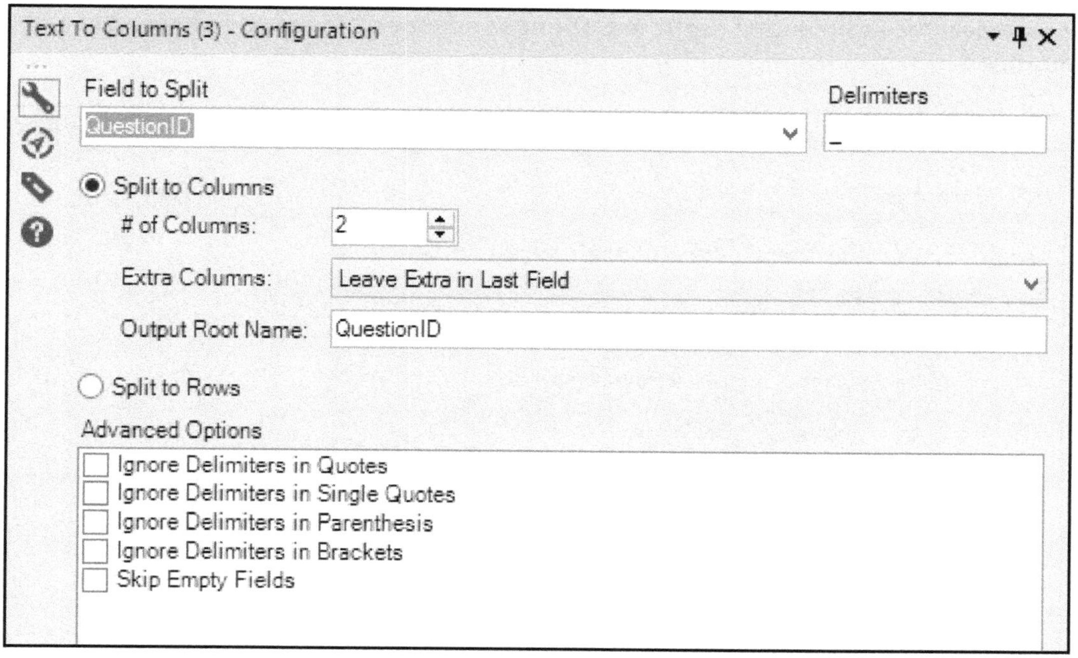

Step 8: Add a Browse tool to the Text to Columns tool.

Step 9: Run the workflow.

The goal here was to split `QuestionID` into two columns using the _ delimiter. The _ delimiter is used to parse the data for anything to the left of _ as its own field and also anything to the right of it as its own field. This leads to the decision to select two for the number of columns to split. If you want to only get the last digit from the `QuestionID` field as its own field, then the `QuestionID2` will contain this.

Text to Columns Example #2: Split the `GeoLocation` field into two columns using the comma `,` delimiter and rename both fields to `Latitude` and `Longitude`. Remove the leading and trailing parentheses for these fields and ensure they do not contain any leading and trailing spaces.

Step 1: Select the Text to Columns tool from the Parse tool palette and drag it onto the canvas. Connect the Text to Columns tool to the Select tool.

Step 2: Select `GeoLocation` from the **Field to Split** drop down and add `,` in the text box under **Delimiters**.

Step 3: Select the radio button, **Split to Columns** and enter `2` in the text box next to **# of Columns**:

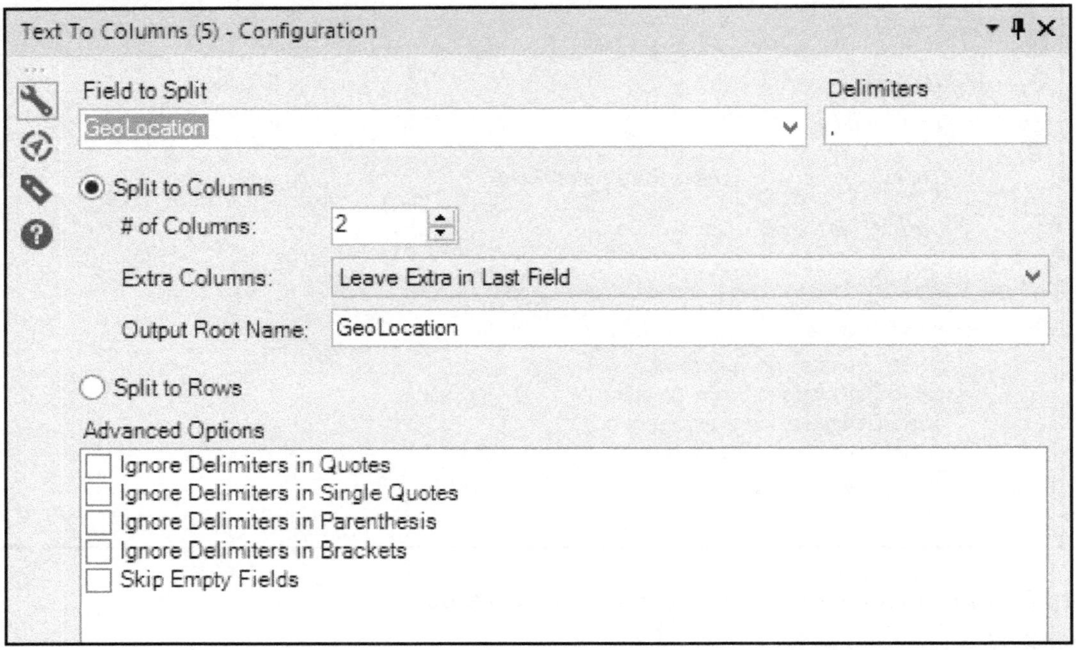

Step 4: Select the Formula tool from the Preparation tool palette and drag it onto the canvas. Connect the Formula tool to the Text to Columns tool.

Step 5: Select **+ Add Column** under the **Output Column** drop down and enter `Latitude`.

Step 6: Add the following formula in the expression window:

```
Trim(Replace([GeoLocation1], "(", ""))
```

Step 7: Select + to add a new column in the Formula tool and select **+ Add Column** under the **Output Column** drop down. Enter `Longitude`.

Step 8: Add the following formula in the expression window, as shown in the following screenshot:

```
Trim(Replace([GeoLocation2], ")", ""))
```

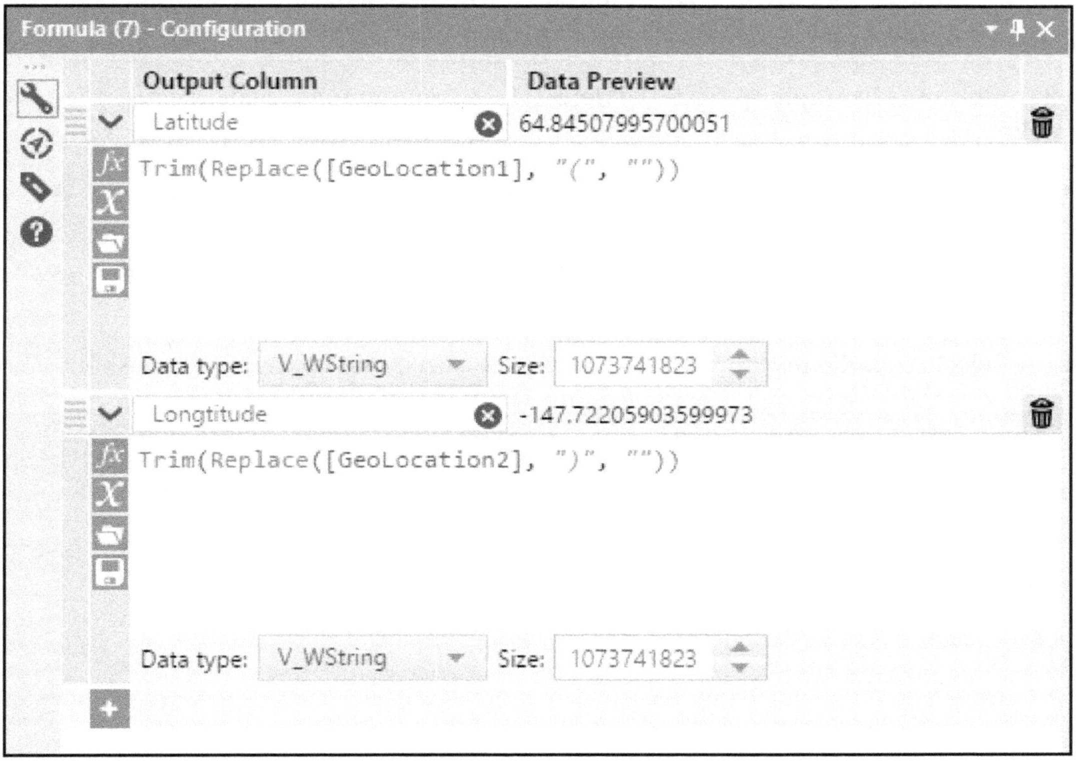

Step 9: Add a Browse tool to the Text to Columns tool.

Step 10: Run the workflow.

This example includes the Split to Columns, as in the previous example, with the desired result of having the Latitude and Longitude as their own fields. A bit of clean up is required after parsing the data. The field to parse in this case is `GeoLocation` and the comma , delimiter would split the fields into Latitude and Longitude. There are only a couple fields of interest, so two would be the number of columns to split. The resulting fields are `GeoLocation1` (Latitude) and `GeoLocation2` (Longitude). The Formula tool is where the renaming and clean up occur. First, the Formula tool is used to rename the fields from `GeoLocation1` to `Latitude` and `GeoLocation2` to `Longitude`.

Second, the Formula tool is used to replace the leading and trailing parentheses using the Replace function. Lastly, the Formula tool is used to remove any unwanted leading and trailing spaces using the `Trim` function wrapped around the `Replace` expression. Notice, the Browse tool will contain the Latitude and Longitude in their own fields. As an example, this dataset can now be brought into Tableau as a Tableau data extract and a map can be created with the `Latitude` and `Longitude` fields.

Text to Columns Example #3: Split the field, `Question` into rows using the space `\s` delimiter.

Step 1: Select the Text to Columns tool from the Parse tool palette and drag it onto the canvas. Connect the Text to Columns tool to the Select tool.

Step 2: Select `Question` from the **Field to Split** drop down and add `\s` in the text box under **Delimiters**.

Step 3: Select the radio button, **Split to Rows** as shown in the following screenshot:

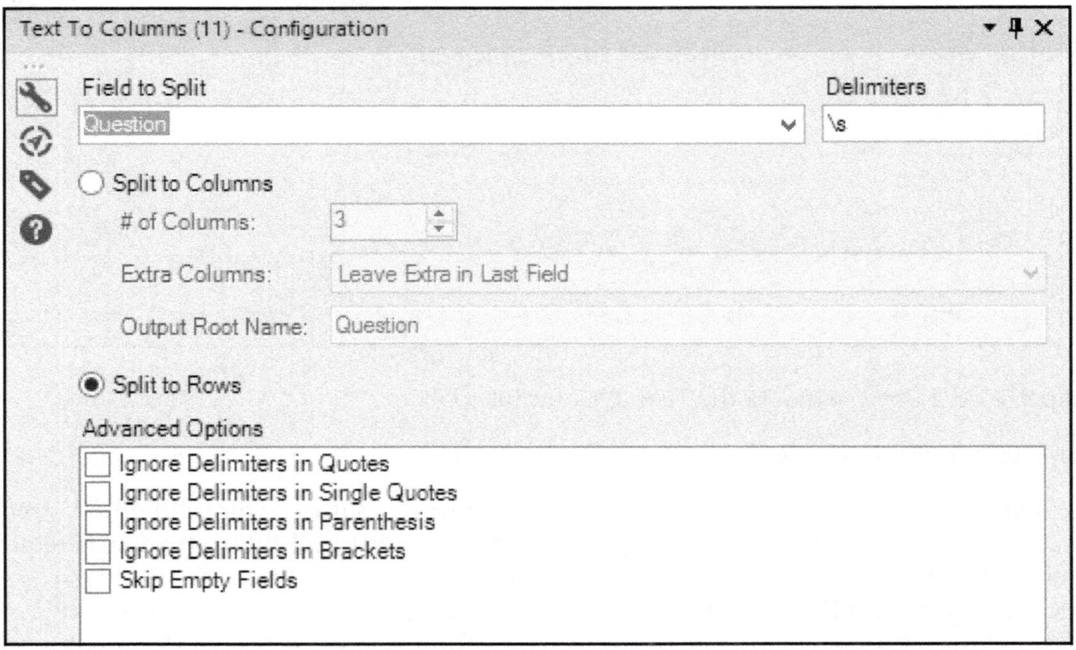

Step 4: Add a Browse tool to the Text to Columns tool.

Step 5: Run the workflow.

This example uses a different approach to parsing data. Rather than using the Split to Columns, it uses the Split to Rows option, where all words contained in the `Question` field are broken out individually. Take a look at the question, `Arthritis among adults aged >= 18 years`. Before the Text to Columns tool, the following snapshot shows question is located in one row:

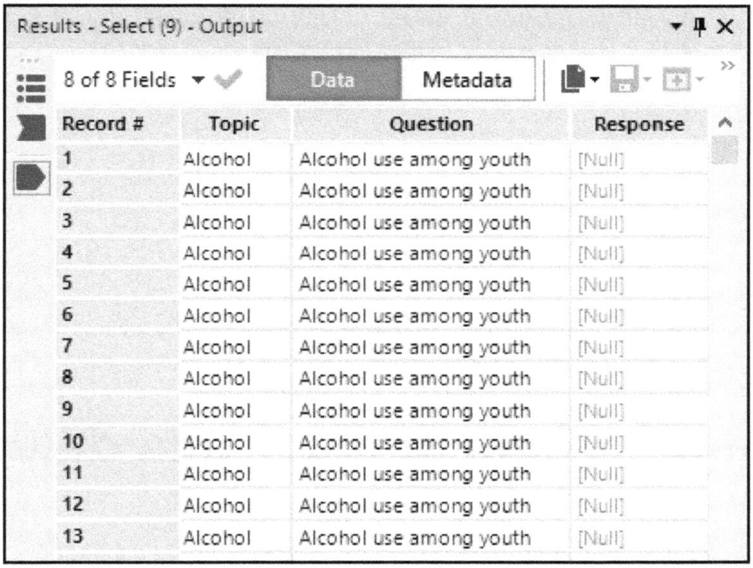

Record #	Topic	Question	Response
1	Alcohol	Alcohol use among youth	[Null]
2	Alcohol	Alcohol use among youth	[Null]
3	Alcohol	Alcohol use among youth	[Null]
4	Alcohol	Alcohol use among youth	[Null]
5	Alcohol	Alcohol use among youth	[Null]
6	Alcohol	Alcohol use among youth	[Null]
7	Alcohol	Alcohol use among youth	[Null]
8	Alcohol	Alcohol use among youth	[Null]
9	Alcohol	Alcohol use among youth	[Null]
10	Alcohol	Alcohol use among youth	[Null]
11	Alcohol	Alcohol use among youth	[Null]
12	Alcohol	Alcohol use among youth	[Null]
13	Alcohol	Alcohol use among youth	[Null]

After the Text to Columns tool is used, by splitting into rows there are now seven rows for this question. All words have been parsed in their own row. A good example of this is reviewing survey data and identifying sentimental words that could identify where to focus on. A key word file containing the sentimental key words can be used to join onto this dataset to find similarities.

The following snapshot shows the output results after using the Text to Columns tool. Note that all words are parsed in their own row.

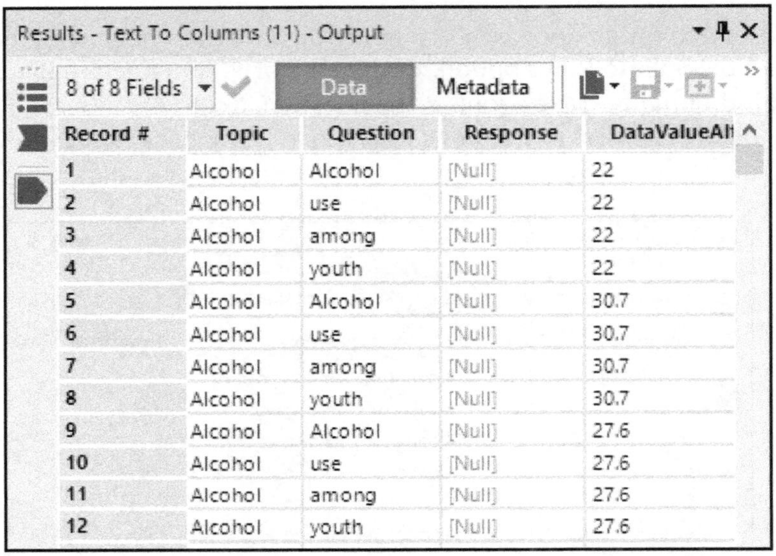

Results - Text To Columns (11) - Output

8 of 8 Fields | Data | Metadata

Record #	Topic	Question	Response	DataValueAlt
1	Alcohol	Alcohol	[Null]	22
2	Alcohol	use	[Null]	22
3	Alcohol	among	[Null]	22
4	Alcohol	youth	[Null]	22
5	Alcohol	Alcohol	[Null]	30.7
6	Alcohol	use	[Null]	30.7
7	Alcohol	among	[Null]	30.7
8	Alcohol	youth	[Null]	30.7
9	Alcohol	Alcohol	[Null]	27.6
10	Alcohol	use	[Null]	27.6
11	Alcohol	among	[Null]	27.6
12	Alcohol	youth	[Null]	27.6

Converting strings to dates and dates to strings

There are a variety of date formats that need to be updated to a data type that meets the needs of the analysis. A string formatted date may need to be updated to a date/time format. On the other hand, a date/time format may need to be updated to a string format. The complexity of updating this can be quite cumbersome and there are formulas available to make these necessary updates. Better yet, there is a DateTime tool in Alteryx that includes options on selecting the format to convert.

The following image shows the DateTime tool located in the Parse tool palette.

The DateTime tool can convert a date/time format to string and vice versa, a string to a date/time format. The flexibility of the format selections is quite helpfully located in just one tool! It contains prestored formats and an option to specify a custom format. Let's go through a few examples using the DateTime tool and looking at how it may benefit you to make the format updates. We will use the U.S. Chronic Disease Indicators workflow from the previous section, along with the resources located in the data folder.

DateTime Example #1: Identify the Unique `QuestionID` values and limit the data only to the Arthritis, Asthma, Cardiovascular Disease, Cardiovascular Disease, and Nutrition, Physical Activity, and Weight Status topics. Join the data to the Survey Question Dates and convert the `QuestionDate` field to a `MM/dd/yyyy` string format.

Step 1: Using an Input Data tool, connect to the file `U.S. Chronic Disease Indicators.csv` located in the `\Learn Alteryx\Chapter` directory.

Step 2: Select the Auto Field tool from the Preparation tool palette and drag it onto the canvas. Connect the Auto Field tool to the Input Data tool. Each string field has now been automatically updated to the smallest field type and size.

Step 3: Select the Select tool from the Preparation tool palette and drag it onto the canvas. Connect the Select tool to the Auto Field tool.

Step 4: Select the following fields in the Select tool:

`LocationAbbr`, `Topic`, `Question`, `Response`, `DataValueAlt`, and `QuestionID`.

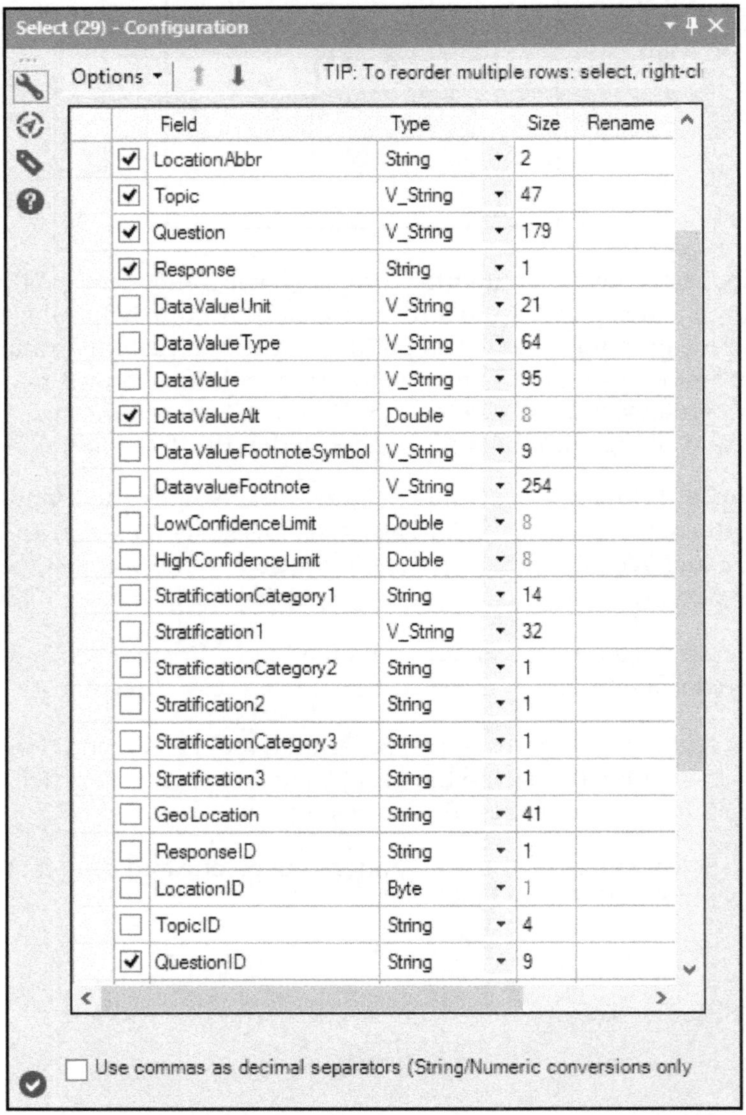

Step 5: Select the Unique tool from the Preparation tool palette and drag it onto the canvas. Connect the Unique tool to the Select tool.

Step 6: Select only the `QuestionID` field within the Unique tool configuration, as shown in the following screenshot:

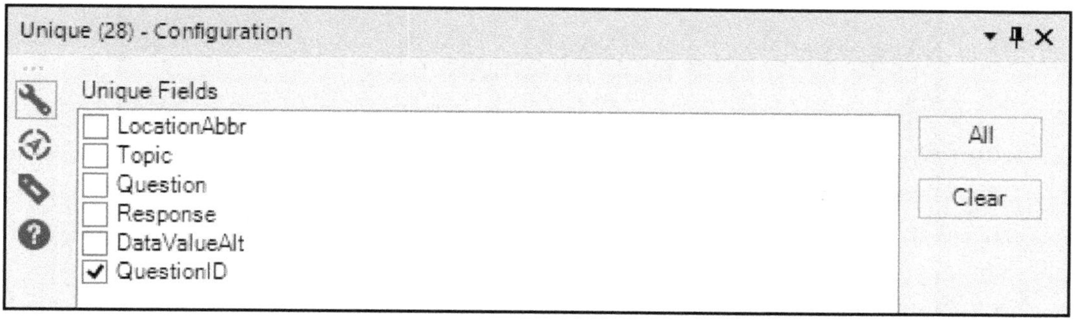

Step 7: Select the Filter tool from the Preparation tool palette and drag it onto the canvas. Connect the Filter tool to the Unique tool (U output).

Step 8: Select the radio button, **Custom Filter** and write the following expression in the expression window:

```
[QuestionID] IN
 (
 'CVD9_1',
 'NPAW10_0',
 'AST4_1',
 'ART2_0',
 'CVD1_2'
 )
```

Step 9: Select the Join tool from the Join tool palette and drag it onto the canvas. Connect the Join tool to the Filter tool (T Output).

Step 10: Select the radio button, **Join by Specific Fields** within the Join tool configuration and select `QuestionID` from the **Left** and **Right** drop downs.

Step 11: Select all the fields within the Join tool configuration, except for the `QuestionID` from the `Right` Input since this already exists in the `Left` Input, as shown in the following screenshot:

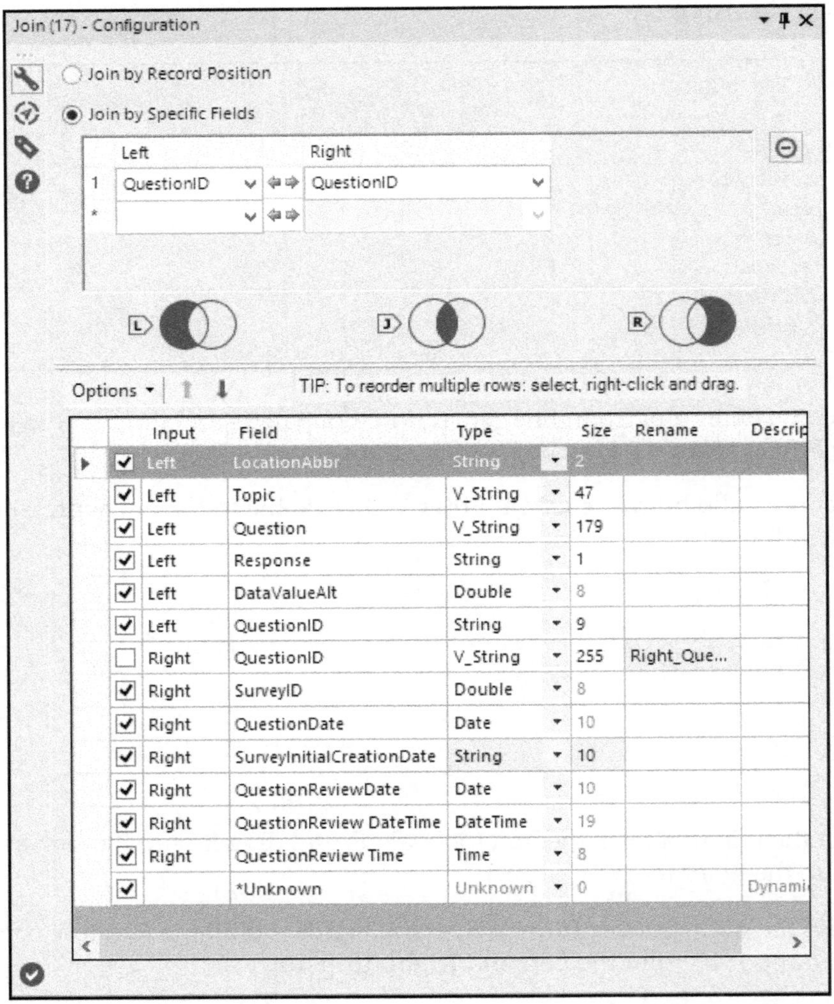

Step 12: Select the DateTime tool from the Parse tool palette and drag it onto the canvas. Connect the DateTime tool to the `J` output from the Join tool.

Step 13: Apply the following selections within the DateTime tool:

- **Select the format to convert:** Date/time format to string
- **Select the date/time field to convert:** `QuestionDate`
- **Specify the new column name:** `QuestionDate_New`
- **Select the format for the new column:** `MM/dd/yyyy`

The following screenshot shows what the `DateTime` Configuration looks like:

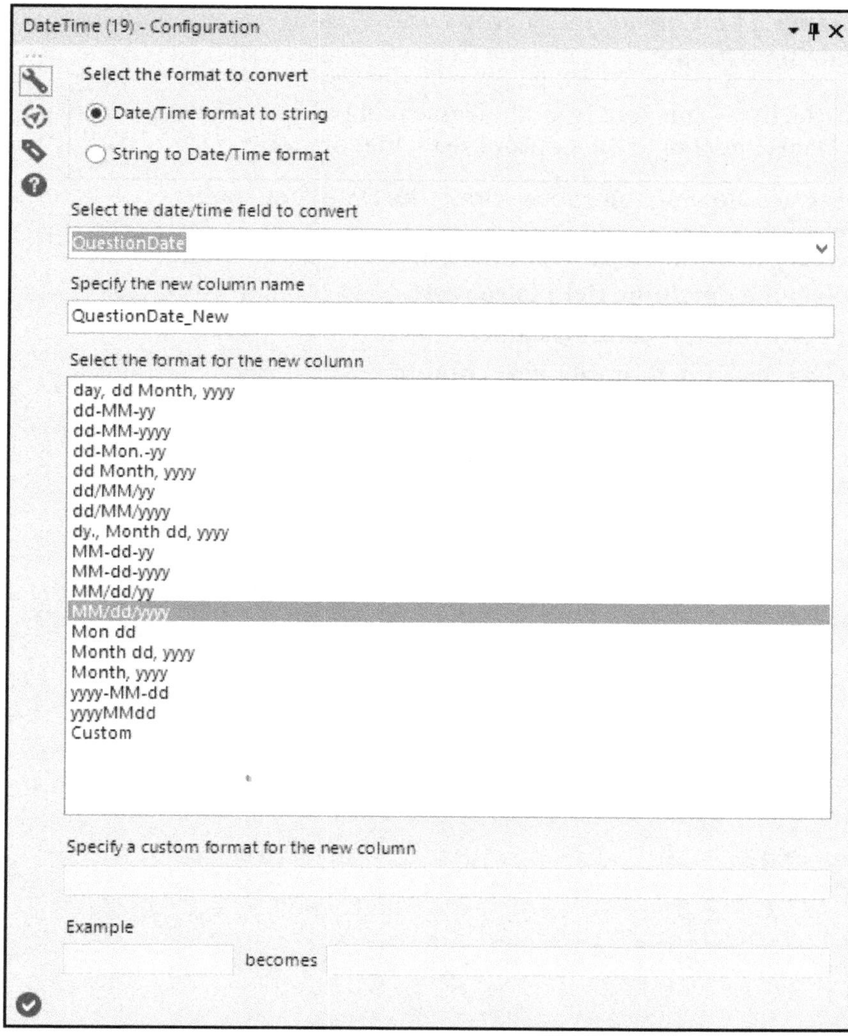

Step 14: Add a Browse tool to the DateTime tool.

Step 15: Run the workflow.

The goal is to identify only one instance of Topic values using the Unique tool and limiting the data to only the specified Topics. The DateTime tool is configured to select the date/time format for string conversion for the `QuestionDate` field. The `MM/dd/yyyy` is a format option available and, by selecting this option, it will give the desired output. This is a great way to update date formatted fields to string formats.

DateTime Example #2: Convert the Survey Initial `CreationDate` field to a `yyyyMMdd` date/time format.

Step 1: Select the DateTime tool from the Parse tool palette and drag it onto the canvas. Connect the DateTime tool to the J output from the Join tool.

Step 2: Apply the following selections within the DateTime tool:

- **Select the format to convert**: date/time format to string
- **Select the date/time field to convert**: `QuestionDate`
- **Specify the new column name**: `QuestionDate_New`
- **Select the format for the new column**: `MM/dd/yyyy`

After applying the selections, your screen will appear as follows; please check if all the selections are applied:

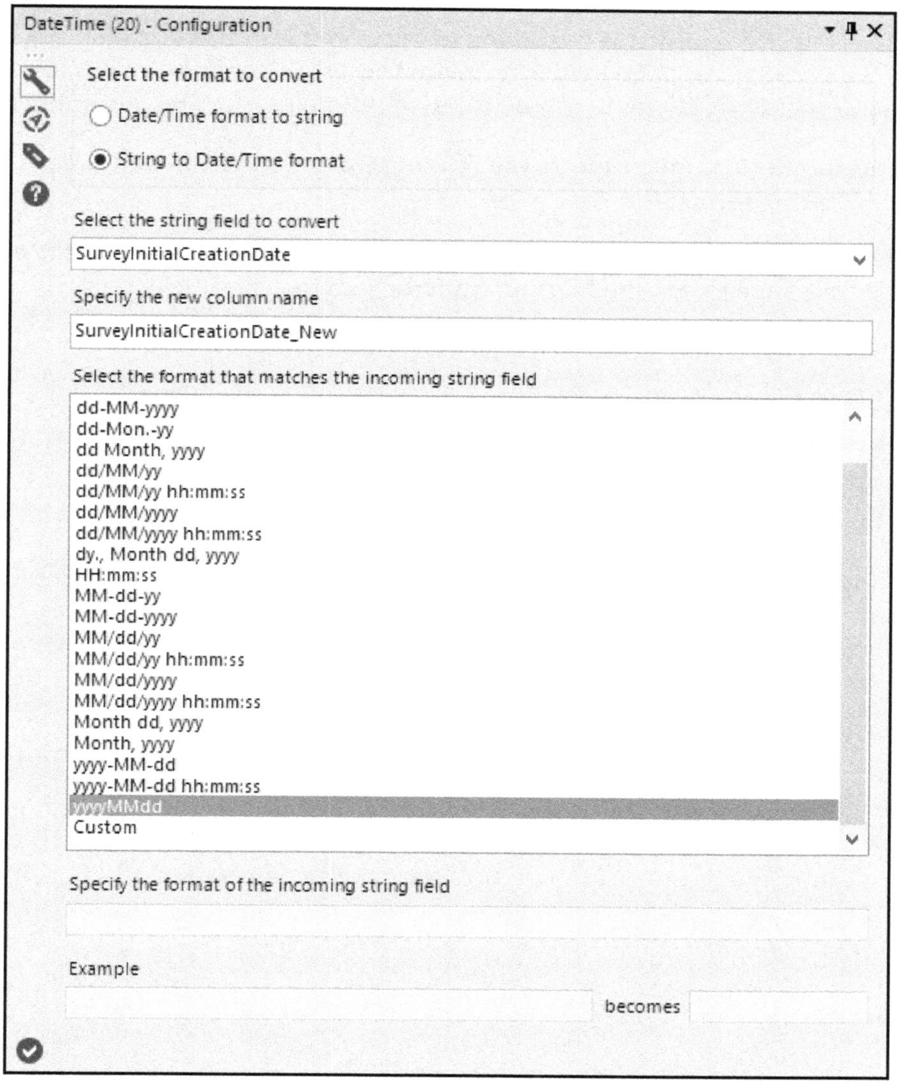

Step 3: Add a Browse tool to the DateTime tool.

Step 4: Run the workflow.

The String to Date/Time format is the option to select in this example, as the `SurveyInitialCreationDate` field is formatted as a string and the goal is to convert it to a date/time format. The `yyyyMMdd` format is the selection to match the incoming field string.

DateTime Example #3: Convert the `QuestionReview DateTime` field to a `day, dd Month, yyyy` string format.

Step 1: Select the DateTime tool from the Parse tool palette and drag it onto the canvas. Connect the DateTime tool to the J output from the Join tool.

Step 2: Apply the following selections within the DateTime tool:

- **Select the format to convert**: `Date/Time format to string`
- **Select the date/time field to convert**: `QuestionReview DateTime`
- **Specify the new column name**: `DateTime_String`
- **Select the format for the new column**: `day, dd Month, yyyy`

The following image shows the DateTime tool options selected based on Step 2:

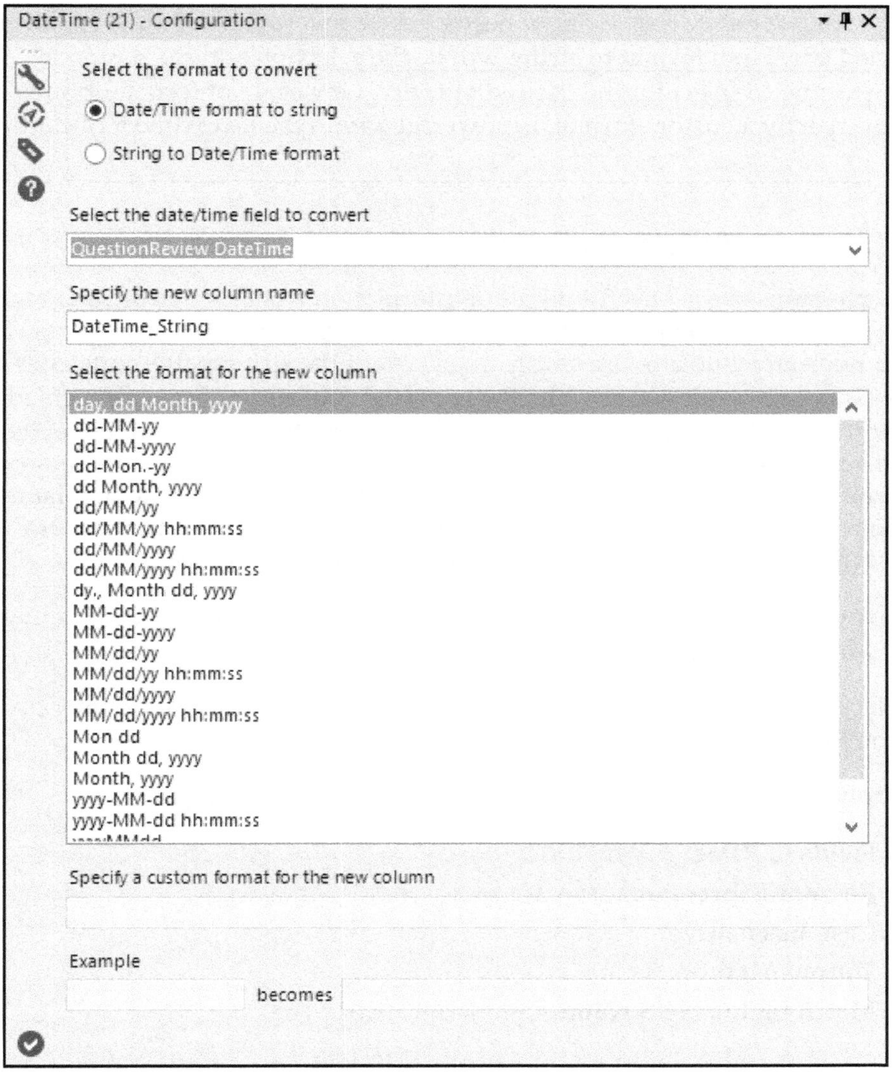

Step 3: Add a Browse tool to the DateTime tool.

Step 4: Run the workflow.

The `QuestionReview DateTime` field needs to be converted to a string; so, like the first example the **Date/Time format to string** will be the selection and the `day, dd Month, yyyy` is the format to select for the desired output. The variety of format options, along with an option to specify a custom format, is powerful within the DateTime tool configuration.

Regular expressions

Regular expressions extract useful pieces of information from strings using matching patterns. They provide robust matching, parsing, or replacement of string data. The Match output is a Boolean value of `true` and `false`. `True` if the string pattern matches the regular expression and `false` if it doesn't. The Parse output returns the groups specified in the regular expression. The Replace output can replace groups specified in the replacement text window. The RegEx tool contains these powerful extraction pieces to obtain important information from strings. Let's go through an example of how versatile regular expressions can be. We will continue using the U.S. Chronic Disease Indicators workflow from the previous section, along with the resources located in the data folder.

Regular Expressions Example #1: Parse the `QuestionID` field to identify if a match is found containing one digit after the underscore _ punctuation.

Step 1: Select the RegEx tool from the Parse tool palette and drag it onto the canvas. Connect the RegEx tool to the Select tool in the top stream.

Step 2: Apply the following selections within the RegEx tool configuration:

- **Fields to Parse**: `QuestionID`
- **Regular Expression**: `.*_\d{1}`
- **Case Insensitive**
- **Output Method**: `Match`
- **Match Status Field Name**: `Contains 1 Digit?`

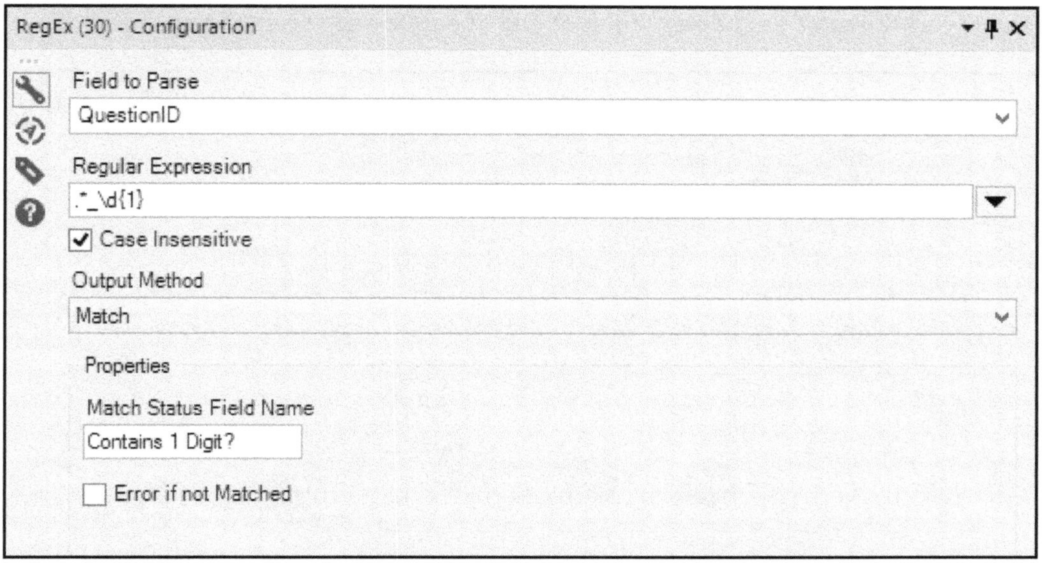

Step 3: Add a Browse tool to the RegEx tool.

Step 4: Run the workflow.

Notice in the new field **Contains 1 Digit?** everything is `True` as every `QuestionID` has one digit after the underscore _ punctuation. Let's breakdown the regular expression to see how it works.

- The `.` located in the `.*_\d{1}` regular expression signifies any single character.
- The `*` identifies zero or more characters.
- The `\d` is used to specify the digit and the `{1}` identifies only one digit.

This method is a great way to solve match cases and the versatile options within the RegEx tool are always handy and ready to parse data the way you want it.

The final workflow in this chapter will look like the following screenshot:

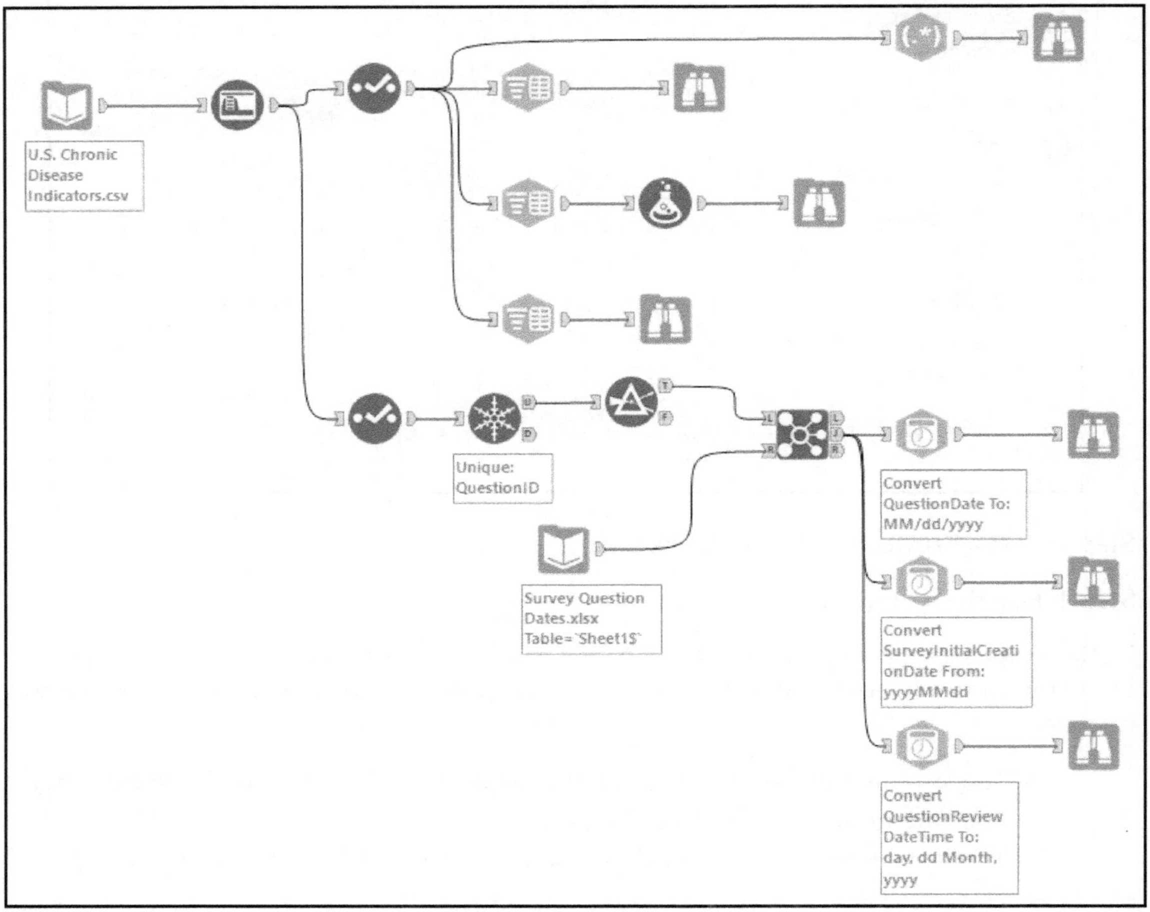

Summary

This chapter provided a variety of parsing methods that will help you parse out data in no time. With the Text to Columns tool, you learned about splitting the data from one field into columns or rows. This is a great way to identify segments of the data for analysis. The DateTime tool was a real force in converting date/time formats to string formats, and vice versa converting string formats to date/time formats. This tool is very handy if dates and times need to be cleaned up quickly. If you're looking for more robust parsing, then the RegEx tool is where a variety of regular expressions can be applied and the Match output method was the desired output. The tools and methods applied in this chapter will provide you with a foundation for parsing data with a variety of specifications.

In the next chapter, you will learn about the reporting tools and how to implement them in your workflow to create custom data-driven reports.

7
Creating Data-Driven Custom Reports

Creating and sending reports across your organization have a vital impact on decision making. An executive can make a business decision at a glance. Developing such reports have to meet the needs of the customer to have a positive impact for continuing to move your organization forward. Alteryx has a suite of reporting tools for creating high quality, data-driven reports to deliver clear and timely reports to customers. The tools are designed with the Alteryx design paradigm in mind, creating snippets in each of the tools. You will create a report from start to finish with the design output that will best help organizations make informed business decisions. Whether it's developing a data table or visual representation, the reporting tools suite will help guide the way to presentation-quality reports. Let's go through developing a data table and charts, which will provide a visual of the data to be analyzed and then combine the snippets to lay them out in a meaningful manner. We'll conclude this chapter by reviewing the variety of options to export and share the report.

This chapter will cover the following topics:

- Data Table
- Charting
- Reporting layout
- Sharing the report

Data Table

The previous chapters you went through data processing through Alteryx by using a wealth of tools and most importantly business questions have been solved. Now, you have to create reports that provide clear representations of areas that are in need of improvement. The suite of reporting tools located in the **Reporting** tool palette will allow you to create quality reports. One tool we'll start with in this section will be the **Table** tool. This creates a table element to output in a report through the **Render** tool. The **Render** tool creates presentation quality reports in a variety of formats, such as `.pdf`, `.html`, `.pptx`, `.xlsx`, `.docx`, `.png`, and many more. The tools within the **Reporting** tool palette are utilized in a workflow to create the presentation output. One tool helps another to get the job done. So, why would you want to use the **Table** tool? The Table tool is a presentation of a data table, that oh-so-favorite crosstab that customers always ask for. There are many times where a data table is helpful because it provides the data without the visualizations. Sometimes, the data has to be drilled down further from the visualizations to get to the data. Let's explore the **Table** tool and how the data table presentation displays that cross tabular format.

In this section, we will use the `U.S. Chronic Disease Indicators.csv` file to build out the workflow, along with the resources located in the data folder.

Table Example #1: Create a data table that displays Location, Topic, Average Data Value ignoring zeros, and Distinct Count of QuestionID for Florida and every Topic. The steps to do so are as follows:

Step 1: Using an **Input Data** tool, connect to the file `U.S. Chronic Disease Indicators.csv` located in the `\Learn Alteryx\Chapter` directory.

Step 2: Select the **Auto Field** tool from the **Preparation tool** palette and drag it onto the canvas. Connect the **Auto Field** tool to the **Input Data** tool. Each string field has now been automatically updated to the smallest field type and size.

Step 3: Select the **Filter** tool from the **Preparation** tool palette and drag it onto the canvas. Connect the **Filter** tool to the **Auto Field** tool.

Step 4: Select **Basic Filter** within the **Filter** tool configuration and select `LocationAbbr` from the field drop down, `Equals` from the operators drop down, and enter `FL` in the text box:

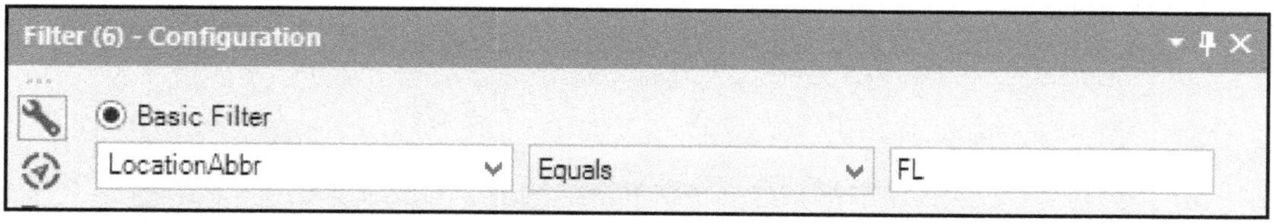

Step 5: Select the **Select** tool from the **Preparation** tool palette and drag it onto the canvas. Connect the **Select** tool to the **Filter** tool (T Output).

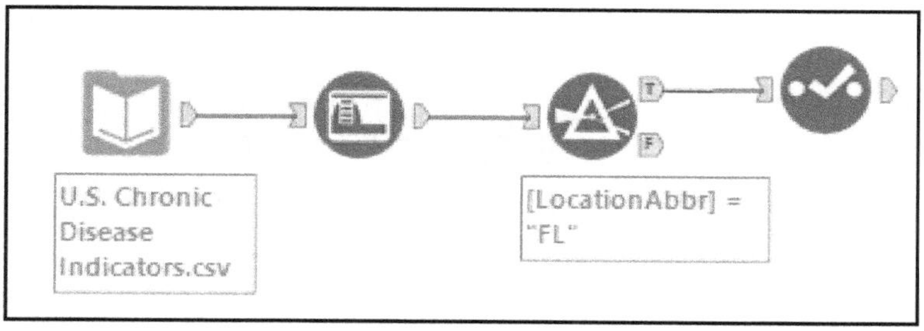

Step 6: Select the following fields within the **Select** tool configuration: `YearEnd`, `LocationAbbr`, `Topic`, `Question`, `DataValueAlt`, and `QuestionID`

Step 7: Select the **Summarize** tool from the **Transform** tool palette and drag it onto the canvas. Connect the **Summarize** tool to the **Select** tool.

Step 8: Select the following fields and select `Add` from the drop down to select their respective actions. Rename the **Output Field Names** to `Location`, `Topic`, `Average Data Value`, and `Distinct Count of QuestionID`. The fields to be selected are shown in the following image:

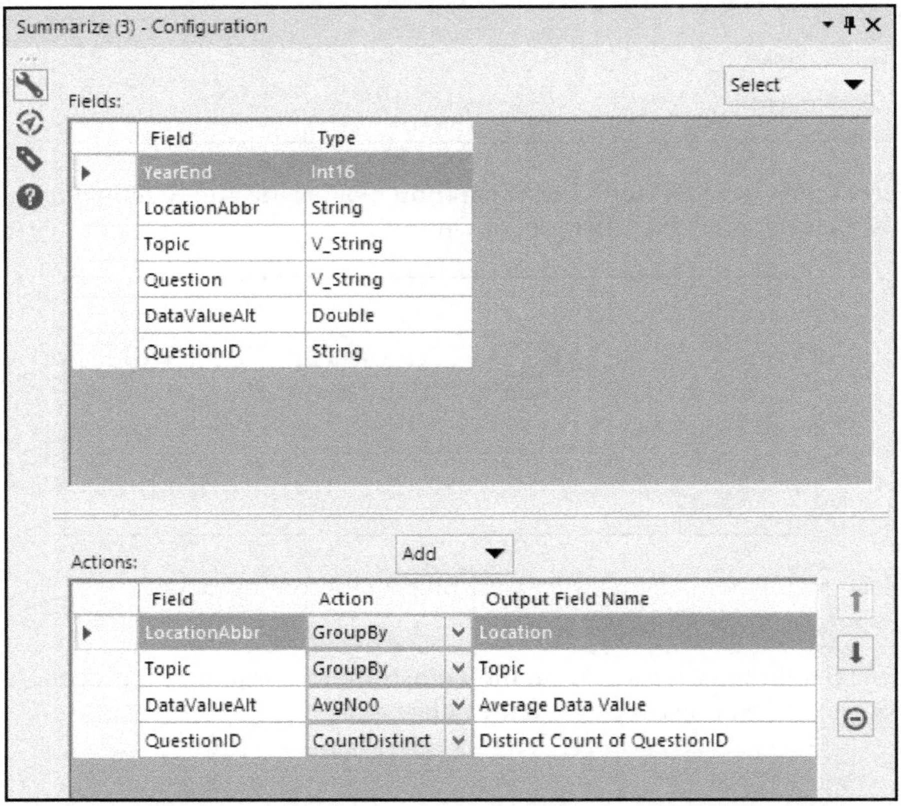

Step 9: Select the **Table** tool from the **Reporting** tool palette and drag it onto the canvas. Connect the **Table** tool to the **Summarize** tool. Leave the options within the **Table** tool configuration as is:

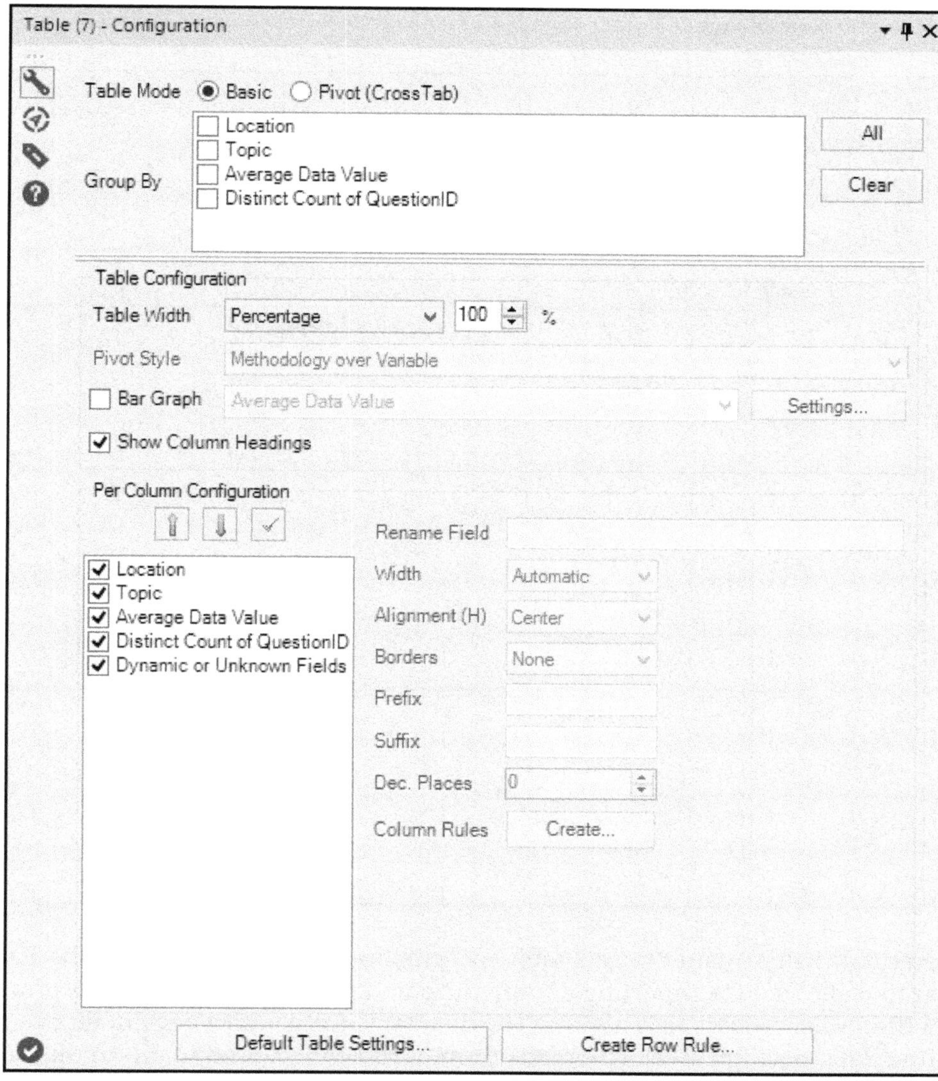

Step 10: Add a **Browse** tool to the **Table** tool.

Step 11: Run the workflow:

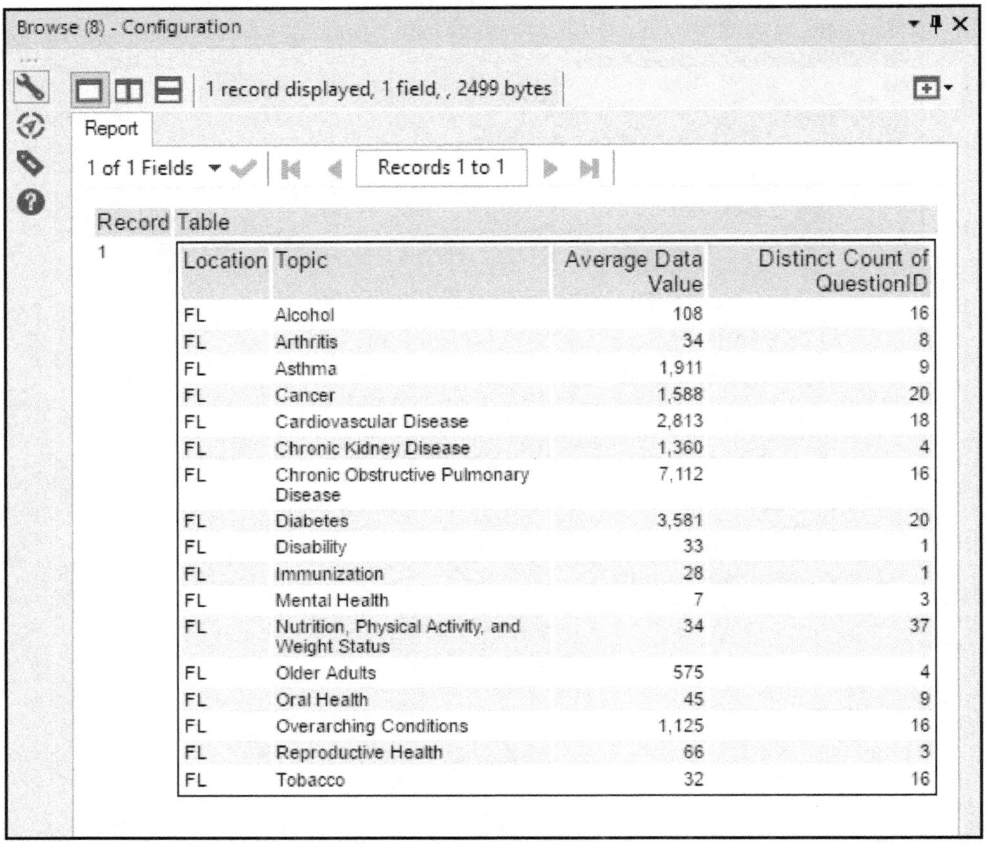

Location	Topic	Average Data Value	Distinct Count of QuestionID
FL	Alcohol	108	16
FL	Arthritis	34	8
FL	Asthma	1,911	9
FL	Cancer	1,588	20
FL	Cardiovascular Disease	2,813	18
FL	Chronic Kidney Disease	1,360	4
FL	Chronic Obstructive Pulmonary Disease	7,112	16
FL	Diabetes	3,581	20
FL	Disability	33	1
FL	Immunization	28	1
FL	Mental Health	7	3
FL	Nutrition, Physical Activity, and Weight Status	34	37
FL	Older Adults	575	4
FL	Oral Health	45	9
FL	Overarching Conditions	1,125	16
FL	Reproductive Health	66	3
FL	Tobacco	32	16

The **Browse** tool will contain the data table presentation that was formed by the **Table** tool. The **Filter** tool allowed the reporting of only the data for Florida, and the **Select** tool provided the selected fields for analysis. The data table format gets developed by aggregating data to a high level, where the **Summarize** tool is used to group the data by `LocationAbbr` and `Topic`. This provides the `17` records that are displayed in the **Browse** tool. The **Summarize** tool also is calculated averaging the data values ignoring zero and finding the distinct count of `QuestionID`. The **Table** tool by default has a **Table Mode of Basic** with the `Show Column Headings` selected and all fields selected. The **Table** tool helps bring the data in a table layout and this can be used to develop a report sent out to stakeholders, which we'll get into in the upcoming sections.

Table Example #2: Create a data table that displays Location, Topic, Question, Average Data Value ignoring zeros, and Max Data Value for every Location and only for *Adults with diagnosed diabetes aged >= 18 years who have taken a diabetes self-management course*. The steps of this process are as follows:

Step 1: We will start this example from the existing **Auto Field** tool from the previous example. Select the **Filter** tool from the **Preparation** tool palette and drag it onto the canvas. Connect the **Filter** tool to the **Auto Field** tool.

Step 2: Select Custom Filter within the **Filter** tool configuration and write the following expression:

```
[QuestionID] = "DIA10_0"
&&
!IsNull ([DataValueAlt])
```

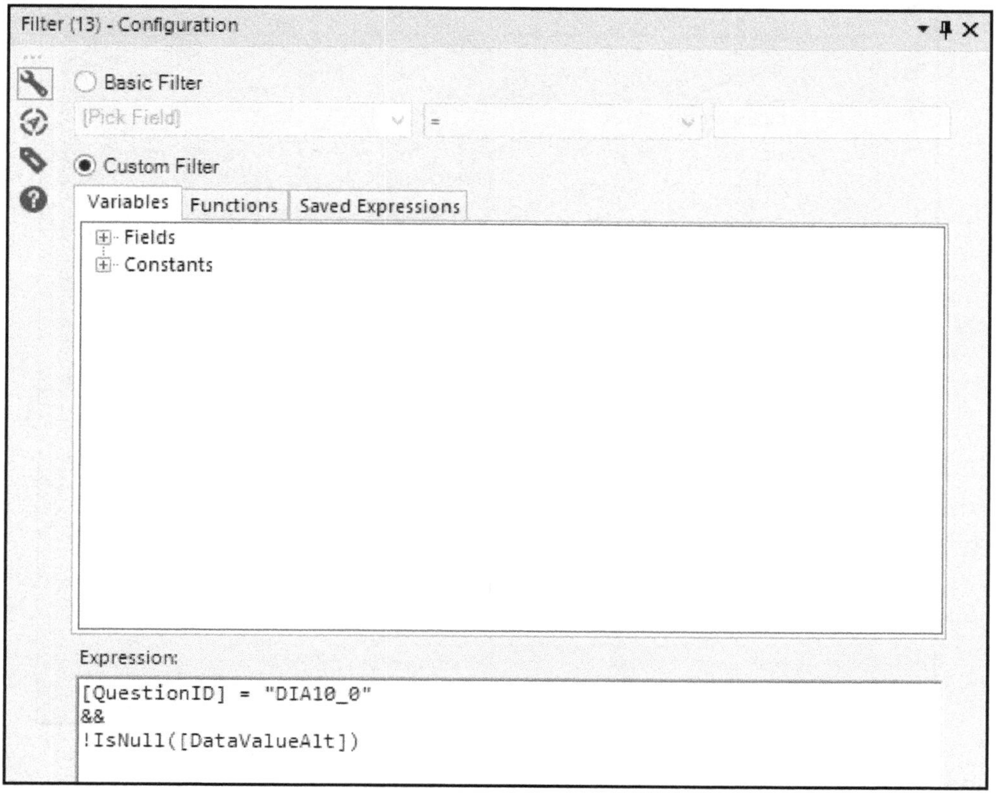

Step 3: Select the **Select** tool from the **Preparation** tool palette and drag it onto the canvas. Connect the **Select** tool to the **Filter** tool (T Output).

Step 4: Select the following fields within the **Select** tool configuration: YearEnd, LocationAbbr, Topic, Question, DataValueAlt, and QuestionID

Step 5: Select the **Summarize** tool from the **Transform** tool palette and drag it onto the canvas. Connect the **Summarize** tool to the **Select** tool.

Step 6: Select the following fields and select **Add** from the drop down to select their respective actions. Rename the Output Field Names to Location, Topic, Question, Average Data Value, and Max Data Value, as shown in the following image:

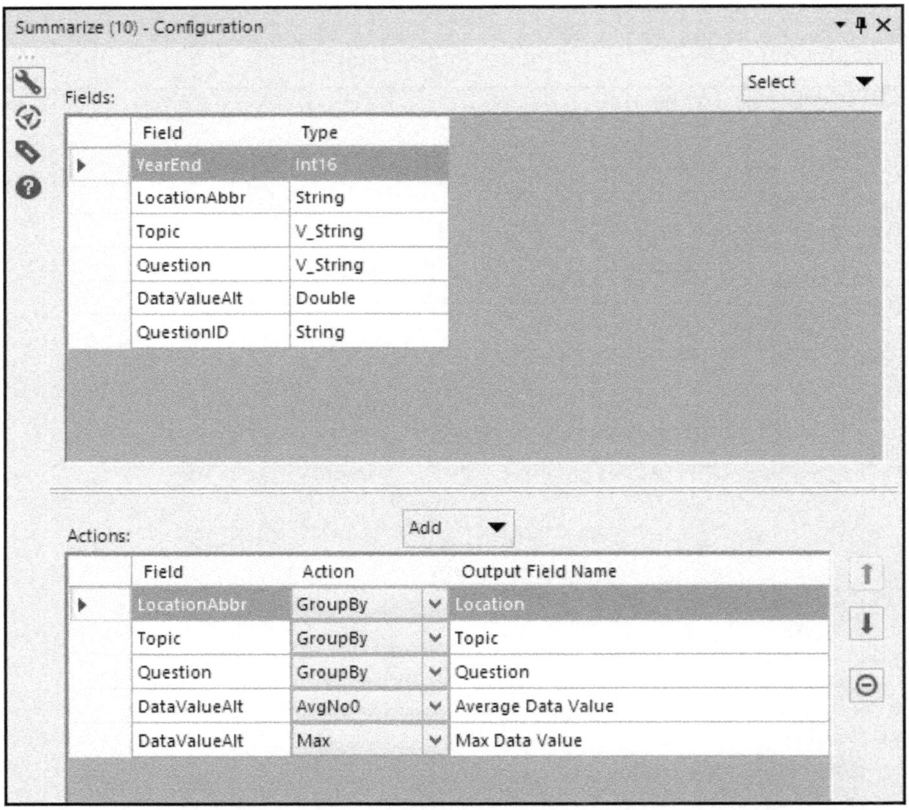

Step 7: Select the **Table** tool from the **Reporting** tool palette and drag it onto the canvas. Connect the **Table** tool to the **Summarize** tool. Leave the options within the **Table** tool configuration as is:

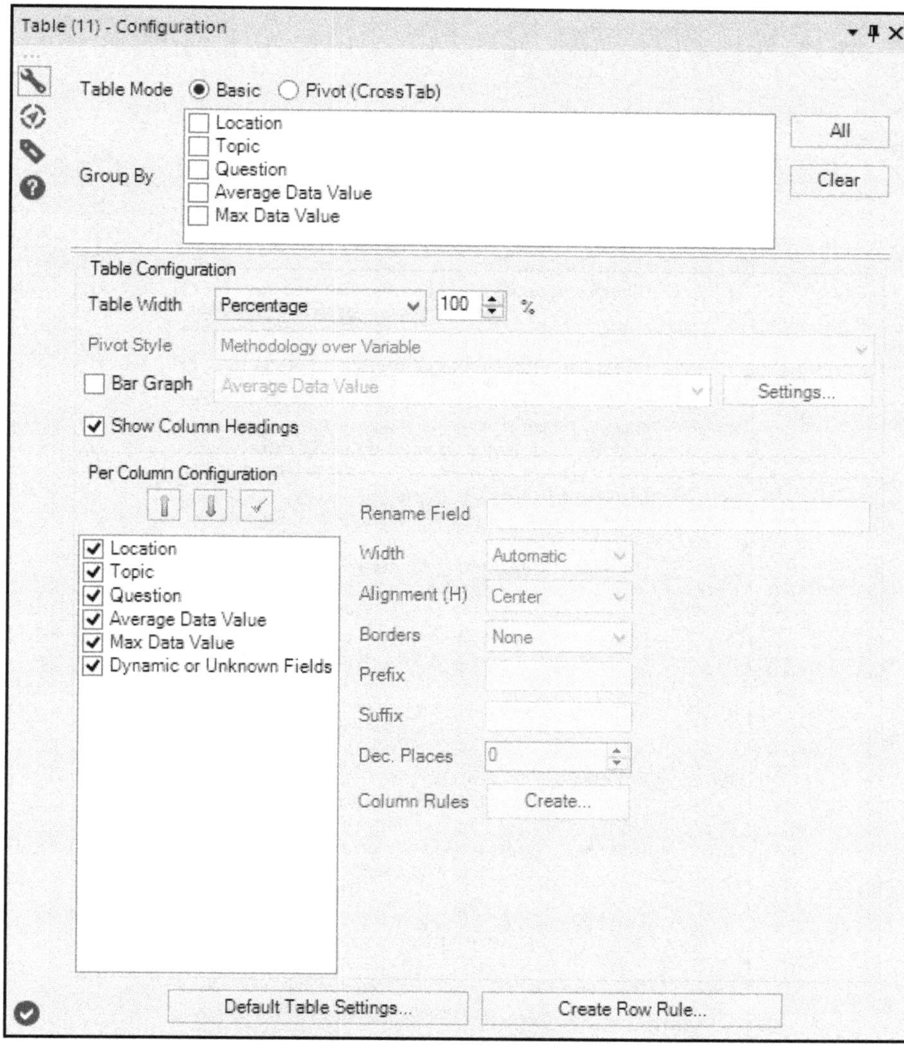

Step 8: Add a **Browse** tool to the **Table** tool.

Step 9: Run the workflow:

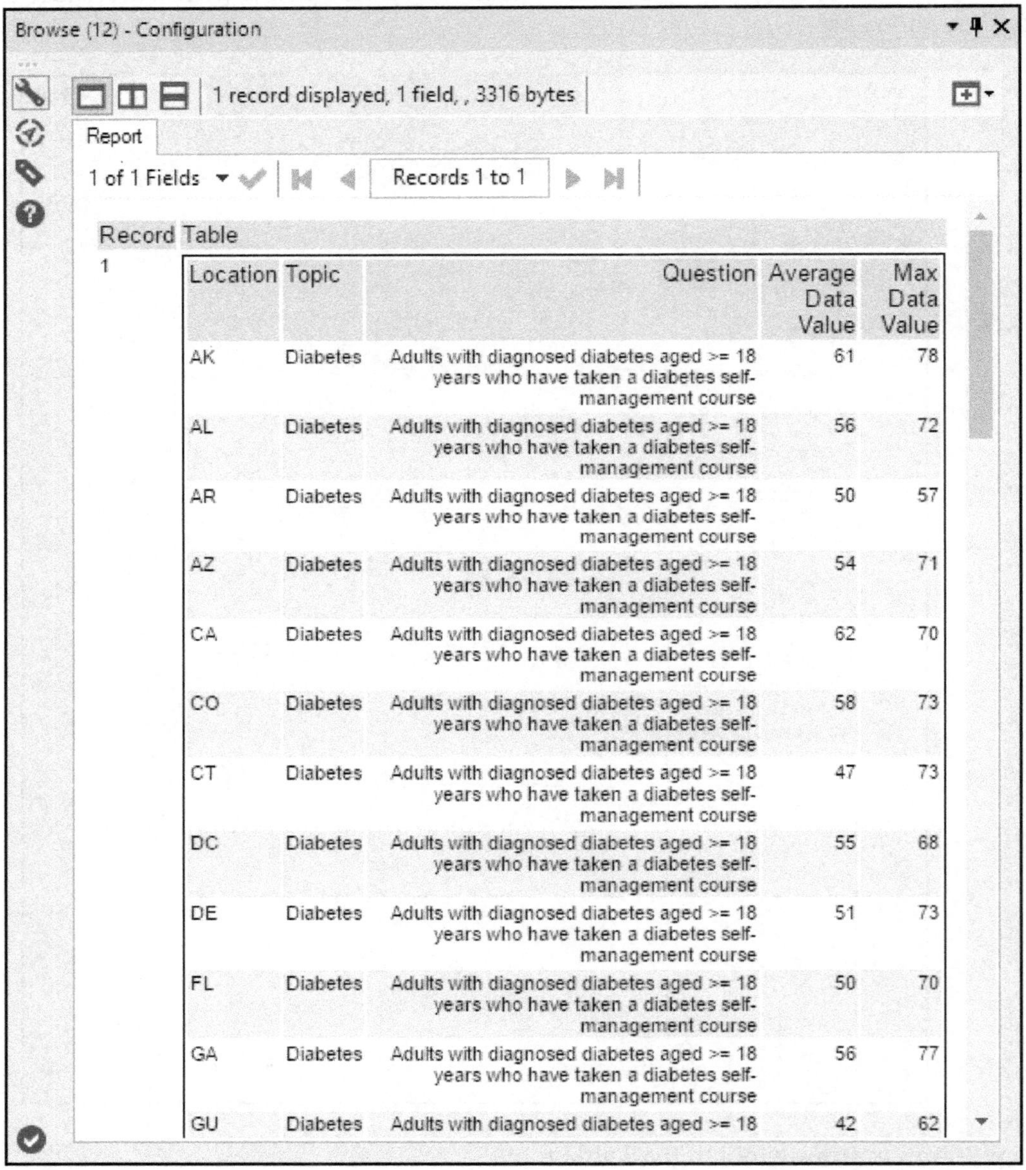

Location	Topic	Question	Average Data Value	Max Data Value
AK	Diabetes	Adults with diagnosed diabetes aged >= 18 years who have taken a diabetes self-management course	61	78
AL	Diabetes	Adults with diagnosed diabetes aged >= 18 years who have taken a diabetes self-management course	56	72
AR	Diabetes	Adults with diagnosed diabetes aged >= 18 years who have taken a diabetes self-management course	50	57
AZ	Diabetes	Adults with diagnosed diabetes aged >= 18 years who have taken a diabetes self-management course	54	71
CA	Diabetes	Adults with diagnosed diabetes aged >= 18 years who have taken a diabetes self-management course	62	70
CO	Diabetes	Adults with diagnosed diabetes aged >= 18 years who have taken a diabetes self-management course	58	73
CT	Diabetes	Adults with diagnosed diabetes aged >= 18 years who have taken a diabetes self-management course	47	73
DC	Diabetes	Adults with diagnosed diabetes aged >= 18 years who have taken a diabetes self-management course	55	68
DE	Diabetes	Adults with diagnosed diabetes aged >= 18 years who have taken a diabetes self-management course	51	73
FL	Diabetes	Adults with diagnosed diabetes aged >= 18 years who have taken a diabetes self-management course	50	70
GA	Diabetes	Adults with diagnosed diabetes aged >= 18 years who have taken a diabetes self-management course	56	77
GU	Diabetes	Adults with diagnosed diabetes aged >= 18	42	62

The output in the **Browse** tool displays the data table by Location, Topic, Question, Average Data Value, and Max Data Value. This table is for every Location, but only for the question *Adults with diagnosed diabetes aged >= 18 years who have taken a diabetes self-management course.* The **Filter** tool limits the data to results that are only for the QuestionID `"DIA10_0"` and that do not contain any null values in `DataValueAlt`. The data is presented in a format where it is easy to identify what the `Average Ignoring Zeros` and `Max Data Value` is per Location.

Table Example #3: Create a data table that displays Location, Topic, Question, Average Data Value, Min Data Value, and Max Data Value. Display each record individually for every Location, Topic, and Question. The steps for this process are as follows:

Step 1: We will start this example from the existing **Auto Field** tool from the previous example. Select the **Filter** tool from the **Preparation** tool palette and drag it onto the canvas. Connect the **Filter** tool to the **Auto Field** tool.

Step 2: Select the **Select** tool from the **Preparation** tool palette and drag it onto the canvas. Connect the **Select** tool to the **Auto Field** tool.

Step 3: Select the following fields within the **Select** tool configuration:
YearEnd, LocationAbbr, Topic, Question, DataValueAlt, and QuestionID

Step 4: Select the **Summarize** tool from the **Transform** tool palette and drag it onto the canvas. Connect the **Summarize** tool to the **Select** tool.

Step 5: Select the following fields and select **Add** from the drop down to select their respective actions. Rename the **Output Field Names** to Location, Topic, Question, Average Data Value, Min Data Value, and Max Data Value, as shown in the following image:

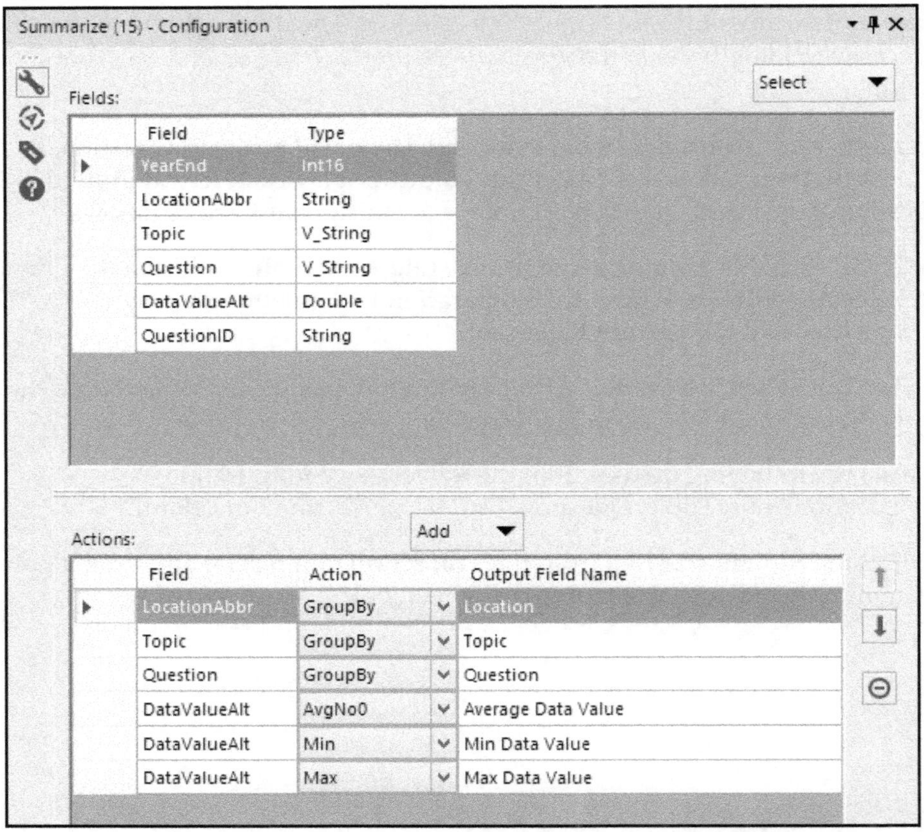

Step 6: Select the **Table** tool from the **Reporting** tool palette and drag it onto the canvas. Connect the **Table** tool to the **Summarize** tool.

Step 7: Select Location, Topic, and Question from the GroupBy selections. Leave all other default options as is:

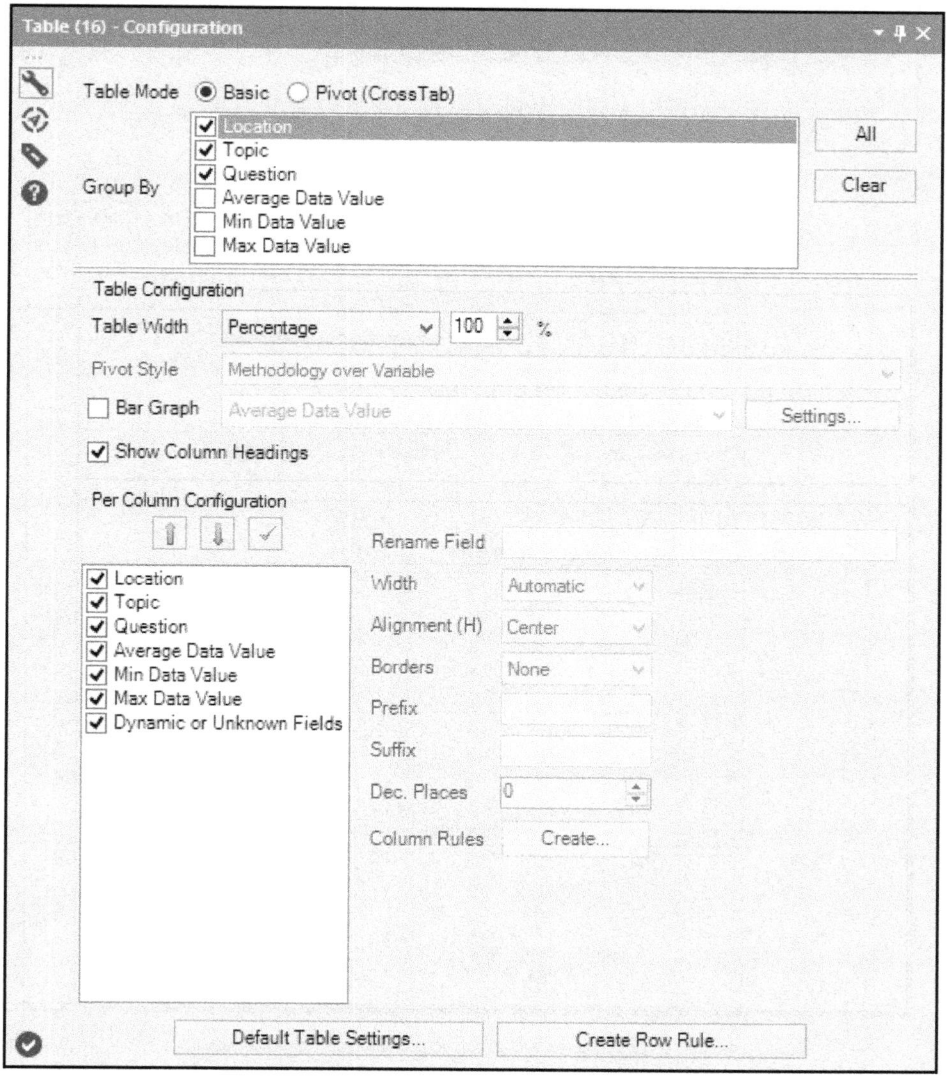

Step 8: Add a **Browse** tool to the **Table** tool.

Step 9: Run the workflow:

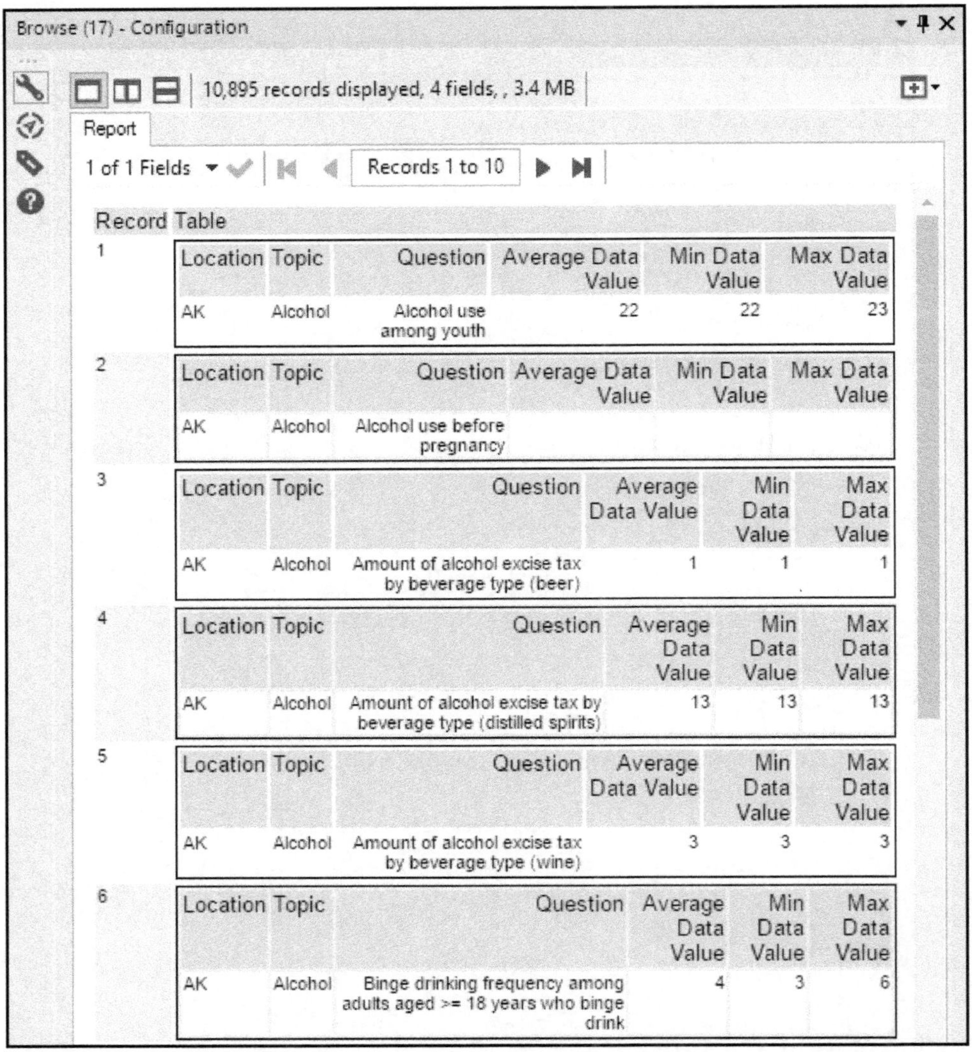

Notice in the **Browse** tool output that each record is displayed individually by Location, Topic, and Question. By selecting the Location, Topic, and Question in the Group By option within the **Table** tool, we allow for each record to be presented separately. The data values aggregated within the **Summarize** tool are Average Ignoring Zeros, Min, and Max. This is another way of displaying data; as you discovered in the previous two examples, all data values were located within one data table, whereas in this example, they are broken down separately. This table layout can be very handy depending on business requests as to how data should be presented.

In the next example, we'll go through creating a Bar Chart using the **Table** tool.

Table Example #4: Create a data table that displays Location, Topic, and a Bar Graph displaying the Average Ignoring Zeros Data Value for every Location, and Topic. The steps are as follows:

Step 1: We will start this example from the existing **Auto Field** tool from the previous example. Select the **Filter** tool from the **Preparation** tool palette and drag it onto the canvas. Connect the **Filter** tool to the **Auto Field** tool.

Step 2: Select **Basic Filter** within the **Filter** tool configuration and select `YearEnd` from the field drop down, Equals from the operators drop down, and enter `2015` in the text box, as shown in the following image:

Step 3: Select the **Select** tool from the **Preparation** tool palette and drag it onto the canvas. Connect the **Select** tool to the **Filter** tool (T Output).

Step 4: Select the following fields within the **Select** tool configuration:
YearEnd, LocationAbbr, Topic, Question, DataValueAlt, and QuestionID

Step 5: Select the **Summarize** tool from the **Transform** tool palette and drag it onto the canvas. Connect the **Summarize** tool to the **Select** tool.

Step 6: Select the following fields and select `Add` from the drop down to select their respective actions. Rename the **Output Field Names** to Location, Topic, and Average Data Value, as shown in the following image:

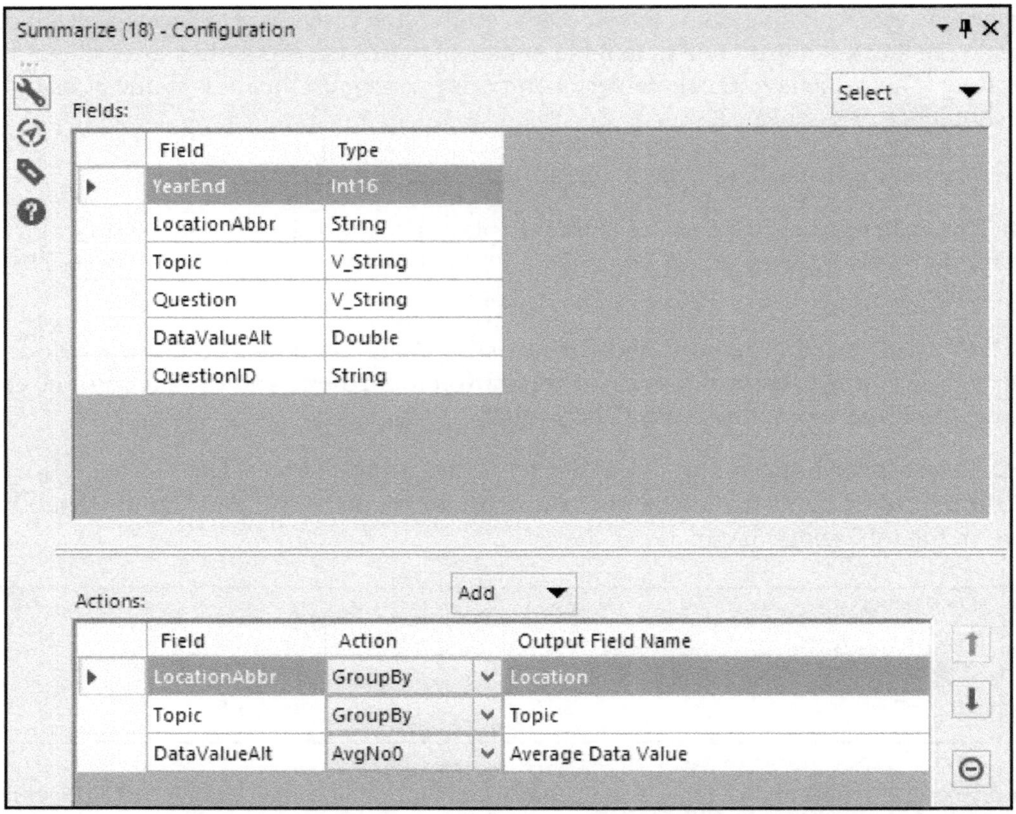

Step 7: Select the **Table** tool from the **Reporting** tool palette and drag it onto the canvas. Connect the **Table** tool to the **Summarize** tool.

Step 8: Select the **Bar Graph** option and deselect the **Average Data Value** option from the available fields:

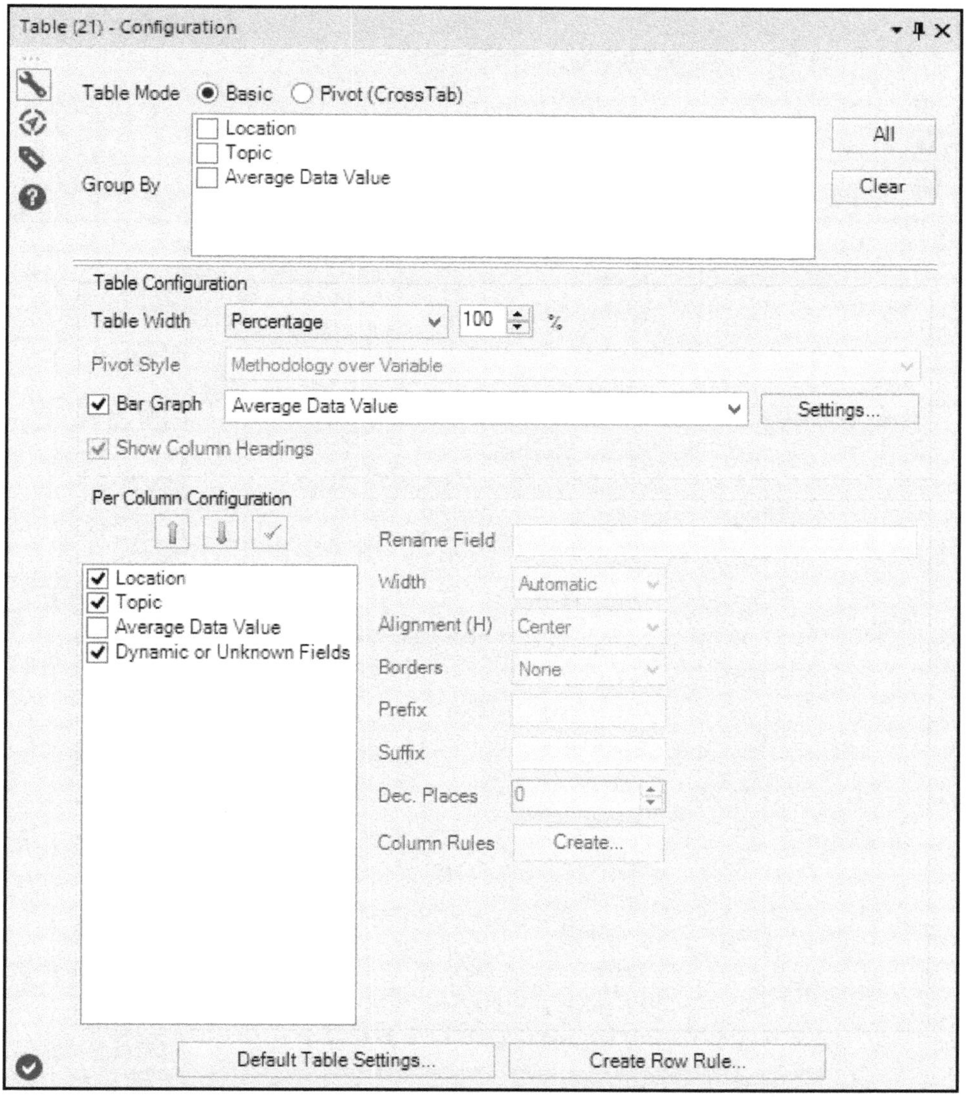

Step 9: Add a **Browse** tool to the **Table** tool.

Step 10: Run the workflow:

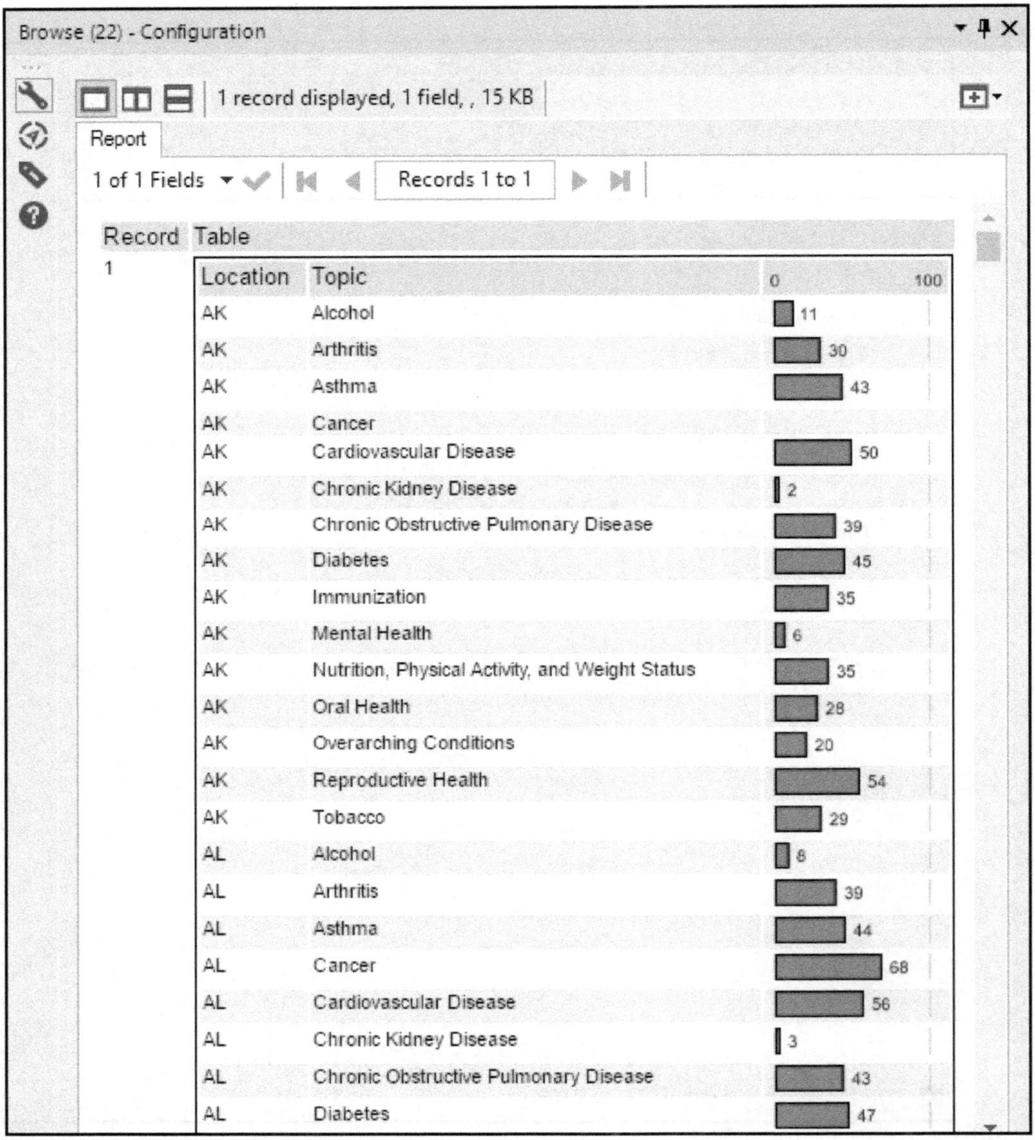

The **Browse** tool output now contains a bar graph visual representation of the data, whereas in previous examples, a data table layout was created. The bar graph shows the Average Ignoring Zeros values for every Location and Topic from 2015 only. The YearEnd was limited to only 2015 within the **Filter** tool, and the Average Ignoring Zeros for every Location and Topic was accomplished within the **Summarize** tool. The **Table** tool has the `Bar Graph` option that was selected to create the desired output, and the **Average Data Value** was deselected because it's not needed, since the bar graph displays the data. This example will provide you a good foundation for discovering the **Charting** tool, which we'll go through in the next section.

Charting

Developing charts is as exciting as it sounds! Charts may be bar charts, comparing dimensions to one another or line charts, visualizing a time-series trend. These charts and many more are available by using the Charting tool located in the Reporting tool palette. The **Charting** tool can be used to create a chart. This includes chart types like Bar, Line, Area, Column, Pie, and many more. This can be a real difference maker when it comes to adding a visualization to go with the data table that you went through in the previous section. Let's go through a couple of examples, and explore the wonders of the **Charting** tool.

Charting Example #1: Create a Line Chart that displays the Average Data Value for each chronic disease only in Florida, and apply a Border around the chart. The steps are as follows:

Step 1: We will start this example from the existing **Summarize** tool, in the top stream within the existing workflow. Select the **Charting** tool from the **Reporting** tool palette and drag it onto the canvas. Connect the **Charting** tool to the **Summarize** tool.

Step 2: Apply the following selections within the **Charting** tool configuration:

- **Chart Type**: `Line`
- **Select Field(s) To Chart (Series 1)**: `Average Data Value`
- **Label Field**: `Topic`
- **Setup Chart Appearance** | **Borders, Backgrounds** | **Border Chart**: `Yes`

The following image shows the selections that are made:

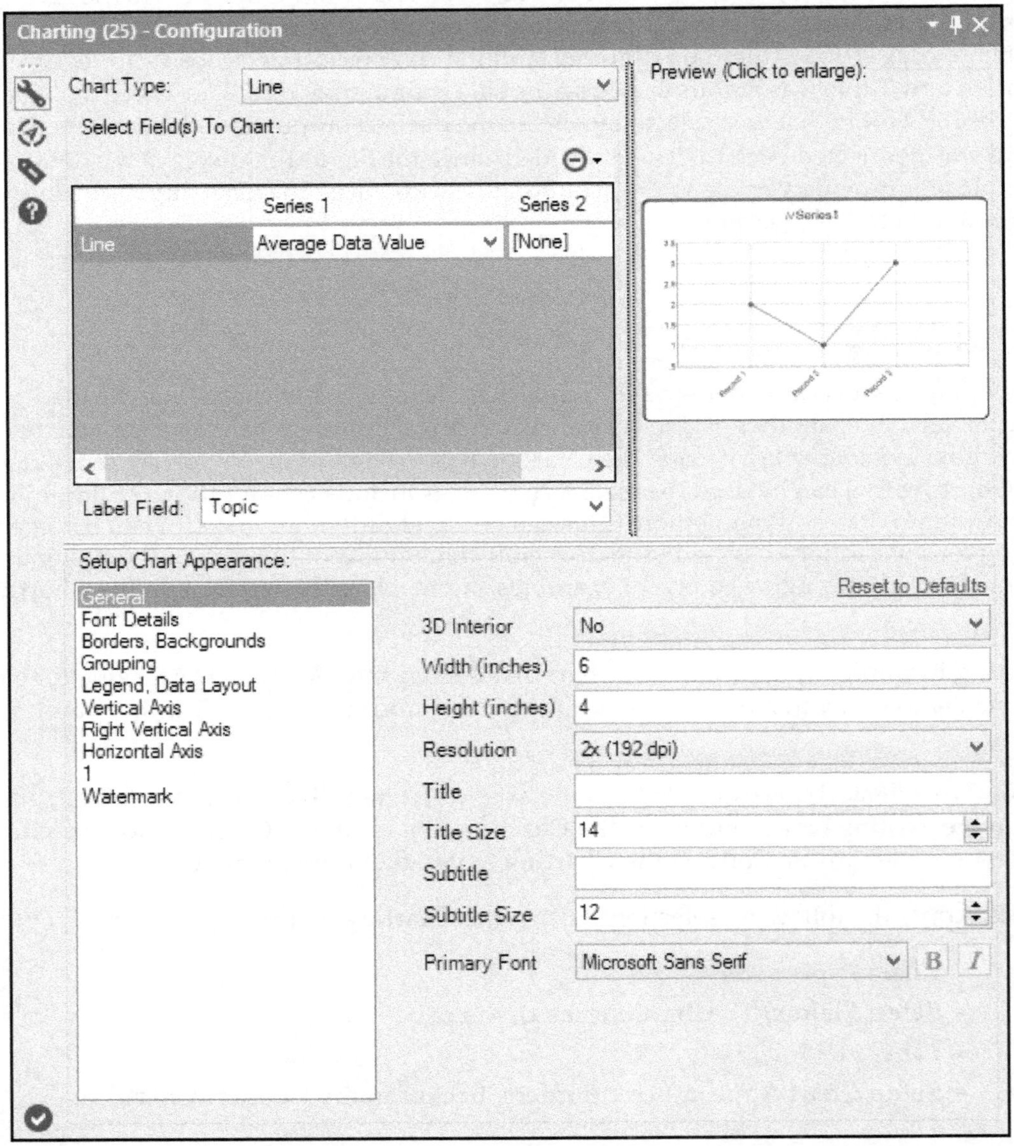

Step 3: Add a **Browse** tool to the **Table** tool.

Step 4: Run the workflow:

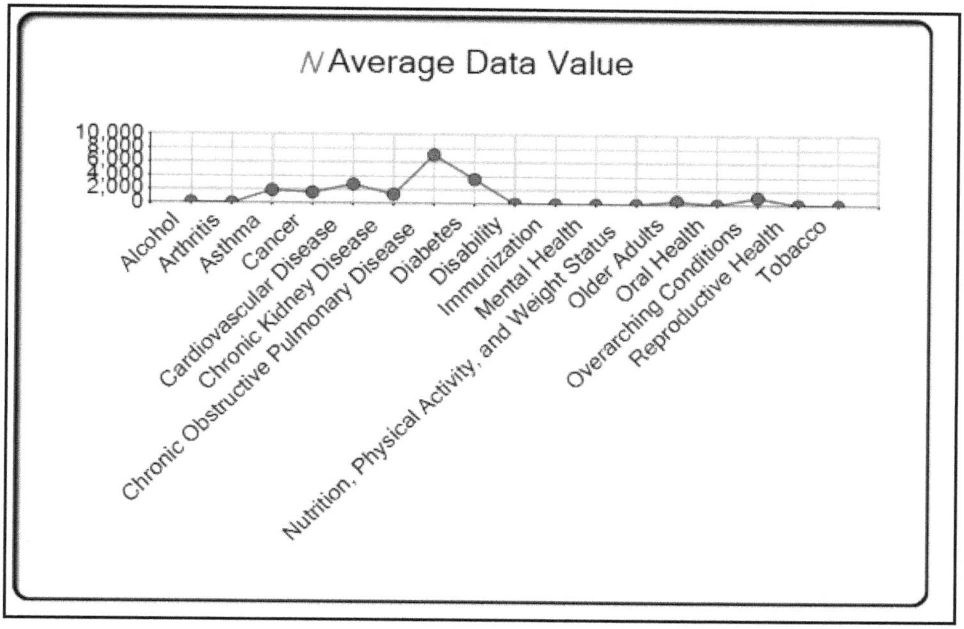

The Line Chart is developed by selecting Line as the Chart Type within the Charting tool configuration, and a border is added under the Setup Chart Appearance selections located in the Borders, Backgrounds options. The Topic field displays each label for every Topic. Very quickly, a trend graph is created, which shows where the chronic diseases stand compared to each other.

Charting Example #2: Create a gradient Bar Chart that displays the Average Data Value for the top 5 chronic diseases only in Florida. Plot the data by chronic diseases and add Winter color palette. Apply a Border around the chart. The steps to do so are as follows:

Step 1: We will start this example from the existing **Summarize** tool in the top stream within the existing workflow. Select the **Charting** tool from the **Reporting** tool palette and drag it onto the canvas. Connect the **Charting** tool to the **Summarize** tool.

Step 2: Select the **Sort** tool from the **Preparation** tool palette and drag it onto the canvas. Connect the **Sort** tool to the **Summarize** tool.

Step 3: Select **Average Data Value** for Name and Descending for Order within the **Sort** tool configuration.

Step 4: Select the **Sample** tool from the **Preparation** tool palette and drag it onto the canvas. Connect the **Sample** tool to the **Sort** tool.

Step 5: Select the radio button **First N Records** and enter `5` in the **N =** text box, as shown in the following image:

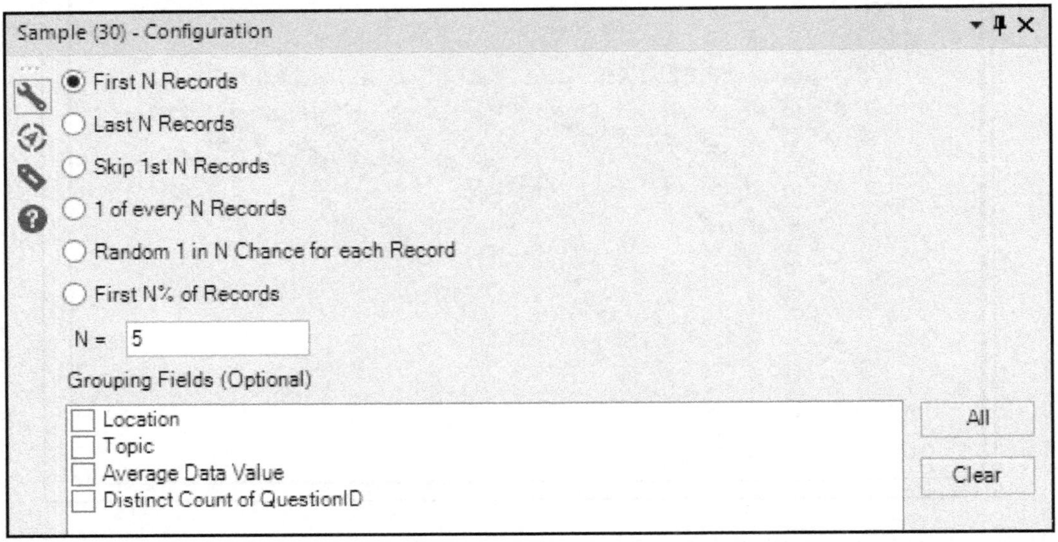

Step 6: Apply the following selections within the **Charting** tool configuration:

- **Chart Type**: `Bar`
- **Select Field(s) To Chart (Series 1)**: `Average Data Value`
- **Label Field**: `Topic`
- **Setup Chart Appearance** | **General** | **Gradient Coloring**: `Yes`
- **Setup Chart Appearance** | **Borders, Backgrounds** | **Border Chart**: `Yes`
- **Setup Chart Appearance** | **Legend, Data Layout**:
    - **Plot Data By:** `Field`
    - **Label Data Points**: `No`
    - **Color Palette**: `Winter`

The following image will give you a better idea of the selections we are making here:

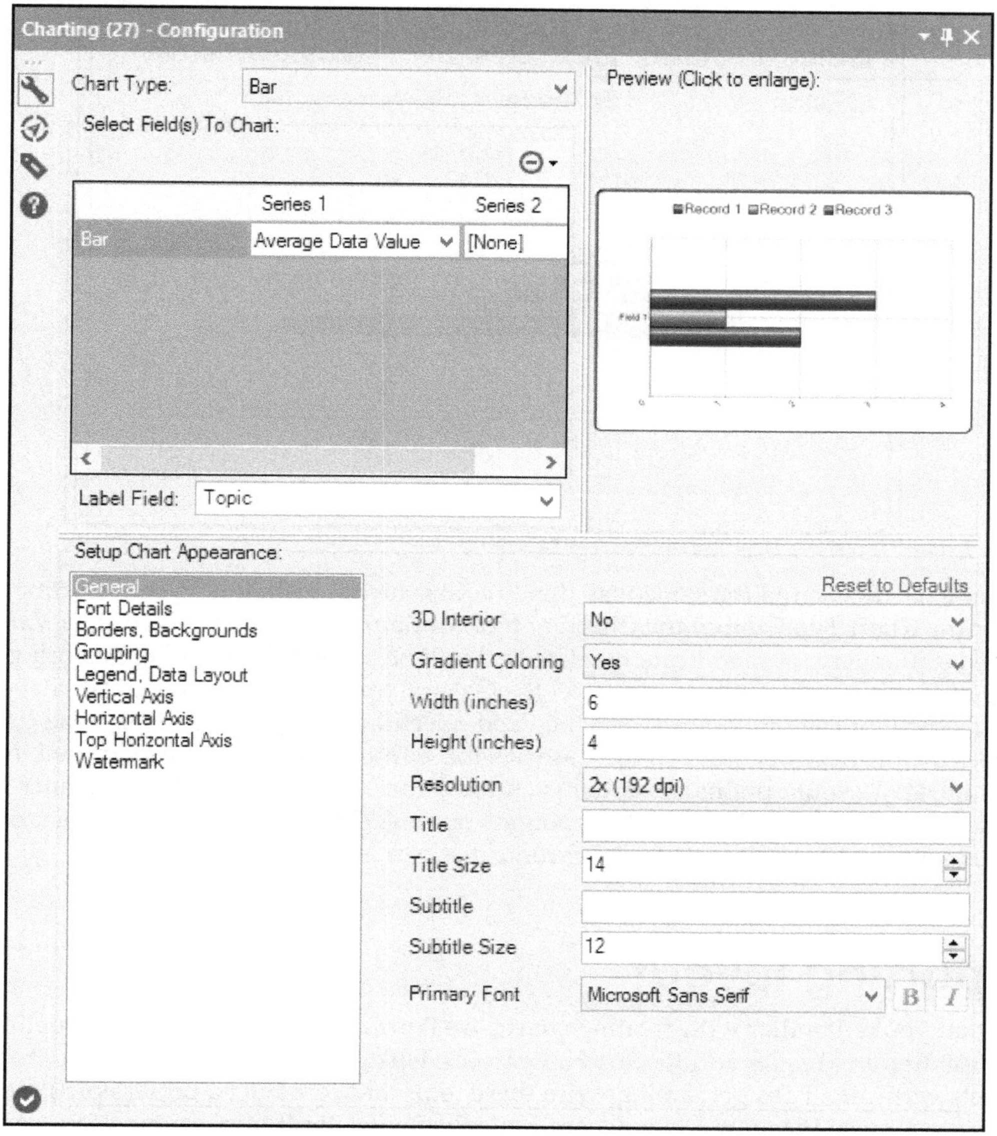

Step 7: Add a **Browse** tool to the **Table** tool.

Step 8: Run the workflow:

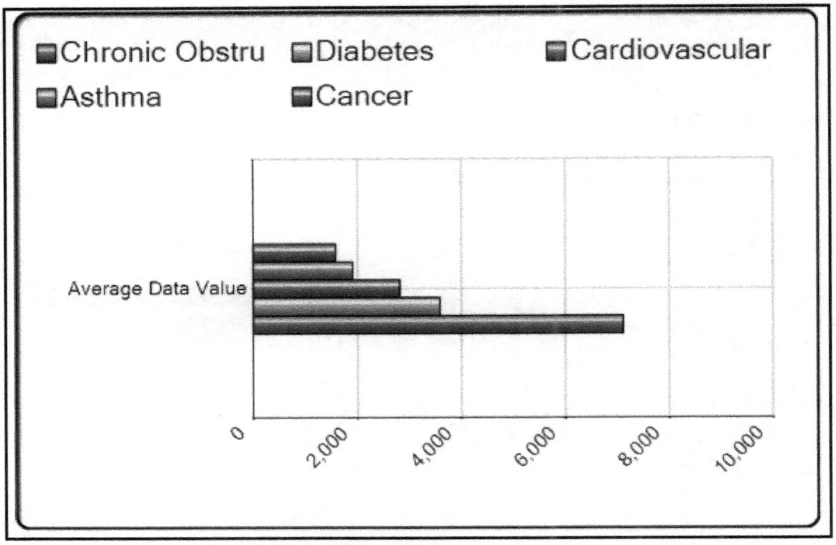

The Bar Chart is created the same way the Line Chart was created, with the selection being Bar for the Chart Type within the Charting tool configuration. The Average Data Value is selected under Series 1 to indicate the data that will be plotted. The gradient coloring is an option under Setup Chart Appearance in the General options. The Legend, Data Layout contains the Plot Data By options and the Field selection is key here to display the chronic diseases by a variety of colors. In this case, it's the Winter color palette also located in the Legend, Data Layout options. A border is added under the Setup Chart Appearance selections located in the Borders, Backgrounds options. The Bar Chart provides a quick visualization for identifying the top 5 chronic diseases in Florida.

Reporting layout

Now that you're familiar with creating charts, we'll move onto laying out the structure using the **Report Header** and **Report Footer** tools. Next, we'll add the **Layout** tool to the snippets vertically. Let's get familiar with these tools and construct a professional report to enhance your visualization. We will continue where we left off from the previous section, where we created a Bar Chart to identify the Top 5 Chronic Diseases in Florida.

Reporting Layout Example 1: Add a report header and name it *Florida: Top 5 Chronic Diseases* and include a date in the report header. Next, add a report footer and add the information *This report was developed using Alteryx*. Lay out the report with the report header at the top, the Bar Chart in the middle, and the report footer at the bottom, all aligned vertically with section breaks. The steps of this process are as follows:

Step 1: Select the **Report Header** tool from the **Reporting** tool palette and drag it onto the canvas. Connect the **Report Header** tool to the **Charting** tool.

Step 2: Apply the following selections within the **Report Header** tool configuration:

- Enter the report title: `Florida: Top 5 Chronic Diseases`
- Include the date in your report header: `Month dd, yyyy`

The following is an image that demonstrates the selections to be applied:

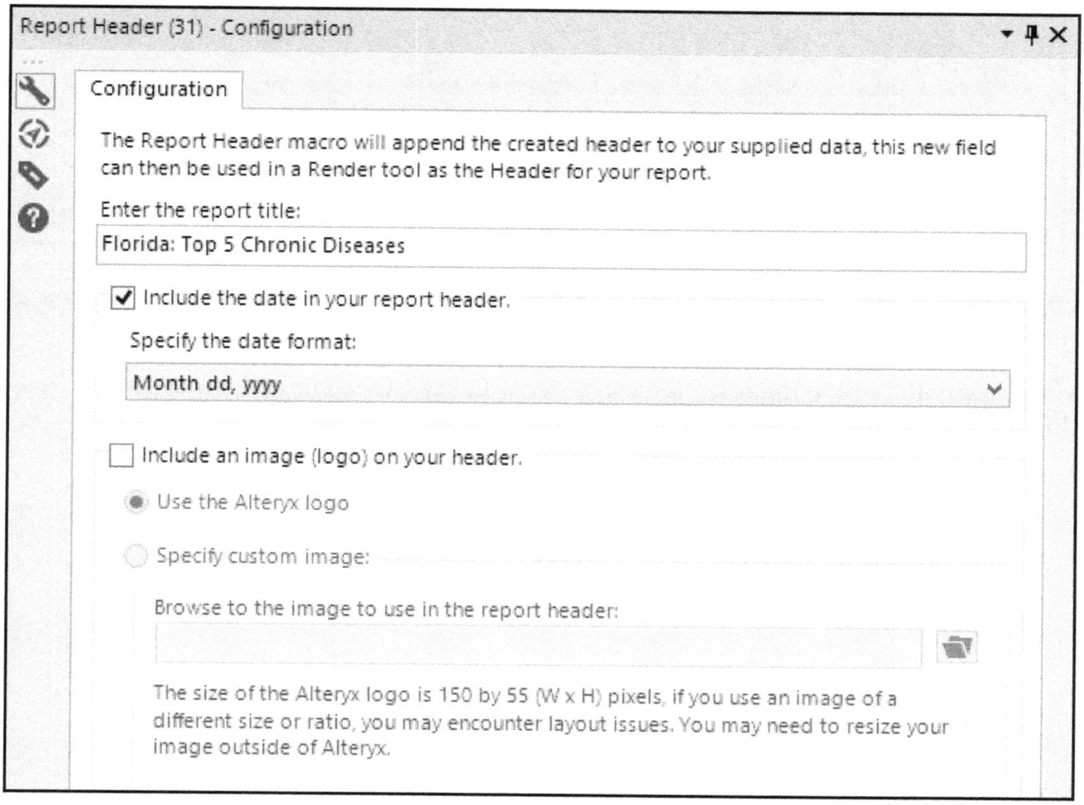

Step 3: Select the **Report Footer** tool from the **Reporting** tool palette and drag it onto the canvas. Connect the **Report Footer** tool to the **Report Header** tool.

Step 4: Apply the following selections within the **Report Footer** tool configuration, as shown in the following image:

Information text: `This report was developed using Alteryx`

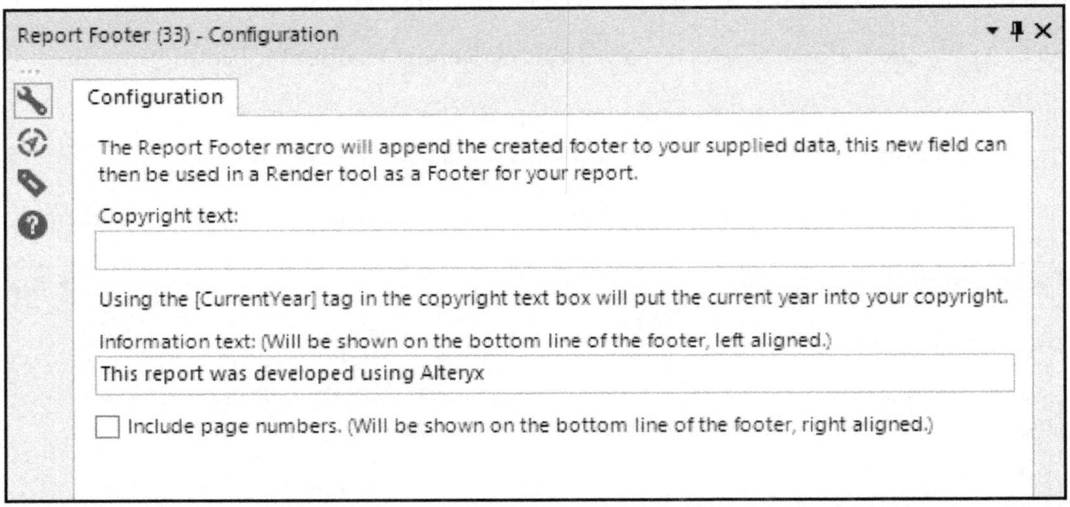

Step 5: Select the **Layout** tool from the **Reporting** tool palette and drag it onto the canvas. Connect the Layout tool to the Report Footer tool.

Step 6: Apply the following selections within the **Layout** tool configuration, as shown in the following image:

- **Layout Mode**: Each Individual Record
- **Orientation**: Vertical with Section Breaks
- **Per Section Configuration**: **Header | Chart | Footer**

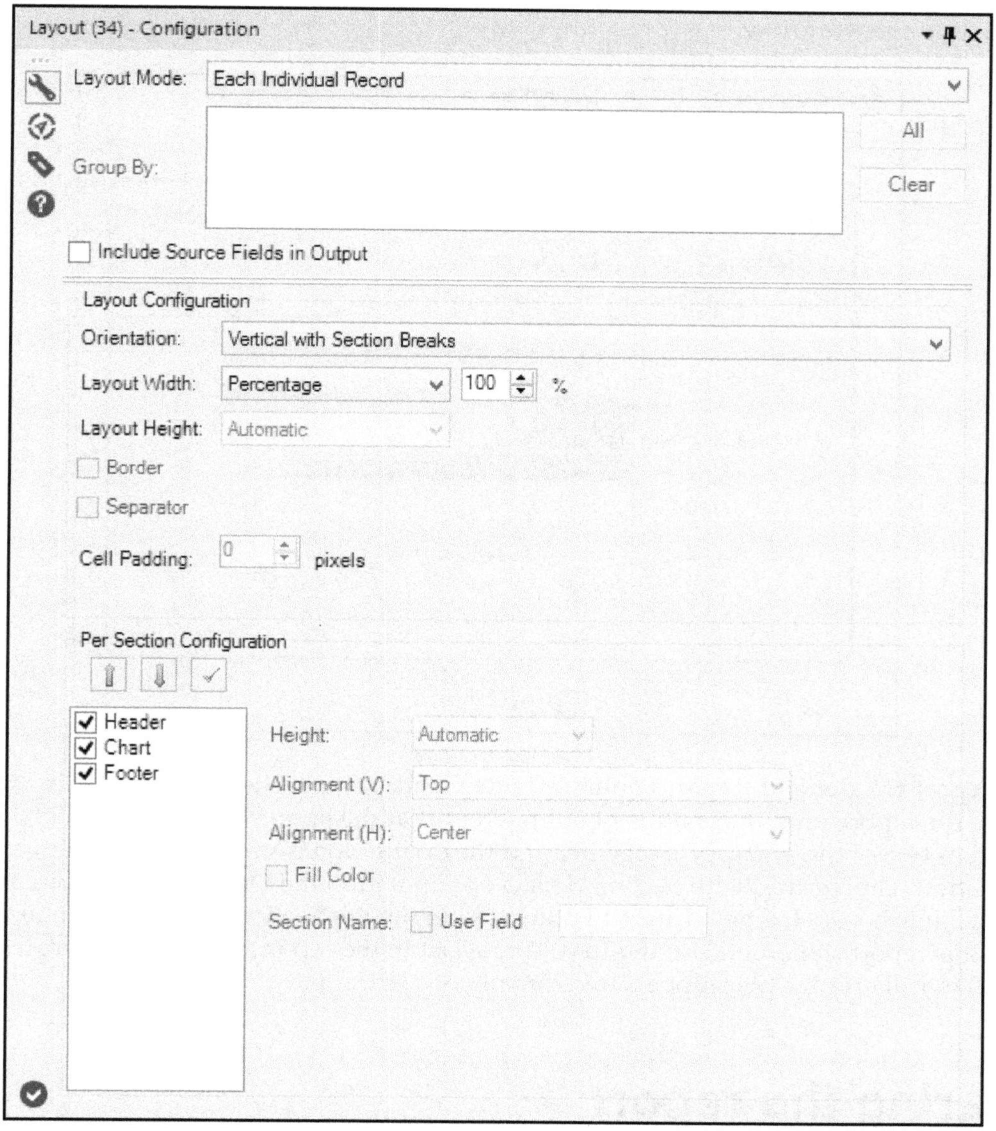

Step 7: Add a **Browse** tool to the **Table** tool.

Step 8: Run the workflow:

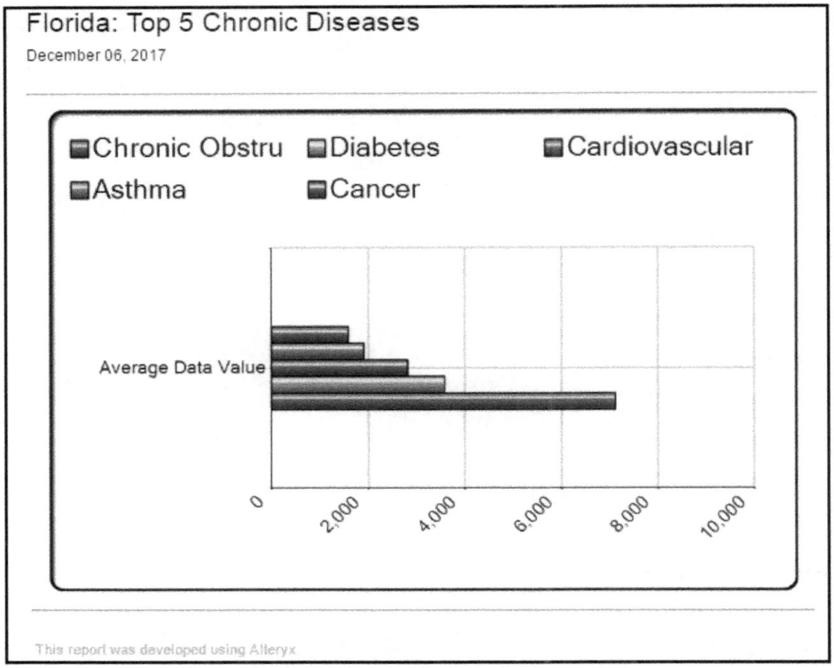

The **Report Header** and **Report Footer** provide details around the report, including the title, date of the report, and information about the report at the bottom. The **Layout** tool combines two or more snippets together and the orientation is vital to lay out the foundation. The Vertical with Section Breaks option within the Orientation options and the order alignment of **Header** | **Chart** | **Footer** within the Per Section Configuration really make this report stand out. Use the **Layout** tool last in the report development process, since this will arrange the snippets horizontally or vertically.

Sharing the report

The final step in the reporting process is to share the report with the stakeholders who will make the important business decisions. With the focus on improving the top 5 chronic diseases in Florida, the stakeholders now want to a visual representation of the top 5 chronic diseases to improve on. This can be quickly accomplished using the **Render** tool in the **Reporting** tool palette. Let's export the *Florida: Top 5: Chronic Diseases* report to a temporary PDF by continuing from the **Layout** tool in the previous section.

Render Example #1: Export the *Florida: Top 5: Chronic Diseases* report to a temporary HTML file. The steps are as follows:

Step 1: Select the **Render** tool from the **Reporting** tool palette and drag it onto the canvas. Connect the **Render** tool to the **Layout** tool.

Step 2: Select `Temporary HTML File` as the **Output Mode** within the **Render** tool configuration. Leave all other defaults as is, as shown in the following image:

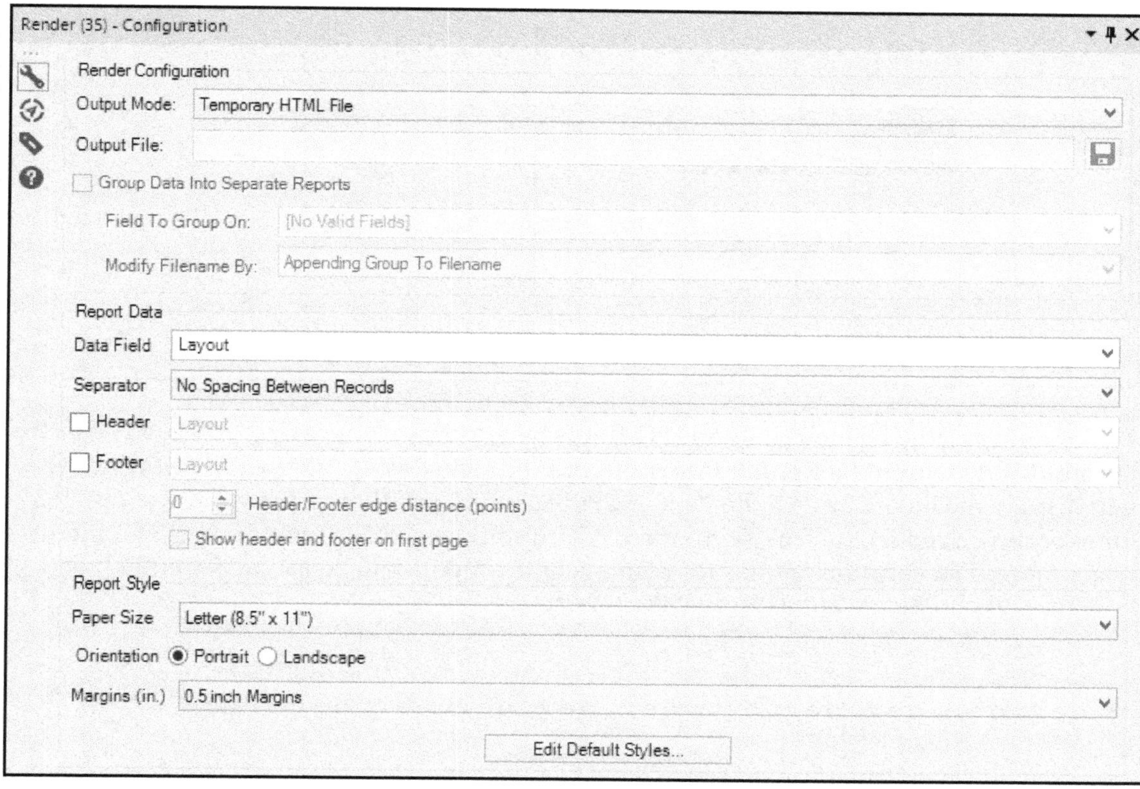

Step 3: Add a **Browse** tool to the **Table** tool.

Step 4: Run the workflow:

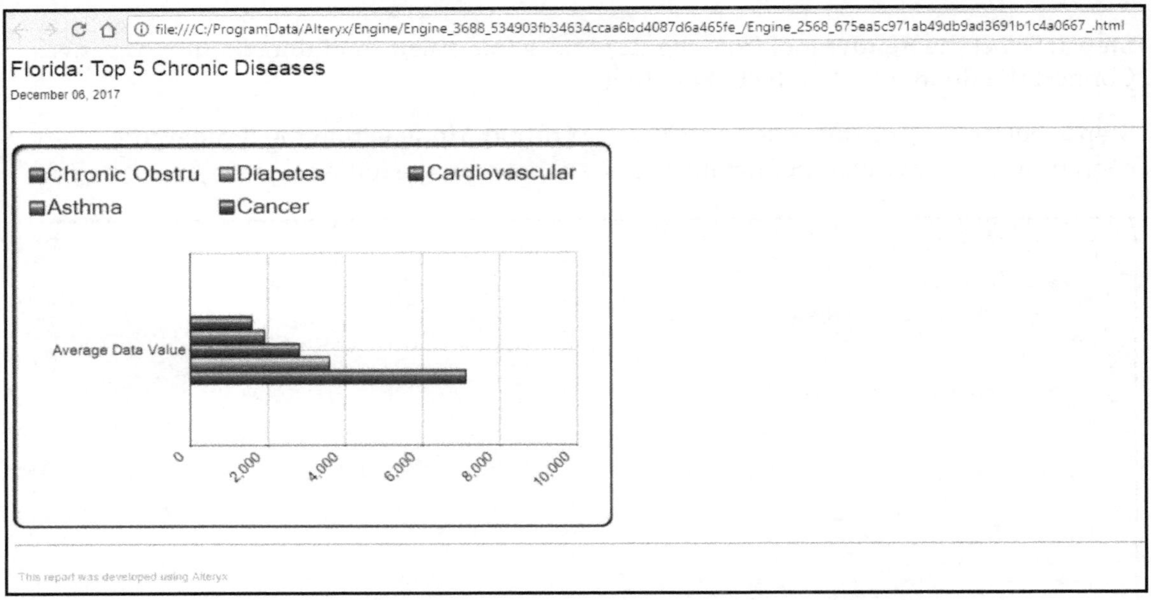

The report can now be viewed as an HTML file by selecting `Temporary HTML File` as the **Output Mode** within the **Render** tool configuration. The Results (*Ctrl* + *Alt* + *R*) window will display the link to launch the `Temporary HTML File`. There are a variety of options for exporting a report, such as Temporary PDF, Temporary RTF, Temporary PNG, and many more. The versatile options for displaying the report will be useful depending on how the stakeholders want to receive the report.

The final workflow will look like the following image:

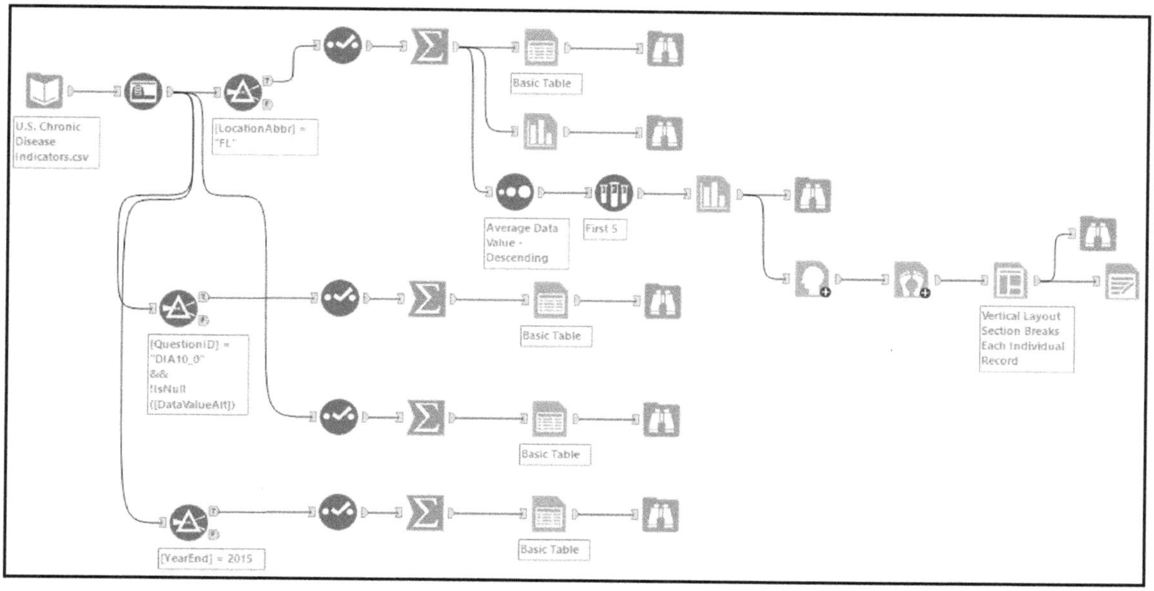

Summary

In this chapter, you learned about the foundation of report development and how it can be combined using multiple tools located in the **Reporting** tool palette. The **Table** tool provided a great way to create a data table in a visual format and the **Charting** tool provided the trend and bar visualizations to identify focus areas of chronic diseases in Florida. The Report Header and Report Footer provided the report title and report information, respectively. These snippets, along with the bar chart, were arranged using the **Layout** tool to display a vertical layout with section breaks. Sharing the report is located within the **Render** tool and you learned that the `Temporary HTML File` is one option for exporting out the report, but there are many options to choose from. This chapter focused on bringing the pieces of data together to create a meaningful report for stakeholders. If you are ever asked to send a report out using the analysis discovered in Alteryx, then the **Reporting** tool palette will contain the tools you'll need to meet this business requirement.

The next chapter will cover developing macros using a collection of tools within Alteryx. These tools are comprised of Interface tools within the Interface tool palette.

8
Using Macros in Workflows

A macro workflow has the flexibility to run as a single tool within another workflow. Macros have capabilities that solve problems quickly and easily than manually up-keeping data processes. There are various macro types that are built by using Interface Tools with the Interface Designer. Batch macros are designed to run repeatedly in the context of a workflow. The next two macros will describe what they are capable of accomplishing. The ability to run a single tool through every record, and loop the records back through the workflow until a condition is met, can be accomplished using an Iterative Macro. The last macro to review is the Location Optimizer Macro, which identifies the best score for each demand location and specifies the amount of locations you would like to add to the Network through an iterative macro. In this chapter, you will learn a variety of macros that will provide you with a foundation for building enhanced workflows using macros.

This chapter will cover the following topics in detail:

- Standard Macro
- Batch Macro

Standard Macro

Before getting into macros, let's define what a macro is. A macro is a collection of workflow tools that are grouped together into one tool. Using a range of different interface tools, a macro can be developed and used within a workflow. Any workflow can be turned into a macro and a repeatable element of a workflow can commonly be converted into a macro.

There are a couple of ways you can turn your workflow into a Standard Macro. The first is to go to the canvas configuration pane and navigate to the Workflow tab. This is where you select what type of workflow you want. If you select *Macro* you should then have Standard Macro automatically selected. Now, when you save this workflow it will save as a macro. You'll then be able to add it to another workflow and run the process created within the macro itself. The second method is just to add a Macro Input tool from the Interface tool section onto the canvas; the workflow will then automatically change to a Standard Macro.

The following screenshot shows the selection of a Standard Macro, under the **Workflow** tab:

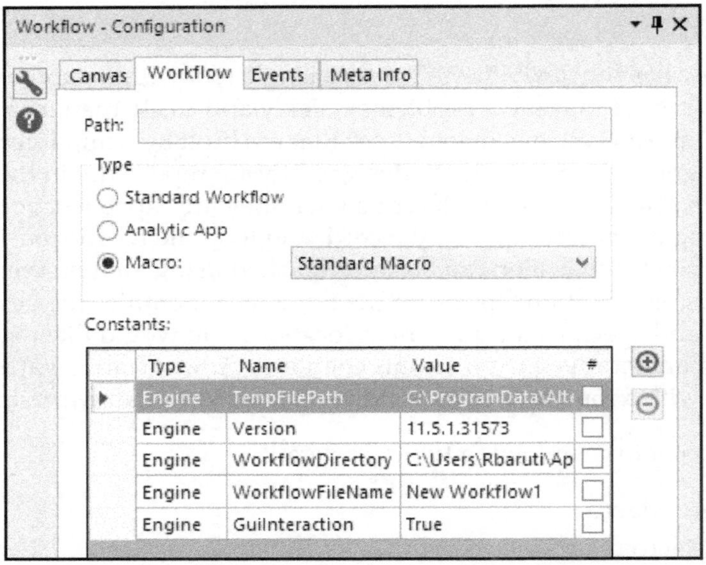

Let's go through an example of creating and deploying a standard macro.

Standard Macro Example #1: Create a macro that allows the user to input a number used as a multiplier. Use the multiplier for the DataValueAlt field. The following steps demonstrate this process:

Step 1: Select the Macro Input tool from the Interface tool palette and add the tool onto the canvas. The workflow will automatically change to a Standard Macro.

Step 2: Select Text Input and Edit Data option within the Macro Input tool configuration.

Step 3: Create a field called **Number** and enter the values: **155**, **243**, **128**, **352**, and **357** in each row, as shown in the following image:

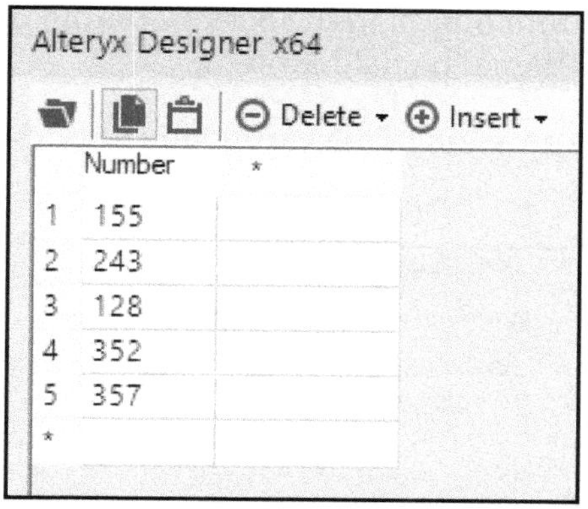

Step 4: Rename the Input Name **Input** and set the Anchor Abbreviation as **I** as shown in the following image:

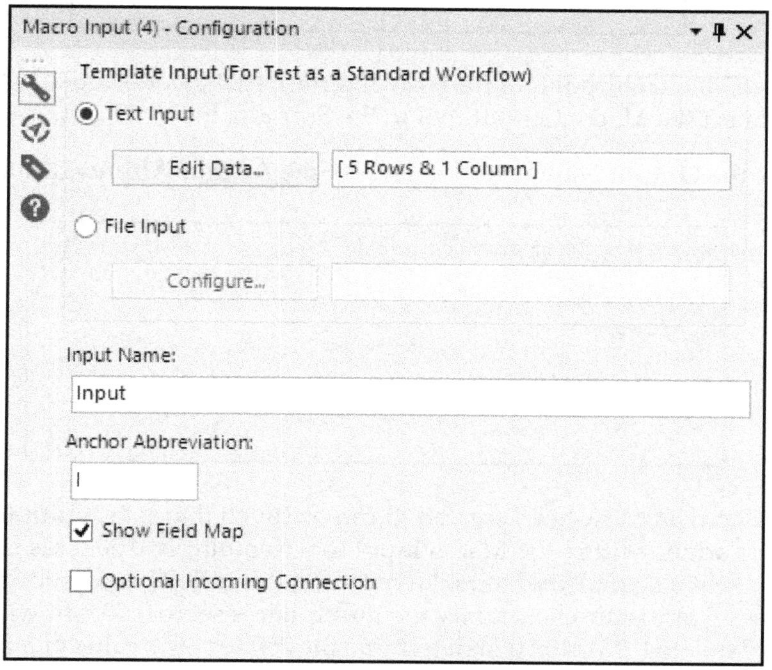

Step 5: Select the Formula tool from the Preparation tool palette. Connect the Formula tool to the Macro Input tool.

Step 6: Select the + Add Column option in the Select Column drop down within the Formula tool configuration. Name the field `Result`.

Step 7: Add the following expression to the expression window:
`[Number]*0.50`

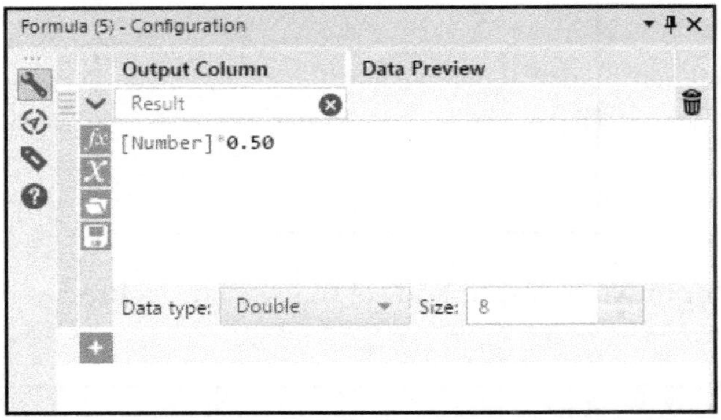

Step 8: Select the Macro Output tool from the Interface tool palette and add the tool onto the canvas. Connect the Macro Output tool to the Formula tool.

Step 9: Rename the **Output Name** `Output` and set the **Anchor Abbreviation** as `O`:

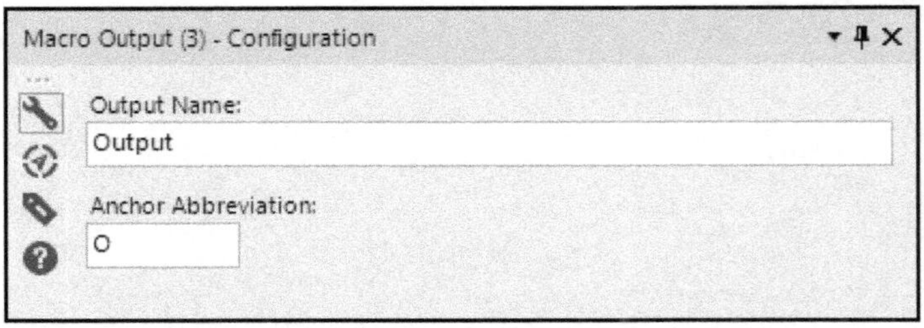

The Standard Macro has now been created. It can be saved to use as multiplier, to calculate the five numbers added within the Macro Input tool to multiply 0.50. This is great; however, let's take it a step further to make it dynamic and flexible by allowing the user to enter a multiplier. For instance, currently the multiplier is set to 0.50, but what if a user wants to change that to 0.25 or 0.10 to determine the 25% or 10% value of a field. Let's continue building out the Standard Macro to make this possible.

Step 1: Select the Text Box tool from the Interface tool palette and drag it onto the canvas. Connect the Text Box tool to the Formula tool on the lightning bolt (the macro indicator). The Action tool will automatically be added to the canvas, as this automatically updates the configuration of a workflow with values provided by interface questions when run as an app or macro.

Step 2: Configure the Action tool that will automatically update the expression replaced by a specific field. **Select Formula | FormulaFields | FormulaField | @expression - value="[Number]*0.50"**. Select the **Replace a specific string:** option and enter `0.50`. This is where the automation happens, updating the `0.50` to any number the user enters. You will see how this happens in the following steps:

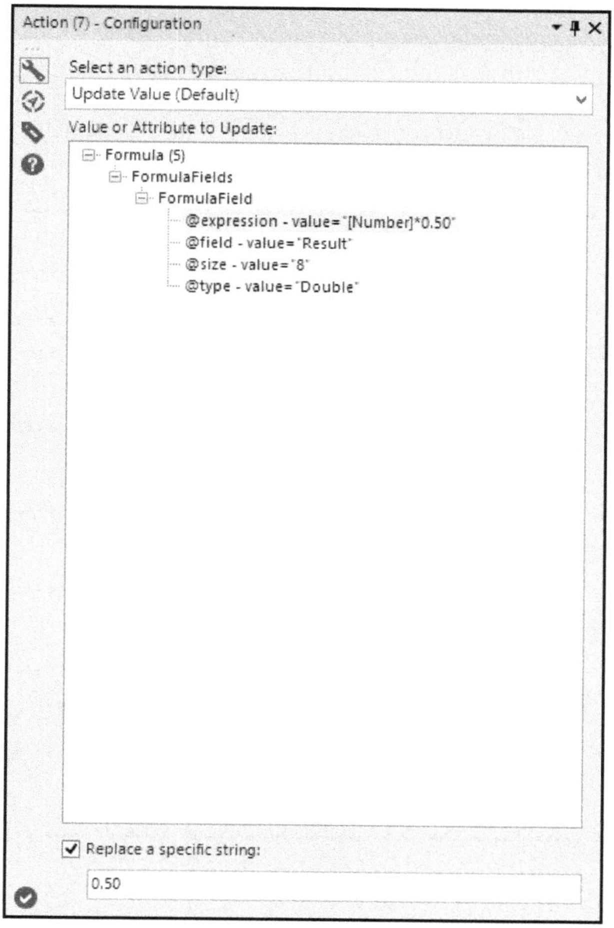

Step 3: In the **Enter the text or question to be displayed** text box, within the Text Box tool configuration, enter: `Please enter a number`:

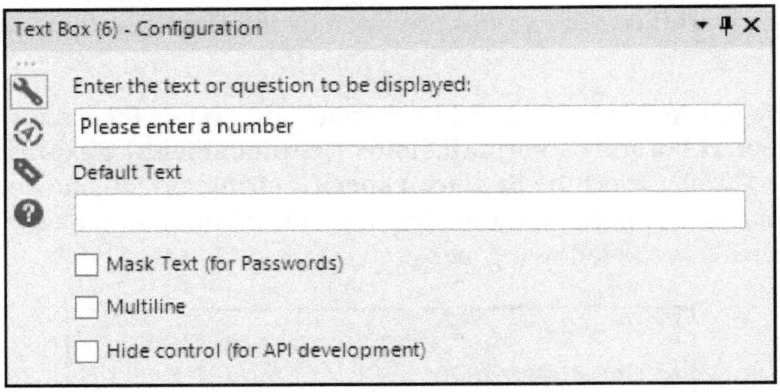

Step 4: Save the workflow as Standard `Macro.yxmc`. The `.yxmc` file type indicates it's a macro related workflow, as shown in the following image:

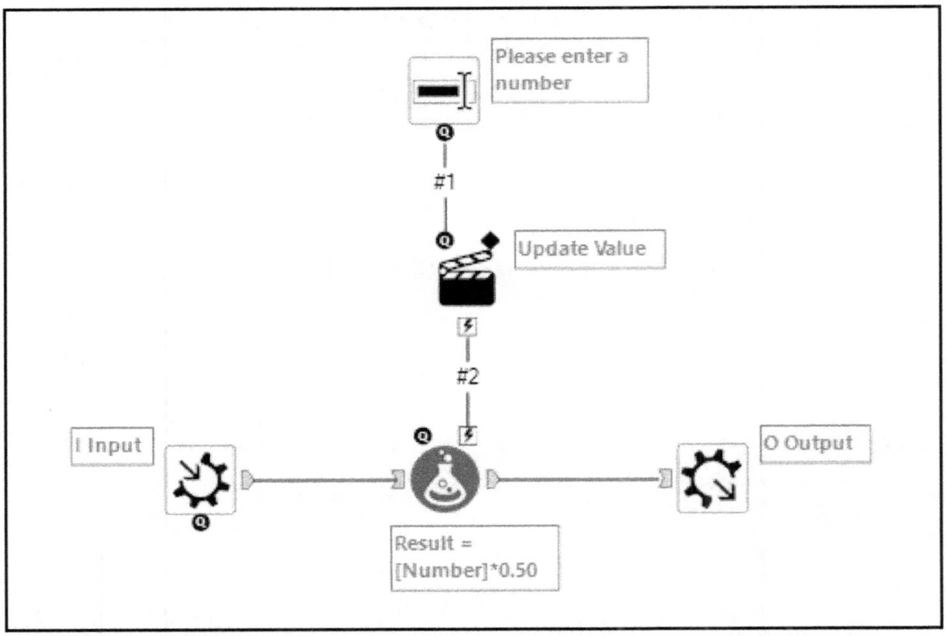

Step 5: Open a new workflow.

Step 6: Select the Input Data tool from the In/Out tool palette and connect to the `U.S. Chronic Disease Indicators.csv` file that you've used in previous chapters.

Step 7: Select the Select tool from the Preparation tool palette and drag it onto the canvas. Connect the Select tool to the Input Data tool.

Step 8: Change the Data Type for the **DataValueAlt** field to Double.

Step 9: Right-click on the canvas and select **Insert** | **Macro** | **Standard Macro**.

Step 10: Connect the Standard Macro to the Select tool.

Step 11: There will be Questions to select within the Standard Macro tool configuration. Select **DataValueAlt (Double)** as the Choose Field option and enter `0.25` in the **Please enter a number** text box:

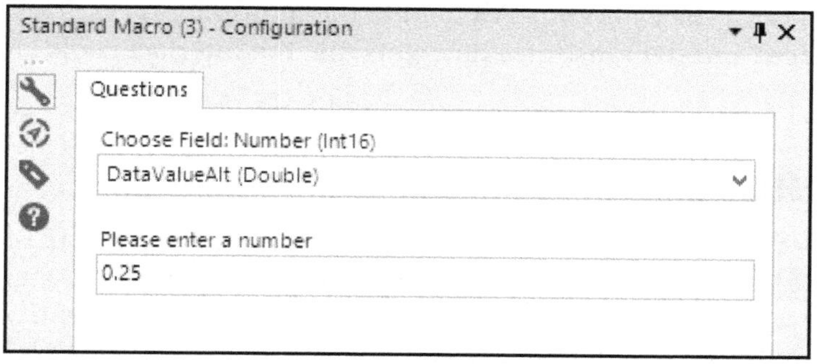

Step 12: Add a Browse tool to the Standard Macro tool.

Step 13: Run the workflow:

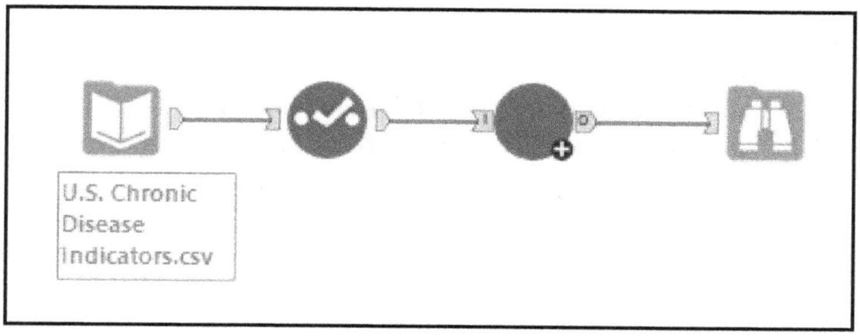

The goal for creating this Standard Macro was to allow the user to select what they would like the multiplier to be rather than a static number. Let's recap what has been created and deployed using a Standard Macro. First, Standard `Macro.yxmc` was developed using Interface tools. The Macro Input (I) was used to enter sample text data for the Number field. This Number field is what is used to multiply to what the given multiplier is - in this case, `0.50`. This is the static number multiplier. The Formula tool was used to create the expression to conclude that the Number field will be multiplied by `0.50`. The Macro Output (O) was used to output the macro so that it can be used in another workflow. The Text Box tool is where the question **Please enter a number** will be displayed, along with the Action tool that is used to update the specific value replaced. The current multiplier, `0.50`, is replaced by `0.25`, as identified in step 20, through a dynamic input by which the user can enter the multiplier. Notice that, in the Browse tool output, the Result field has been added, multiplying the values for the DataValueAlt field to the multiplier `0.25`. Change the value in the macro to 0.10 and run the workflow. The Result field has been updated to now multiple the values for the DataValueAlt field to the multiplier `0.10`. This is a great use case of a Standard Macro and demonstrates how versatile the Interface tools are.

Batch Macro

A Batch Macro is a special kind of macro that is used to process a group of records based on a control parameter. The group of records processed within the macro logic is determined by the control parameter. The control parameter is where you will identify the input fields from the control input you want to use to configure the macro. The Batch Macro is run from beginning to end for each control parameter. This applies to each record, where the entire macro will be reconfigured and run. Records that go in the control input will not form as streams inside the macro like regular inputs. Let's go through a Batch Macro and how it can help in a repeatable process.

Batch Macro Example #1:

Step 1: Select the Macro Input tool from the Interface tool palette and add the tool onto the canvas. The workflow will automatically change to a Standard Macro.

Step 2: Select Text Input and Edit Data option within the Macro Input tool configuration.

Step 3: Create a field called **Number** and enter the values: **155**, **243**, **128**, **352**, and **357**, as shown in the following image:

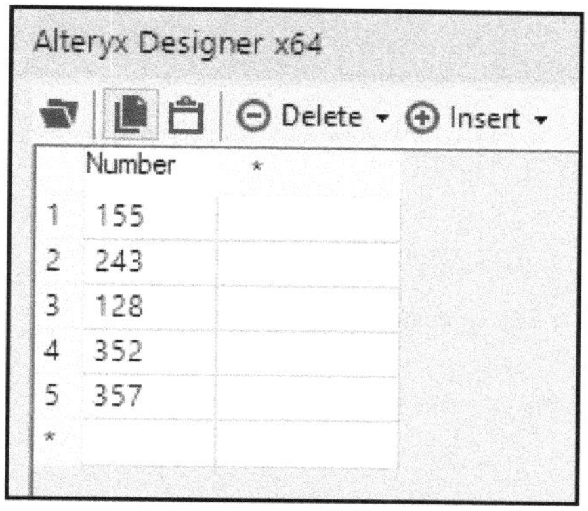

Step 4: Rename the Input Name **Input** and set the Anchor Abbreviation as **I**, as shown in the following image:

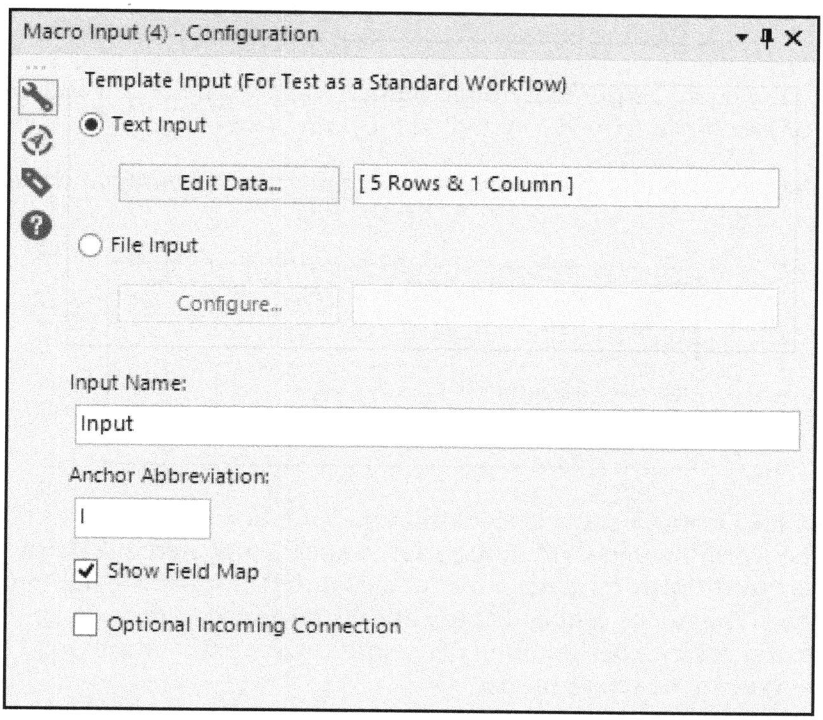

Step 5: Select the Formula tool from the Preparation tool palette. Connect the Formula tool to the Macro Input tool.

Step 6: Select the + Add Column option in the Select Column drop down within the Formula tool configuration. Name the field *Result*.

Step 7: Add the following expression to the expression window:
`[Number]*0.50`

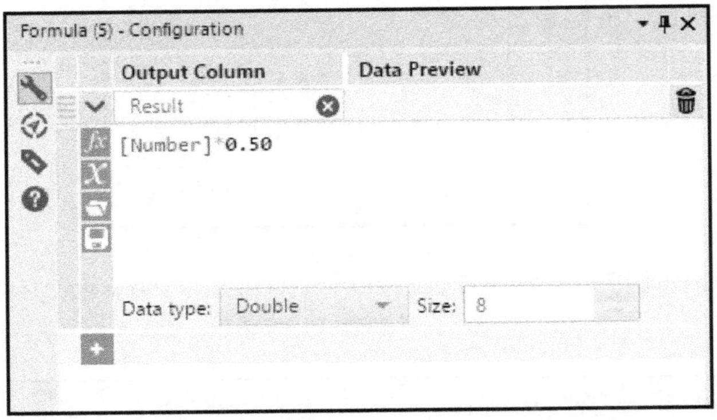

Step 8: Select the Macro Output tool from the Interface tool palette and add the tool onto the canvas. Connect the Macro Output tool to the Formula tool.

Step 9: Rename the Output Name **Output** and set the Anchor Abbreviation as **O** as seen in the following image:

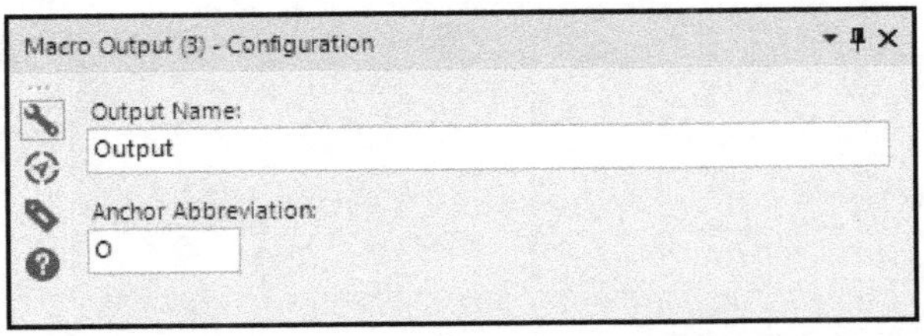

Step 10: Select the Control Parameter tool from the Interface tool palette and drag it onto the canvas. The workflow type will now be automatically updated to a Batch Macro. Connect the Control Parameter tool to the Formula tool on the lightning bolt (the macro indicator). The Action tool will automatically be added to the canvas, as this automatically updates the configuration of a workflow with values provided by interface questions when run as an app or macro.

Step 11: Configure the Action tool that will automatically update the expression replaced by a specific field. Select **Formula** | **FormulaFields** | **FormulaField** | **@expression - value=[Number]*0.50**. Select the **Replace a specific string:** option and enter: `0.50`. The following image demonstrates this process:

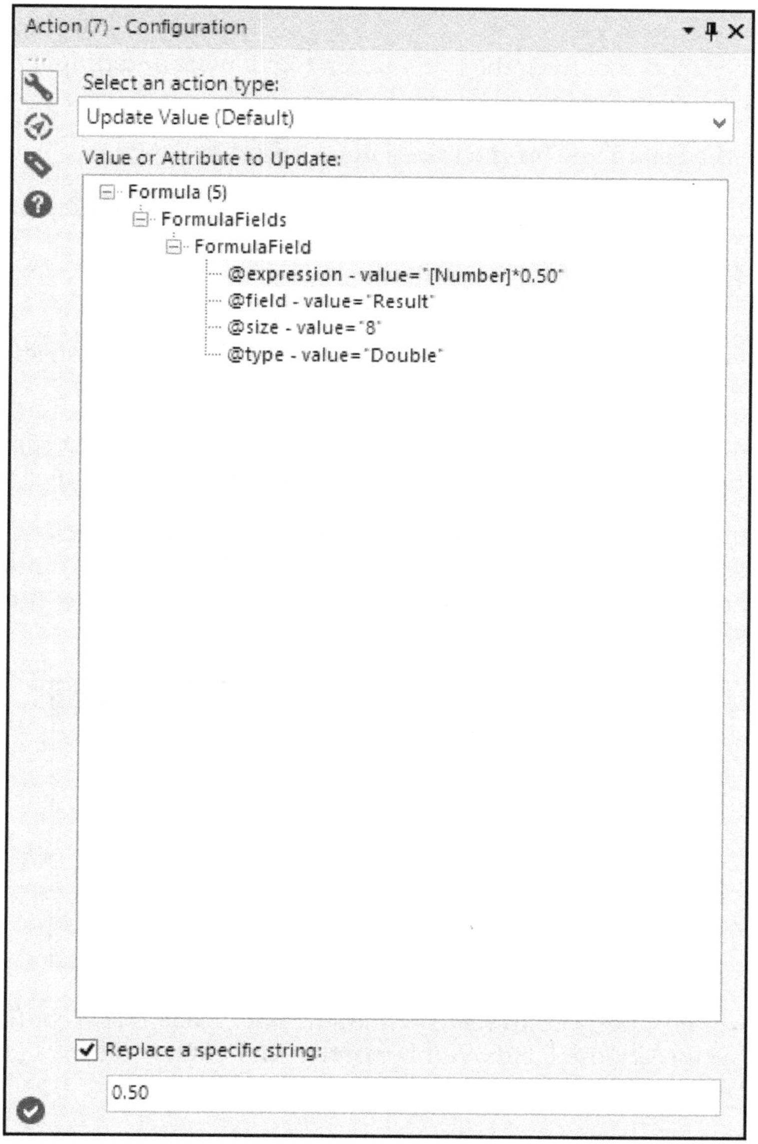

Step 12: Save the workflow as Batch `Macro.yxmc`.

Step 13: Open a new workflow.

Step 14: Select the Input Data tool from the In/Out tool palette and connect to the `U.S. Chronic Disease Indicators.csv` file.

Step 15: Select the Select tool from the Preparation tool palette and drag it onto the canvas. Connect the Select tool to the Input Data tool.

Step 16: Change the Data Type for the DataValueAlt field to Double.

Step 17: Right-click on the canvas and select **Insert** | **Macro** | **Batch Macro**.

Step 18: Connect the Input Data tool containing the `U.S. Chronic Disease Indicators.csv` file to the Input of the Batch Macro.

Step 19: Select the Input Data tool from the In/Out tool palette and connect to the QuestionID `Indicators.xlsx` file.

Step 20: Connect the Input Data tool containing the `QuestionID Indicators.xlsx` file to the upside question mark. This is where or how we're going to define that batch.

Step 21: There are **Group By** and **Questions** tabs within the Batch Macro tool configuration. Select the QuestionId field from both the **Control GroupBy Field** and **Input GroupBy Field**. This is where we define what field we want to group by combing through the Input data stream, as shown in the image that follows:

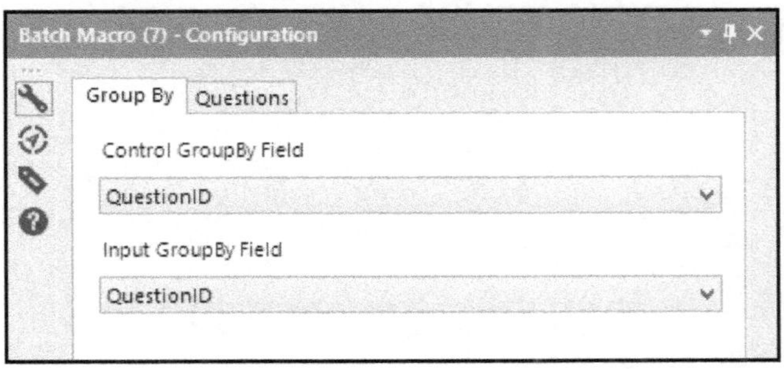

Step 22: There will be Questions to select within the Batch Macro tool configuration. Select `DataValueAlt` as the Choose Field: Number option and enter `Multiplier` as the Choose Field: Control Parameter option.

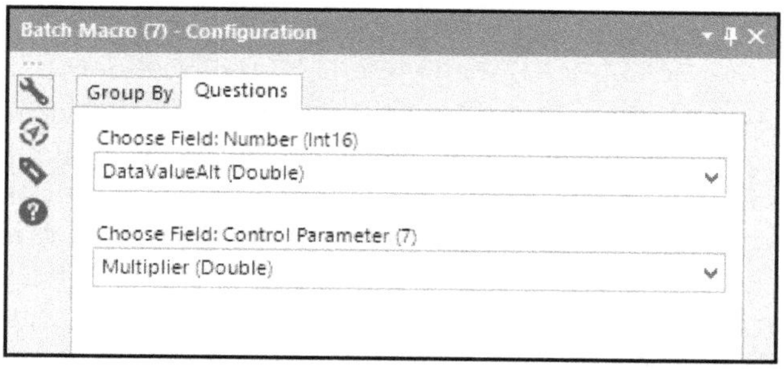

Step 23: Add a Browse tool to the Standard Macro tool.

Step 24: Run the workflow:

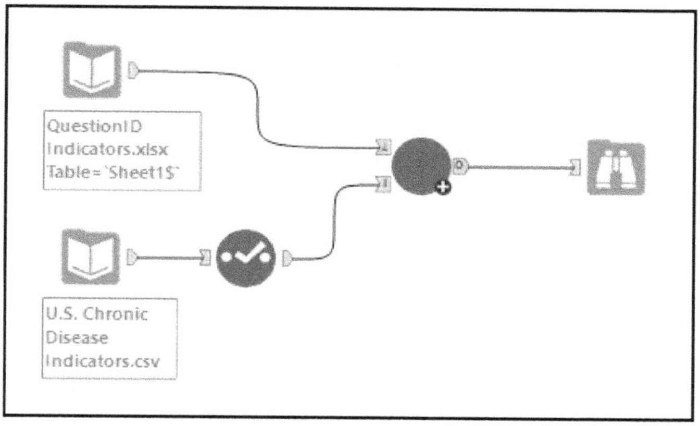

The Result field in the Browse tool output will show the data value multiplied by the multiplier for a particular QuestionID. The Batch Macro will have two inputs describing what file to input and where or how to define the batch through the upside-down question mark input. The Batch Macro will run all records that meet the condition specified by the Control Parameter, which uses an expression within the Action tool to replace the specific string with the multiplier. This type of macro is great when the goal is to process a group of records and it's significantly helpful if you have millions of records that must be processed based on the multiplier.

Summary

In this chapter, you learned about macros and their dynamic use within workflows. A Standard Macro was developed to allow the end user to specify what they want the multiplier to be. This is a great way to implement the interactivity within a workflow. The Batch Macro was created to run a batch specified by the Control Parameter and process the records to a file with given multipliers. There are other macros that can be created and deployed by using an Iterative Macro and Local Optimizer Macro. An Iterative Macro will run through every record and loop the records back through the workflow as many times as is specified or until a condition is met and a Local Optimizer Macro runs multiple iterations to determine the best locations to add or remove from an existing location network. These powerful macros will take your self-service analytics to the next level by identifying areas of data processing. This collection of tools creates an output that can be used anywhere within a workflow to enhance and optimize workflows. In the next chapter, you will learn about Alteryx Server and Alteryx Analytics Gallery. Workflows can be automatically scheduled through Alteryx Server and they can be shared across your team through the Alteryx Analytics Gallery.

9
Sharing Your Insights

Alteryx Server is the easiest and fastest way to deploy data intensive analytics across your organization. You can avoid potential security issues and costly business interruptions using Alteryx Server. Furthermore, you can publish, schedule, and share workflows through the Alteryx Server and Alteryx Public Gallery to provide self-service analytics. Alteryx Server empowers teams to collaborate on data-driven decisions quickly, and easily all through a scalable platform. You'll identify how data can be deployed through an effective and secure collaboration across teams. The Alteryx Public Gallery is an analytics cloud platform that delivers a consumer-based analytics experience. Organizations look to cloud business intelligence to deliver faster deployment.

This chapter will cover the following topics:

- Alteryx Server
- Alteryx Analytics Gallery

Alteryx Server

Alteryx Server provides a scalable platform for deploying and sharing analytics. This is an effective and secure establishment when deploying data rapidly. You can integrate Alteryx processes directly into other internal and external applications from the built in macros and APIs. Alteryx Server can help you speed up business decisions and enable you to get answers in hours, not weeks. You will learn about these powerful features that revolutionize data processing using Alteryx Server:

- Speed time-to-insight with highly scalable workloads
- Empower every employee to make data-driven decisions
- Reduce risk and downtime with analytic governance

Before learning about these powerful features, review the Server Structure illustration so you have a solid understanding of how the server functions, as shown in the following image:

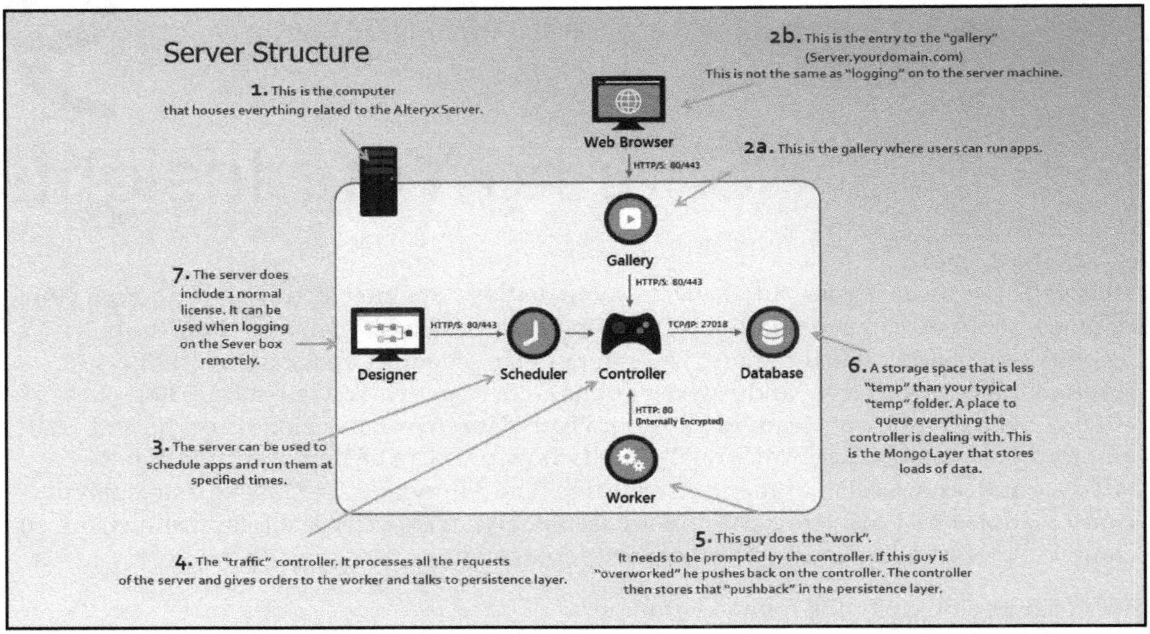

Enterprise scalability

Enterprise Scalability allows you to scale your enterprise analytics that will speed time to insight. Alteryx Server will compute the data processing by scheduling and running workflows. This reliable server architecture will process data intensive workflows at your scalable fashion. Deploy Alteryx Server on a single machine or in a multi-node environment, allowing you to scale up the number of cores on your existing server or add additional server nodes for availability and improved performance as needed.

Ultimate flexibility and scalability

Highly complex analytics and large scale data can use a large amount of memory and processing that can take hours to run on analysts' desktops. This can lead to a delay in business answers and sharing those insights. In addition, less risk is associated with running jobs on Alteryx Server, due to system shutdowns and it being less compressible compared to running on desktop. Your IT professionals will install and maintain Alteryx Server; you can rest assured that critical workflow backups and software updates take place regularly. Alteryx Server provides a flexible server architecture with on-premise or cloud deployment to build out enterprise analytic practice for 15 users or 15,000 users.

Alteryx Server can be scaled in three different ways:

- **Scaling the Worker node for additional processing power**: Increase the total number of workflows that can be processed at any given time by creating multiple Worker nodes. This will scale out the Workers.
- **Scaling the Gallery node for additional web users**: Add a load balancer to increase capacity and create multiple Gallery nodes to place behind a load balancer. This will be helpful if you have many Gallery users.
- **Scaling the Database node for availability and redundancy**: Create multiple Database nodes by scaling out the persistent databases. This is great for improving overall system performance and ensuring backups.

More hardware for Alteryx Server components may need to be added and the following table provides some guidelines:

	Worker	Gallery	Database
Redundancy needed	✓	✓	✓
High availability needed	✓	✓	✓
Workflow execution time increases	✓		
Number of simultaneous users increases	✓	✓	
Number of backend jobs increases	✓		
Workflows sit in queue for long periods of time	✓		
Memory or CPU consumption is high on web nodes		✓	

Scheduling and automating workflow execution to deliver data whenever and wherever you want

Maximize automation potential by utilizing built-in scheduling and automation capabilities to schedule and run analytic workflows as needed, refresh data sets on a centralized server, and generate reports so everyone can access the data, anytime, anywhere. This will allow you to focus more time on analytic problems, rather than keeping an eye on your workflows running on the desktop. Let the server manage the jobs on a schedule.

You can schedule workflows, packages, or apps to run automatically through the company's Gallery, which we'll discuss in more detail in the next section, or to a controller. Also, you can schedule to your computer through Desktop Automation (Scheduler). To schedule a workflow, go to **Options** | **Schedule Workflow** and to **View Schedules** go to **Options** | **View Schedules** as shown in the following image:

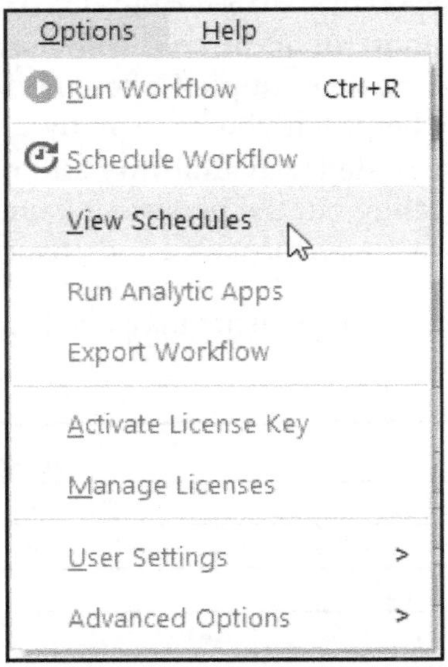

If you want to schedule to your company's Gallery, you will need to connect to your company's Gallery first. Add a Gallery if you aren't connected to one. To add a **Gallery**, select **Options** | **Schedule Workflow** | **Add Gallery**. Type the **URL** path to your company's Gallery and click **Connect**. The connection is made based on built-in authentication by adding your Gallery email and password or Windows authentication by logging in through your user name. The following screenshot shows the URL entry screen:

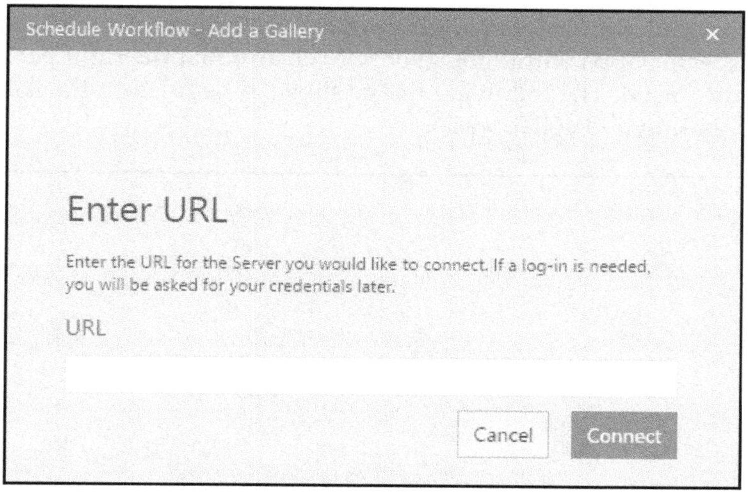

Schedule your workflow to run on a controller. A controller is a machine that runs and manages schedules for your organization. A token is needed to connect to the controller once the Alteryx Server Administrator at your company sets up the controller. To add a controller, select **Options** | **Schedule Workflow** | **Add Controller**. The following illustration is where you will add the server name and the controller token to proceed with connecting to the controller:

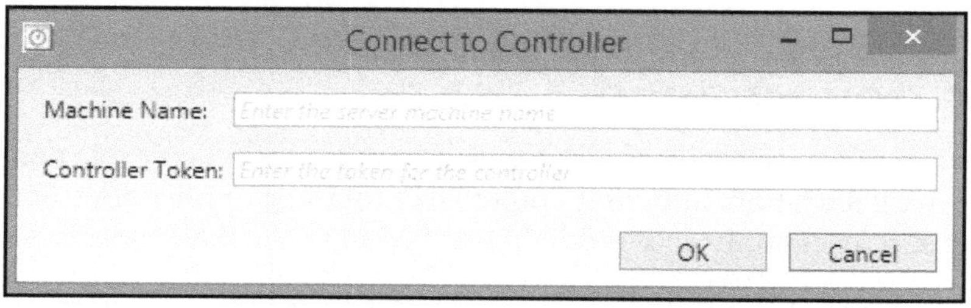

Sharing and collaboration

Data Analysts spend too much time customizing existing reports and rerunning workflows for different decision-makers instead of adding business value by working on new analytics projects. Alteryx Server lets you share macros and analytic applications, empowering business users to perform their own self-service analytics. You can easily share, collaborate on, and iterate workflows with analysts throughout your organization through integrated version control for published analytic applications.

The administrators and authors of analytic applications can grant access to analytic workflows and specific apps within the gallery to ensure that the right people have access to the analytics they need. The following image shows schedules on the Alteryx Analytics Gallery for easy sharing and collaboration:

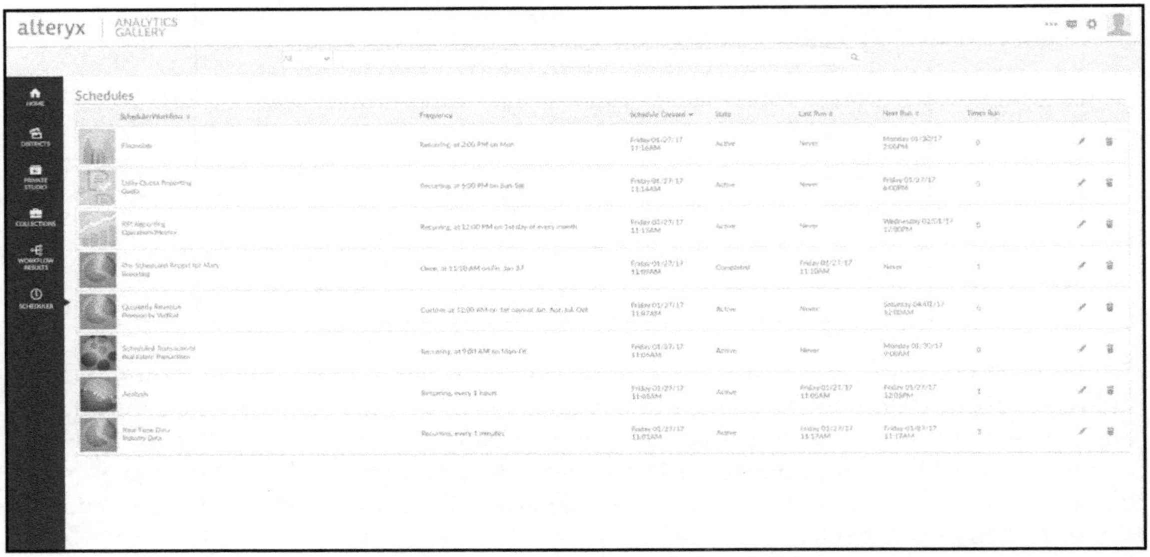

Analytic governance

Alteryx Server provides a built-in secure repository and version control capabilities to enable effective collaboration, allowing you to store analytic applications in a centralized location and ensure users only access the data for which they have permissions.

The following screenshot shows the permission types to assign for maintaining secure access and sharing deployment:

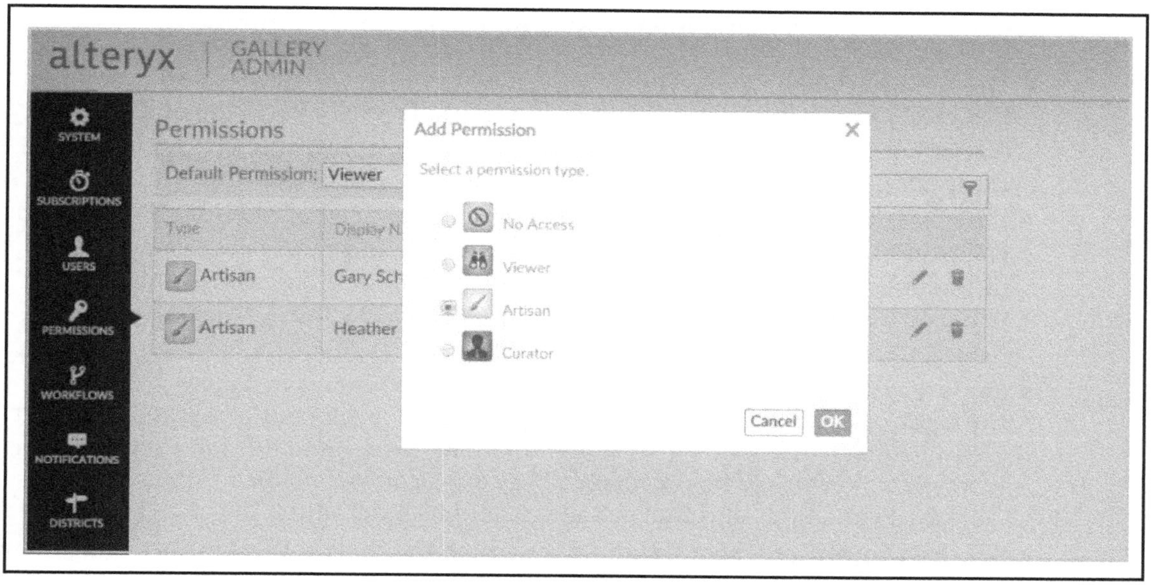

The goal of managing multiple teams collaborating together and deploying enterprise self-service analytics is to reduce downtime and risk, while ensuring analytic and information governance. Many organizations have become accustomed to a data-driven culture, enabling every employee to use analytics and helping business users to leverage the analytic tools available. You can meet service-level agreements with detailed auditing, usage reporting, and logging tools, and your system administrators can rest assured that your data remains safe and secure.

Alteryx Analytics Gallery

The **Alteryx Analytics Gallery** is a web-based environment that allows users to publish, share, and run analytic applications. Through Alteryx Server, companies can offer a private Gallery to their internal users hosted on their own server infrastructure. Also, Alteryx uses Alteryx Server to offer a public Gallery, so any user can sign up and have access to sharing workflows, macros, and apps.

Let's review some details about the Alteryx Analytics Gallery architecture:

- **Host**: With Amazon EC2, Alteryx can launch as many virtual servers (known as instances) as required, manage storage, and configure networking and security. Amazon EC2 (Amazon Elastic Compute Cloud) provides scalable computing capacity in the Amazon Web Services (AWS) cloud.
- **Load balancer**: The web pages and API functionality is served up using the load balancer in front of the Gallery web server nodes, and can easily manage the different levels of web requests. Incoming application traffic across multiple Amazon EC2 instances is automatically distributed by the AWS Elastic Load Balancing.
- **Gallery web gallery web server nodes**: Three web server instances work across the Alteryx Analytics Gallery. The load balancer has incoming web requests that are pulled from the web server nodes and pass them on to the Service Controller when there is work to be processed. They are also responsible for the sharing of workflows and apps and the management of user accounts.
- **Service Controller**: The delegation of work to the Service Workers is managed by the Controller. Only one of the servers acts as a Controller, even though Alteryx Server is deployed across multiple servers. The web server communicates to the Controller to schedule the job to be run instantly when a user wants to run a workflow or app published to the Gallery.
- **Service Workers**: The Service Workers Controller provides work to the Worker and is responsible for retrieving the output and executing workflows and apps. In order to run more concurrent jobs, Alteryx has four Worker servers and each is configured with two processing threads (one thread per physical core for a total of eight threads). Map tile requests are processed using two workers.
- **Database**: Alteryx Server stores information such as the job queue, application files, and result data through a persistence Database layer. A three node replica set is configured in Alteryx by a standalone MongoDB Enterprise database for the Alteryx Analytics Gallery. Data is read from either the primary or one of two secondary nodes and is written to the primary node.

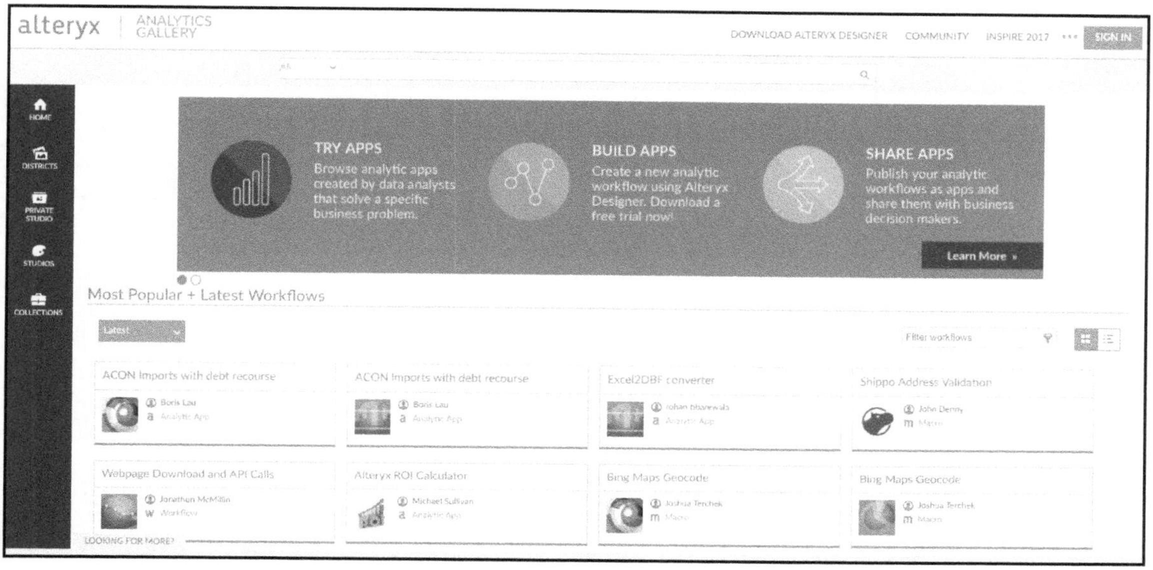

Summary

Alteryx Server has powerful abilities to schedule and deploy workflows and share them with your team. You learned in this chapter how the scheduler is used to process workflows and helpful for running nightly jobs, since the server is always on. The Gallery can be accessed to run workflows through a web-based platform, whether it's privately for your company or publicly to share with other users. Your company can push out workflows to users on the team and they can run the workflows via the Gallery. You can save time with Alteryx Server by letting the server run the jobs, so you can focus on analytical insights to solve complex business problems. Think about the time saved for every workflow ran through Alteryx Designer compared to Alteryx Server, and how you can best utilize that time saved. This gives you and your organization the power to succeed in eliminating time consuming processes and increasing speed time for insights to minutes, not hours.

In the upcoming chapter, you will learn about best practices around structuring and organizing your workflows to make them even more efficient. In addition, speedy and handy tips and tricks that will save you time during your workflow development will be covered.

10
Best Practices

The data necessary for making critical business decisions is best consumed by streamlined workflows. The workflow layout can help you visually build workflows faster. Ensuring autosave is always set to save at faster incremental minutes will help make sure you don't lose that powerful workflow created. Apply data profiling throughout your workflow to visualize the data quality. In this chapter, you will learn best practice solutions for building efficient workflows, reviewing data exploration techniques, and handling data sources. These best practice guidelines, along with their associated tips and tricks, will save you valuable time in the business decision making process.

This chapter will cover the following topics:

- The ultimate guide to workflow design
- Tips and tricks

The ultimate guide to workflow design

By now, you have a solid base on why Alteryx is so powerful for data blending, data cleansing, joining and aggregating data to help solve complex business problems accurately and quickly. This section will focus on how you can make your workflow designs more efficient and intuitive for you. Designing efficient workflows can not only speed up processing but also help with faster troubleshooting. More clarity around your workflows will lead to less time spent going through a scavenger hunt finding that favorite tool of yours. Let's go how to design your workflow layout, save your workflow more frequently, and apply data profiling to ensure you have optimal data quality.

Workflow layout

Design your workflow orientation horizontally or vertically. Whether you prefer to work from left to right or from top to bottom, the tools added to your workflows will be included based on the **Layout Direction** selection. Click anywhere in the canvas and in the Workflow - Configuration window, select the **Canvas** tab and select **Layout Direction**. `Horizontal` and `Vertical` options are available, so select your layout preference, as shown in the following image:

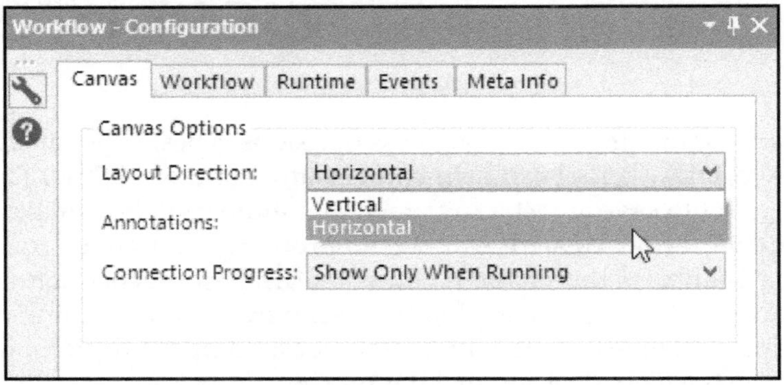

The **Annotation** option under the **Canvas** tab includes the **Hide**, **Show**, and **Show w/ Tool Names**. While building out your workflows, you may add many tools and sometimes it may be difficult to translate which tool is which. You could try to remember the Multi-Field Formula tool as a milkshake or the Multi-Row Formula tool as the Burger King crown. This may work for some tools, but with the number of tools in Alteryx it's best to show the tool names and the **Show w/ Tool Names** option is helpful. It can be activated, as shown in the following image:

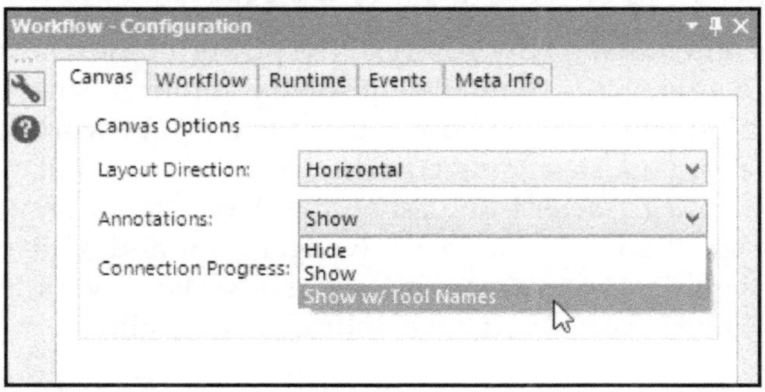

The **Connection Progress** will have three options; **Hide**, **Show**, or **Show Only When Running**. If you prefer not to view the **Connection Progress**, then the **Hide** option suits you best. If you want to catch a glimpse of the **Connection Progress** as your workflow is processing, then the **Show Only When Running** option is your choice. The **Show** option may fit you best if you would like to display the number of records that were processed even after the operation is finished; this option is great for troubleshooting. You can select from these options, as shown in the following image:

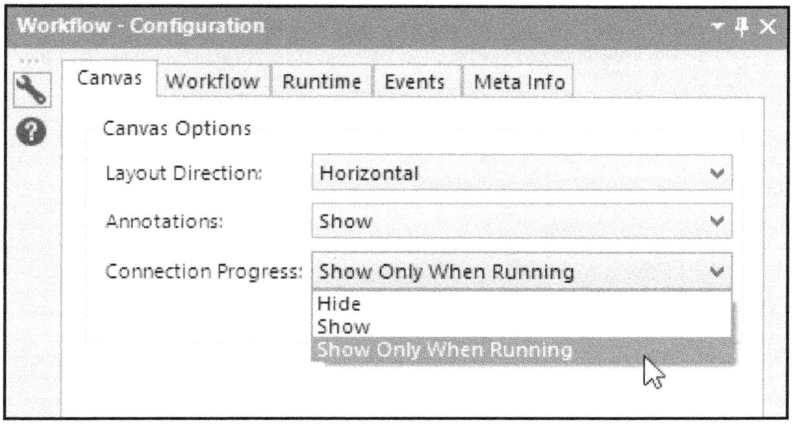

Autosave workflows

Imagine this: you are building a beautifully designed workflow and the pop-up `Upgrade finished: Computer will now restart` appears out of nowhere! Uh oh, quick, *Ctrl* + *S* is racing through your mind. Thankfully, the Autosave feature saves the hassle by selecting time intervals to save the workflow you are working on.

The Autosave option is located under **Options** | **User Settings** | **Edit User Settings** | **Advanced:**

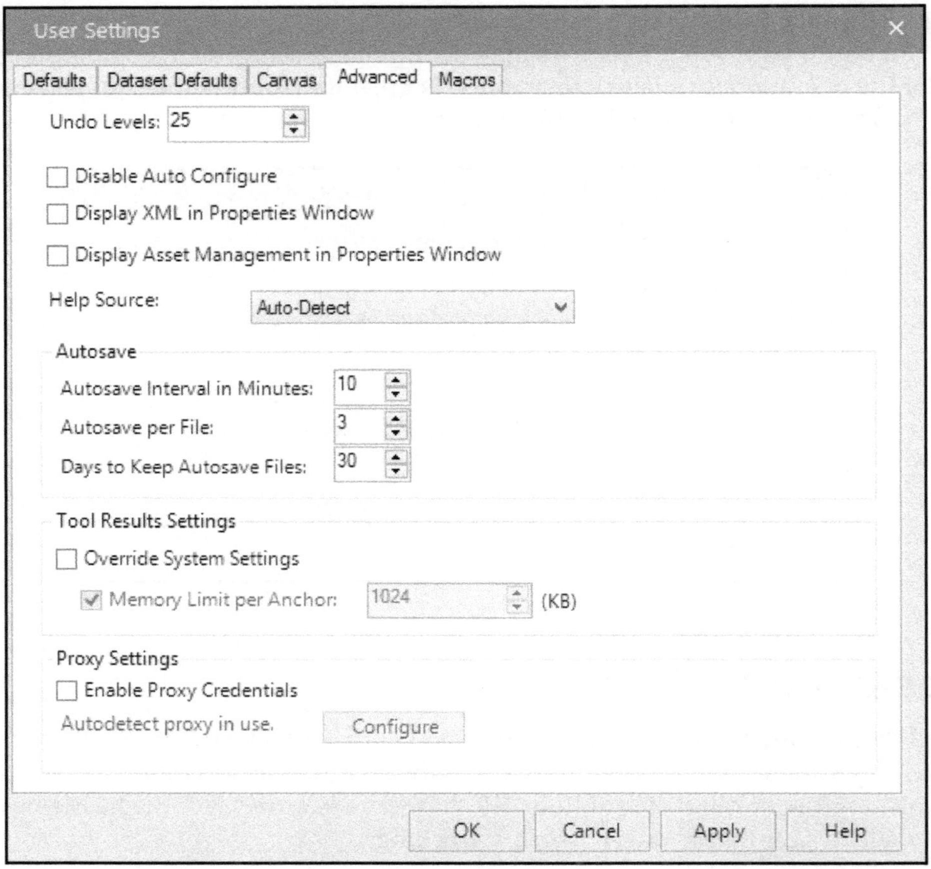

The Autosaved files can be accessed by going to **File** | Open Autosaved files. The available files are listed and can be opened or saved as a different file.

Data profile information

The Browse tool contains Data profiling information that provides you with details on the quality of the data. Data profiling can be turned on or off by deselecting **Collect and display data profile information** under the **Options** | **User Settings** | **Edit User Settings** | **Default** tab. There will be various metadata and charts displayed depending on the data type of the column selected. The quality of data is color coded by the following in the Browse tool:

- **Red**: Not OK (white spaces possible)
- **Yellow**: Null, due to no data
- **Gray**: Empty
- **Green**: Good, quality of data is healthy

The following snapshot shows where, under the **Defaults** tab, the Collect and display data profile information option can be turned on or off:

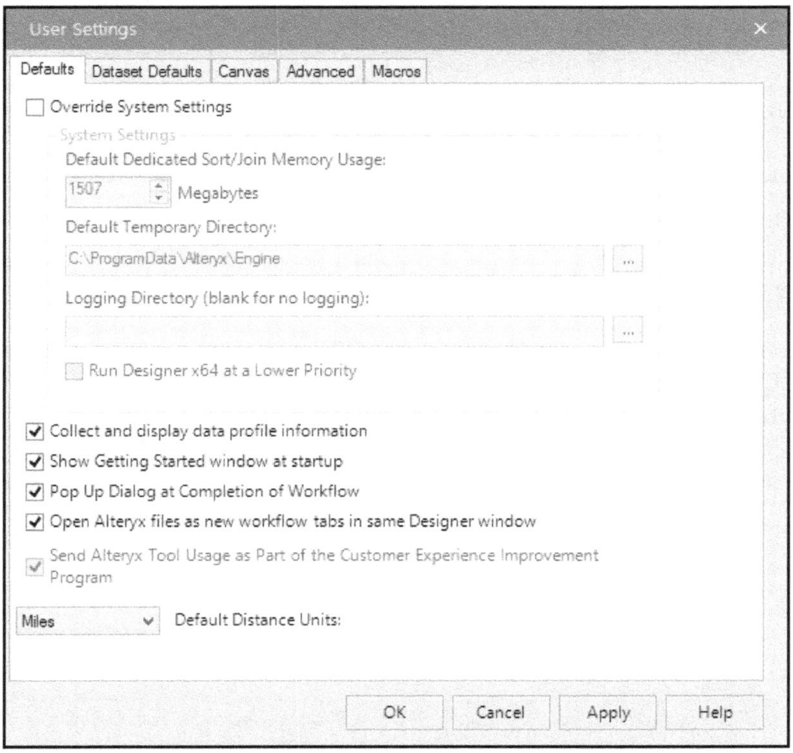

Explorer box

The Explorer box is a great way to quickly open workflows while Alteryx is already open. The workflow file can be dragged from Windows Explorer and dropped on the canvas. The workflow will open in the same window on a new tab. This reduces the amount of time a new instance of Alteryx needs to open each time. The Explorer Box tool can be found under the Documentation tool palette:

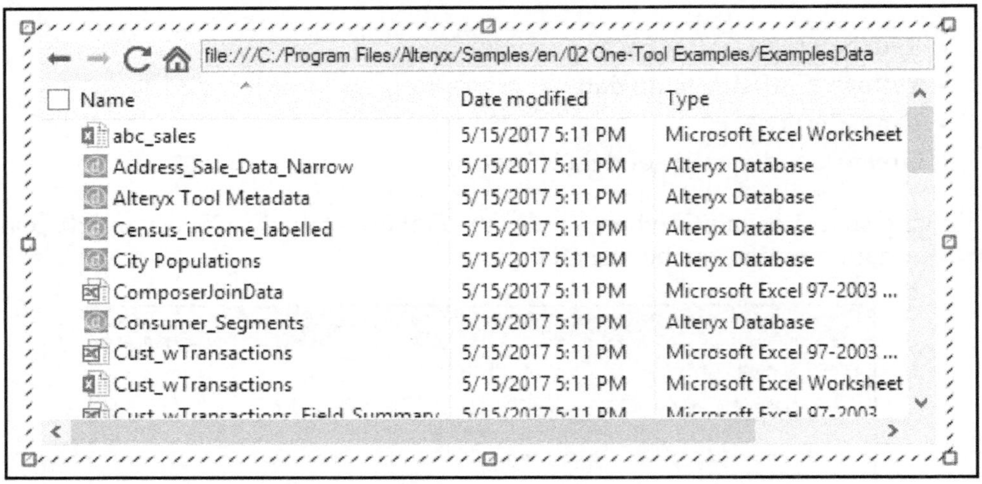

Tips and tricks

This section focuses on the tips and tricks that are handy time savers during the workflow development. Designing an optimal workflow is the first step for downstreaming data efficiency by utilizing the right tools in the right areas of your workflow. The quick tips and tricks are something that you want to stay with you forever, to help you quickly maneuver through the workflow within seconds. Let's take a look at these handy dandy tips and tricks.

Browse data

The Browse Everywhere option was introduced in Version 11 of Alteryx. This is where you can click on the output anchor of a tool and view the results without having to add a Browse tool to view your data! Sounds like a win win to me. The best part is the Browse tool contains more hidden gems, in one of the most used tools in Alteryx. Let's say you have many columns, and scrolling through the Browse tool to locate the columns may not be very easy. Within the Results - Browse configuration, you can select the down area next to the available fields - in this case, 4 0f 35 Fields. Select the fields you want to view within the tool configuration. This saves you time scrolling through data and also saves you from needing to add a new tool, such as the Select tool, to narrow down the number of fields; therefore it also optimizes performance. Interested in finding information on the fields available in the tool configuration? Select the Metadata option to view the Name, Type, Size, Source, and Description of your metadata, as shown in the following image:

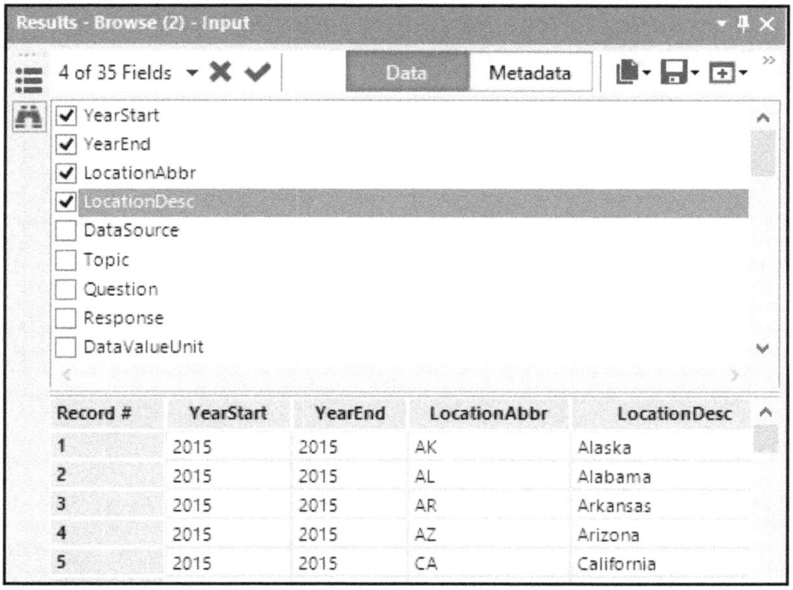

Data organization

Organizing your data comes with a few tips and tricks that will help polish and shine your workflow to be brighter than ever. The **Add to New Container** option was added in Version 11 of Alteryx. This great option allows you to group tools into a container by selecting one or more tools. This can be quickly accomplished by selecting one or more tools, right-clicking, and selecting **Add to New Container**. Instantly, your tools are organized in a container that can be enabled or disabled. If your focus is in one specific area of the workflow and another section of the workflow is in a container, the container can be disabled and, when the workflow is running, the processing time is reduced, as records won't be processed for tools within the disabled container:

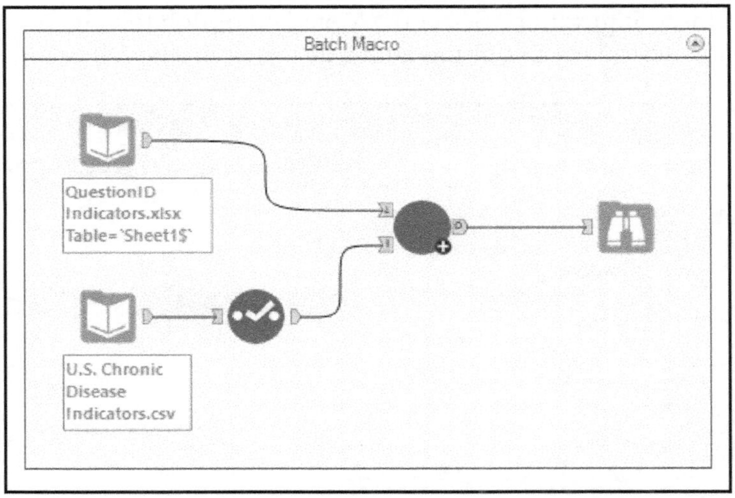

Tool alignment

Sometimes, with the number of tools in your workflow, they may be scattered around and not as perfectly aligned as you would like. The tools can be aligned in the canvas horizontally or vertically. This is a very handy option when it comes to some tools not structured in a linear line downstream. This can be done by selecting the tools you're interested in aligning, right-clicking, and select either **Align Horizontally** or **Align Vertically**. The shortcut favorites for this are *Ctrl* + *Shift* + - to align horizontally and *Ctrl* + *Shift* + + to align vertically. The following screenshot shows the tools not aligned horizontally:

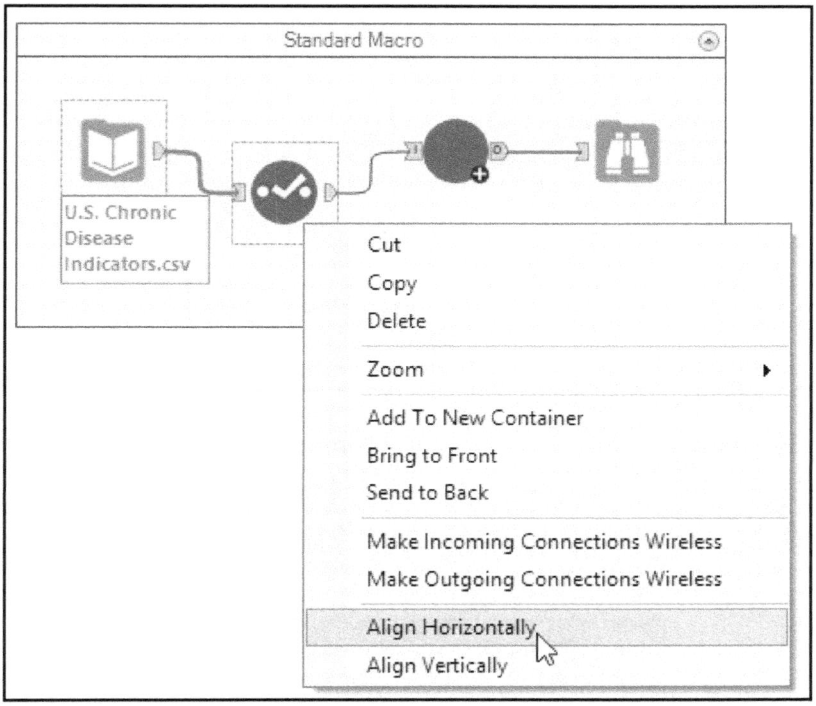

The following screenshot now shows the results of applying the **Align Horizontally** option; just like that, your workflow is the same pattern and we've saved time, rather than aligning tool by tool to get that tool linearity pattern.

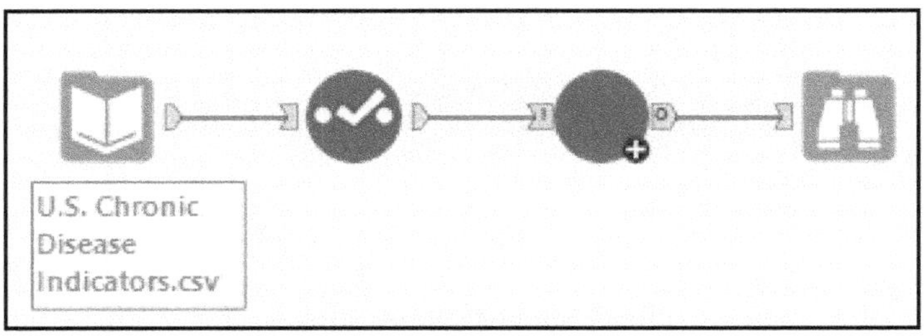

Time savers

These time savers will help you rapidly update your workflow. Using the same tool palette over and over again may indicate you're a fan favorite of those tools! Right-click on a tool palette and select **Pin** [Tool Category Name]. In the following example, the **Preparation** tool palette has been pinned and will appear to the front of the tool palette:

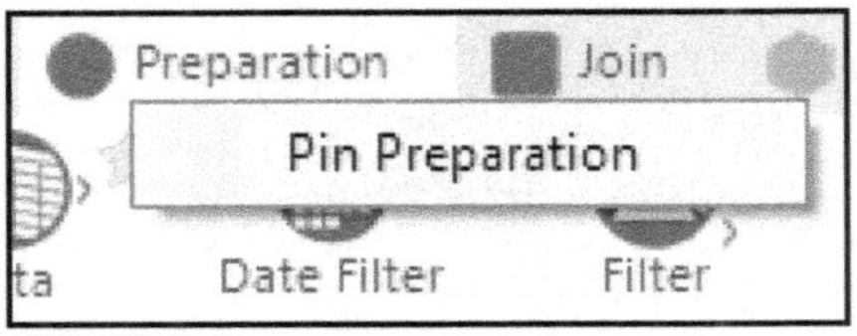

There are times where new fields are brought through the **Input Data** tool and old fields have been removed, whether that's using a local file or from the database. The fields will appear as missing within the tool and aren't necessary to keep for downstream processing. There is a quick fix for this using the **Forget All Missing Fields** option in a tool configuration under the **Options** tab, as shown in the following image:

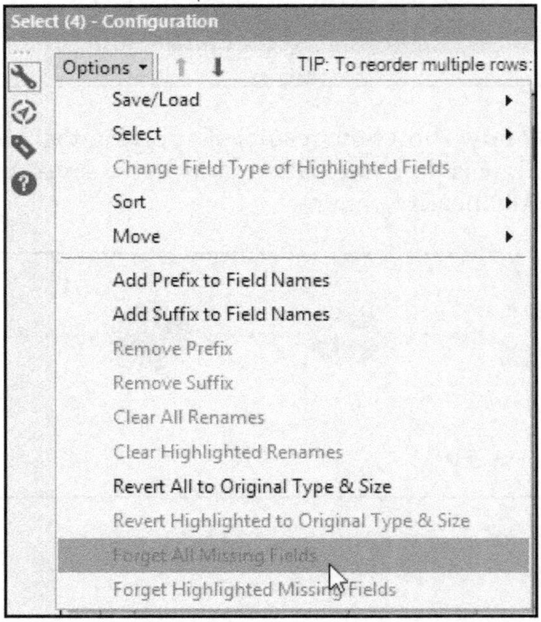

Summary

In this chapter, you learned about workflow design and how it can help you during your self-service analytics endeavors. Select a layout that meets your preferences, autosave your workflow to ensure all the new enhancements made are saved, and apply data profiling to gather information about your data quality. View which columns are looking good and not so good. Apply necessary updates to your data, as the better your data quality, the better your analysis. You also explored tips and tricks that are very handy. Browse results shows data results the way you want to see them and can be viewed without adding a Browse tool. You learned about structuring your data in tool containers to enable and disable as needed, providing clarity and optimization to your workflow. The tool alignment saves time by quickly aligning tools horizontally or vertically. The chapter capped off with time savers that will save you precious time to use on analysis, rather than updating and fixing your workflow. Pin frequently used tool palettes as favorites and forget missing fields with a click away rather than selecting each field to remove in downstream processing.

This book covered the foundation of Alteryx and how complex business problems can be solved. You now have a solid foundation on which to comfortably build workflows and answer the questions of your data analysis rapidly. You can now cleanse, prep, blend, and join data, which will grant you the power to quickly deliver and share insights with decision makers. I hope you enjoyed this book and came away learning something new and useful that you can apply towards your business needs and build efficiently designed and optimized workflows.

Index

Lightning Source UK Ltd.
Milton Keynes UK
UKHW050855020321
379650UK00005B/205

9 781788 392655